Managing Defence in a Democracy

Although each state is unarguably unique, it is possible to identify certain common problems and issues with respect to defence governance and management. This volume introduces the reader to the basic principles of governance and management through the identification of these key commonalities.

It also shows that if individuals are keen to reform practices within their defence establishment they also need to be aware of the various constraints and obstacles that may challenge them. Written by acknowledged experts in the field, the contributions presented here identify examples of good practice from across the world and analyse the steps that need to be taken to implement that practice. The book is designed to support teaching, so each chapter includes prompts for reflective activity and short vignettes to enhance accessibility.

This book will be essential reading for students of defence management, and of great interest to students of security studies in general.

Laura R. Cleary joined Cranfield University in July 2002 as a Senior Lecturer in the Department of Defence Management and Security Analysis. She is currently the Academic Director for the UK MoD's sponsored Defence Diplomacy courses and is the Director of Research for DMSA.

Teri McConville holds a PhD for a project concerning the discursive formation of managerial decisions and specializes in organization theory. She is co-editor of *Defence Management in Uncertain Times* (Cass 2003) and co-ordinator for the Cranfield Defence Management conferences. She is deputy director of research for the Department of Defence Management and teaches research method to doctoral candidates.

Cass Military Studies

Intelligence Activities in Ancient Rome
Trust the gods, but verify
Rose Mary Sheldon

Clausewitz and African War
Politics and strategy in Liberia and Somalia
Isabelle Duyvesteyn

Strategy and Politics in the Middle East, 1954–60
Defending the Northern Tier
Michael Cohen

The Cuban Intervention in Angola, 1965–1991
From Che Guevara to Cuito Cuanavale
Edward George

Military Leadership in the British Civil Wars, 1642–1651
'The Genius of this Age'
Stanley Carpenter

Israel's Reprisal Policy 1953–1956
The dynamics of military retaliation
Ze'ev Drory

Bosnia and Herzegovina in the Second World War
Enver Redzic

Leaders in War
West point remembers the 1991 gulf war
Frederick Kagan and Christian Kubik (eds)

Khedive Ismail's Army
John Dunn

Yugoslav Military Industry 1918–1991
Amadeo Watkins

Corporal Hitler and the Great War 1914–1918
The list regiment
John Williams

Rostóv in the Russian Civil War 1917–1920
The key to victory
Brian Murphy

The Tet Effect
Intelligence and the public perception of war
Jake Blood

The US Military Profession into the 21st Century
War, peace and politics
Sam C. Sarkesian and Robert E. Connor, Jr (eds)

Civil–Military Relations in Europe
Learning from crisis and institutional change
Hans Born, Marina Caparini, Karl Haltiner and Jürgen Kuhlmann (eds)

Strategic Culture and Ways of War
Lawrence Sondhaus

Military Unionism in the Post Cold War Era
A future reality?
Richard Bartle and Lindy Heinecken (eds)

Warriors and Politicians
U.S. civil–military relations under stress
Charles A. Stevenson

Military Honour and the Conduct of War
From ancient Greece to Iraq
Paul Robinson

Military Industry and Regional Defense Policy
India, Iraq and Israel
Timothy D. Hoyt

Managing Defence in a Democracy
Laura R. Cleary and Teri McConville (eds)

Managing Defence in a Democracy

Edited by
Laura R. Cleary and
Teri McConville

Routledge
Taylor & Francis Group

LONDON AND NEW YORK

First published 2006
by Routledge
2 Park Square, Milton Park, Abingdon, Oxon OX14 4RN

Simultaneously published in the USA and Canada
by Routledge
270 Madison Ave, New York, NY 10016

*Routledge is an imprint of the Taylor & Francis Group,
an informa business*

Typeset in Sabon by
Newgen Imaging Systems (P) Ltd, Chennai, India
Printed and bound in Great Britain by
MPG Books Ltd, Bodmin

British Library Cataloguing in Publication Data
A catalogue record for this book is available
from the British Library

Library of Congress Cataloging in Publication Data
    Managing defence in a democracy / edited by Laura R. Cleary
and Teri McConville.
        p. cm. – (Cass military studies)
    Includes bibliographical references and index.
        1. Armed Forces – Management. 2. Military administration.
I. Cleary, Laura Richards II. McConville, Teri, 1954–
III. Title. IV. Series.

UB146.M35 2006
355.6–dc22   2006004543

ISBN10: 0–415–39563–1   ISBN13: 978–0–415–39563–2 (hbk)
ISBN10: 0–415–40887–3   ISBN13: 978–0–415–40887–5 (pbk)
ISBN10: 0–203–96853–0   ISBN13: 978–0–203–96853–6 (ebk)

This book is dedicated to our students:
those in the past, who taught us so much,
those of the future, from whom we have much to learn.

Contents

Figures

Tables

Contributors

Mr Alex Alexandrou is a freelance consultant specializing in HR developments. He has worked with a range of organizations, including the UN, EU, the UK Home Office, the Police Federation of England and Wales and the RAF. He is currently Chair of the International Professional Development Association.

Dr David Chuter has worked for the UK MoD since 1976 in a variety of posts, which have given him a knowledge and expertise of arms control, European integration, defence exports and war crimes. He is currently seconded to the French Ministry of Defence.

Dr Laura R. Cleary is a Senior Lecturer and Academic Director for Cranfield University's UK MoD sponsored short courses on Managing Defence in a Democracy. A prize-winning University lecturer, she specializes in defence and security sector reform, with a special interest and expertise in Eastern Europe.

Dr Roger Darby is a lecturer in HRM at Cranfield University. He has taught and acted as a consultant on the subject throughout Central and Eastern Europe and in South Africa and China. His most recent research is on the cross-cultural effects on knowledge management.

Prof Jeff Haynes is a Professor of Politics at London Metropolitan University. He has more than 100 publications, including 15 books, 40 articles and 45 book chapters. His current research interests include comparative politics and globalization, religion and politics and development issues.

Dr Sylvie Jackson is a Senior Lecturer in Defence Management at Cranfield University. She specializes in quality management, and has acted as a consultant for a number of organizations in both the public and private sectors. She is a member of the Chartered Management Institute and the Chartered Institute of Marketing.

Dr Teri McConville has practical experience of public sector management, in the Princess Mary's Royal Air Force Nursing Service and the National

Contributors

Health Service. She teaches organizational behaviour and other aspects of defence management at Cranfield University and within the Defence Academy of the United Kingdom.

Ms Annie Maddison is Deputy Director of the Masters in Defence Administration at Cranfield University. She lectures on the management of information systems and is currently completing a PhD on that subject.

Dr Derrick J. Neal is a Senior Lecturer in Strategic Management at Cranfield University and also Dean of Faculty of Military Science, Technology and Management. He has worked in the defence industry with Vickers and SMEs, both in technical roles and as a Marketing Director. He works as a consultant within the UK defence sector on matters of Strategic and Change Management.

Mr Len Nockles is a lecturer in logistics at Cranfield University. Prior to joining the University he worked for Exel Logistics in a number of roles including Logistics Director. He maintains his links with the logistics industry by acting as a consultant for a number of forwarders.

Prof Trevor Taylor is a Professor and Head of Department for DMSA at Cranfield University. He takes a close interest in the UK SMART Acquisition initiative and teaches defence acquisition on a number of courses. He has published extensively on European Security and defence industrial issues.

Preface

In 1998, as part of a broad-based Strategic Defence Review, the UK Ministry of Defence established Defence Diplomacy as one of eight military missions. A component of that mission was the development of a Defence Diplomacy Scholarship Scheme, through which politicians, civil servants and military personnel from developing democracies could be educated in the governance and management of defence. Cranfield University at the Defence Academy of the United Kingdom has been privileged to make a significant contribution to that scheme through means of its MSc in Global Security and its seven and two-week courses on Managing Defence in a Democracy (MDD).

The initial intent of the MDD courses was to introduce participants to the way in which Britain governs and manages defence. Over time, however, the aim and content of the course have evolved. Course instructors are facilitators rather than educators, because it is ever more apparent that we share common problems and, potentially, common solutions in the governance and management of defence, regardless of whether we reside in a developed or developing democracy.

This book provides us with an opportunity to take stock of what we have learned in delivering the MDD courses and to share those insights with others. This is by no means an exhaustive treatment of the subject; that would be impossible to achieve in one volume. There is a great deal more that we would have liked to discuss, and, in all honesty, the editorial decision on what to include has been a difficult one. The topics gathered in this volume should be viewed as headline issues, or as points for initial discussion.

We have enjoyed and valued all of the discussions that we have had with our students from Central and Eastern Europe, South America, South and Southeast Asia, and Africa. As a result of that dialogue we have learned a great deal and this book is an attempt to share that knowledge with future students. We look forward to continuing our discussions with them.

Laura R. Cleary and Teri McConville

Acknowledgements

A book such as this is not produced without the efforts of many people. There are too many to name individually but we would like to single out the following people for special thanks:

Our secretaries, Anne Harbour and Anne Smith, have cheerfully taken on the extra work that editorial duties generated, protected us from interruptions and walked the second mile to help us with our research.

Our colleagues at Cranfield, and Andrew Humphrys at Routledge, for sharing our vision so that this book could become a reality.

The UK MoD and US DOD; and publishers: Financial Times/Pearson Educational; Wiley; and RAND corporation for their kind permission to reproduce material for which they hold the copyright.

Our families for patiently enduring our absence, physical or mental, during the editing phase; especially Christina who coped admirably with her mum being constantly busy.

Part I
Defence governance

1 Commonalities and constraints in defence governance and management

Laura R. Cleary and Teri McConville

It has been argued that the armed forces have an inherent 'need to be different' (Dandeker and Freedman 2002: 465). This need stems from the basic fact that soldiers, sailors and airmen are willing to forfeit that most fundamental of human rights: the right to life. In many countries around the world, in democracies and authoritarian regimes, this need to be different has given rise to a perceived right: the right of the military, as an institution, to be immune from wider political pressures to ensure good governance.

That assumption of immunity is increasingly being challenged. As those countries which were carried along by the third wave of democratization attempt to consolidate their gains, and a new group of states succumb to the fourth wave of democratization, there is growing recognition that democracy will falter unless the principles of good governance are applied equally and impartially across all sectors of government, including, and especially, the defence and security services.[1]

In the West this process has been underway for the past twenty-five years. Under the guise of New Public Management, attempts have been made to make the defence sector more efficient, effective, transparent and accountable. Democratizing countries, from South Asia to South America, are focussing on these same goals but under the rubric of good governance and security sector reform.[2]

The security paradigm has shifted significantly since the end of the Cold War. Despite the United States' assertion that national interest and state security should be of primary importance over all other considerations, a growing number of states believe that there can be no state security without human security.[3] This truth was made evident by the riots in France in October and November 2005. President Jacques Chirac acknowledged that the 'profound malaise' in society and the 'poison' of racial discrimination would need to be addressed if stability and security were to be re-established (*The Guardian* 15 November 2005: 17). The guarantee of opportunities for, and the rights of, the individual are the critical factor in the attainment of security.

Such thinking is increasingly reflected in a range of policy documents from around the world. For example, the Bulgarian *National Security Concept* (1998) states that:

> We can speak of national security when the major rights and liberties of the Bulgarian citizens are protected as well as the state borders, the territorial integrity and independence of the country, when there is not any danger of armed attack, violated political dictate or economic compulsion for the state and the democratic functioning of the state and civilian institutions is guaranteed in result of which the society and the nation preserve and increase their prosperity and develop.

In Colombia, the concept of national security has been rejected in favour of a new concept, that of *democratic* security. Within the Colombian Defence Policy (2003) the case for democratic security is clearly articulated:

> Democratic security differs from the notions of security expounded by authoritarian regimes, which are based on ideological hegemony and political exclusion. The Government rejects the idea of 'National Security'…which considered certain ideological groups or political parties as the 'enemies within'. We believe that all are welcome in a democracy.

These are very different countries, with distinct histories and cultures which, nevertheless, share a desire to achieve human security within a democratic framework.

Process and goal: democratic, civil and civilian control

The state is understood as being a 'human community that (successfully) claims the monopoly of the legitimate use of physical force within a given territory' (Weber 1946). A question which all democracies must address is how they intend to control the means of violence (Giddens 1994). It is a pertinent question for all democracies, regardless of length of establishment, and it pertains in equal measure to considerations of both internal and external security. It has long been recognized that, for democratic states, the control and use of that physical force may pose challenges so severe that they threaten democracy itself. This was a topic of concern for Alexis de Tocqueville in his work on *Democracy in America* and for Edmund Burke who observed that 'an armed, disciplined body is, in its essence, dangerous to liberty' (Cited by Kemp and Hudlin 1992). When confronted with crime, urban violence, political insurrection or terrorism, democratic governments do not tend to emphasize the democratization of institutions; they favour instead the implementation of authoritarian measures (Tedesco 2000). Examples of such behaviour can be seen in Argentina in the 1990s as the government and police tried to contend with an increase in criminal activity; in Ethiopia following the contested elections of May 2005; and in the proposals for new anti-terrorism legislation tabled by the British Labour government in 2005.

For decades, governments and academics have been in search of the most appropriate means by which to manage civil-military, and now civil-security relations. Leading works within this field include Samuel Huntington, *The Soldier and the State* (1957), Morris Janowitz, *The Professional Soldier* (1961), and Samuel E Finer, *The Man on Horseback* (1976). These authors centred their arguments on either the professionalism of the armed forces or the political maturity of the society. While certain elements of their theories remain relevant for civil-military relations in the twenty-first century, there is a growing body of literature which calls for a more holistic approach to the issue of defence governance and management. This book should be viewed as an initial attempt to respond to that call.

For many new democracies, whether they are transitioning away from a communist, authoritarian or military regime, the armed forces will have been a critical support to the regime. The challenge, therefore, is to develop a new, more balanced relationship between the civil society and the military. Democratic, civil and civilian control is viewed in the West as the most appropriate framework to adopt, but for many within developing democracies there is either confusion over the terms or concern about the way they are applied. For example, Serbians sometimes understand democratic and civil control to mean the same thing, while Ukrainians and Russians understand control as *kontrol*: the monitoring or checking of activities. Within their language *kontrol* does not imply direction (*upravlinia*) or supervision (*nadzor*) concepts which are encompassed within the English usage of control (Sherr 2001: 2).

Democratic, civil and civilian control is a highly nuanced concept. Each element within it is distinct, but they are all dependent. The application of one element without the others may lead to unbalanced and fraught civil-military relations. For example, in Macedonia, the too-literal application of civilian control of the armed forces, without scope for military contributions to policy formation, has led to an antagonistic relationship.

Within this book, democratic control will be understood to mean the subordination of the armed forces to democratically elected political authorities, who are responsible for taking all decisions concerning the defence of the country (Rose 1994: 1). It should be noted, however, that democracy is a process, not an end state. As a result, it cannot be assumed that democratic control of the armed forces is a fixed attribute. It is something which must be fought for; bearing in mind that some of the greatest democratic deficits occur within the security sector (Luckham 1996). Democratic control needs to be underpinned by other principles and supported by certain activities.

Civil control, sometimes referred to as civil supremacy, is defined by David Chuter as 'the obedience which the military owes to the civis, the state' (Chuter 2000: 27; Finer 1976: 24). This concept implies an allegiance to a group larger than the government of the day; it is an allegiance to the citizen body in its entirety. While it is important that the military should adhere to such a principle, it is equally important that the politicians and civil servants believe in this same principle. An understanding of shared values and allegiance is one element of Rebecca Schiff's concordance theory. Schiff argues that when the military, the political leadership and citizenry view each others as partners in the delivery of security, military involvement in politics is less likely to occur (Schiff 1995).

As in the case of democratic control, civil control too can prove problematic, particularly in those countries in which state and regime security have previously been equated. For many African states, constructing a broader notion of citizenship, and thus partnership, is a challenge that must be addressed if appropriate mechanisms for democratic, civil control are to be devised.

The final element of the equation is civilian control. Ideally, civilian control should be viewed as a critical component of democratic, civil control, rather than as an independent variable. Civilian control is achieved through the appointment of civilian politicians to positions of responsibility over the armed forces, as well as by means of granting decision-making powers to civil servants. The extent to which the latter will occur varies between political systems. It is vital, however, that both politicians and civil servants operate within the framework of their constitutional authority and subject to the rule of law.

In some Central and East European states the assertion of civilian control has proven problematic, because it has not been linked to broader policy initiatives. In a number of instances, civilians were appointed as ministers of defence without any thought being given to the reporting chains within that ministry, or between the ministry and the General Headquarters, or other branches of government. The result was that ministers were left isolated and ignorant of what was actually going on. When a highly professional military force is coupled with poor or weak civilian control, it can result in the forces becoming increasingly politicized; which is not a good outcome for a fledgling democracy.[4]

In combination, then, democratic, civil and civilian control is understood to mean the subordination of the armed forces to democratically elected political authorities, who are responsible for taking all decisions concerning the defence of the country. Politicians, military personnel and civil servants undertake an oath of obedience to the state and are equally bound to operate within the constitutional framework and under the rule of law. It is this concept which pervades the arguments advanced in the following chapters. There is an assumption made that in an ideal form of governance or management politicians, civil servants and military personnel will be working in partnership. It is also recognized, however, that political and managerial systems frequently fall short of this ideal. While there is no perfect form of governance or management, there are some universally recognized principles, which if applied can potentially make existing systems more efficient, effective and responsive. The purpose of this book is to identify those principles and to illustrate how they may be applied in those democracies undergoing defence reform. Each chapter contains a series of reflective questions to encourage the reader to consider whether the approaches being discussed are relevant to their circumstances and how they might be applied.

Governance and management: inter-linking variables

Although this book has been, perhaps artificially, divided into sections on governance and management, we are of the firm belief that the two topics are inextricably intertwined. This belief stems from the very definition of governance, which '(1) describes the process of governmental decision-making and (2) the manner in which decisions are put into practice' (Haynes, chapter 2). In our experience, the vast majority of literature on civil-military relations focuses on the strategic policy level – what the politicians have decided; very little attention is paid to the mechanics of how those decisions are subsequently implemented, or the reasons why they are not. As a Ghanaian civil servant once said, 'In Ghana we are fabulous at formulating policy, but lousy at implementing it.' This critique could be applied to a range of countries in Central and Eastern Europe (CEE), South America and South Asia, indeed any country which has had to conform to conditions set by international financial institutions (IFIs), international organizations (IOs), or donor states, but which has never generated its own internal motors for reform. If good governance, or at least better governance, is to be achieved, however, then a range of management expertise and tools will need to be brought to bear.

We do not wish to prescribe a particular model of governance or management within this volume for there is sufficient evidence around the world that prescriptions from external actors are foolhardy at best, significantly damaging to fledgling democracies at worst. Proposals for reform must be desired, designed and owned by those who will initiate and be subject to them. The purpose of this book is to highlight certain considerations and introduce particular concepts and methods which may prove useful in the reform of the defence sector. Within this volume, the defence sector is taken to include the armed forces, civil servants, defence industries and agencies (whether in public or private ownership) and their political leaders.

Commonalities and constraints

We understand that history, culture, economics, geopolitical position and the intervention of external actors, whether they are other states or international financial institutions, have a bearing on the political and defence structures and procedures which are established in democratizing states. Nevertheless, whether a state is moving away from a communist or military regime there are certain issues which repeatedly come to the fore. The most common problems evidenced are:

- a form of civil-military relations which is confrontational rather than cooperative;
- the assumption that regime and state security are synonymous;
- a legislature which has the power to check the executive in theory, but not in practice;
- defence policies which are either antiquated or absent;
- civil-servants who are unable to provide objective direction or meaningful support to decision-makers because they have been either politicized or militarized;
- distrust of and amongst politicians, the military, civil servants, the media and civil society itself.

That being the case, the aims of this book are to increase security literacy amongst those responsible for the delivery of security; to encourage ownership of existing systems and proposed changes to them, and of the means of managing the change process as well as the new systems.

As a result of the growing globalization of governance and security, most countries recognize that they need to ensure greater oversight and accountability of their defence and security related activities. They are hampered in doing so, however, by a lack of political direction or will, inappropriate institutional designs, hostile political and organizational cultures, and a lack of resources.

Overcoming these shortfalls requires clear strategic direction articulated within an appropriate policy framework. Without external guidance, however, many countries struggle to formulate their policy architecture. Although external assistance may be available, it may not always be appropriate, especially when there is no local ownership of the proposals. Two examples, one from Eastern Europe and the other from West Africa, serve to illustrate this point. In the first case an analysis of the security sector and environment was conducted by a US sponsored academic institution. On the basis of that analysis, a proposal for restructuring the defence sector was put forward, and was, in turn, accepted by the generals and politicians of the recipient state. Those responsible for implementing the proposal, colonels and civil servants alike, believed it to be unworkable, because it was relevant for a defence sector the size of that in the United States, not one serving a population of just over three million. A second externally conducted analysis confirmed the conclusions of those who opposed the programme, but to no avail; the military and political elite persisted with the plan because it had been sanctioned by the United States.

There are now concerns that meaningful defence reform will be delayed indefinitely.

In the West African case, a private security firm advocated a new structure for ministerial responsibility for defence. Although initially adopted, it was subsequently deemed to run counter to the broader political culture and system. As a result, yet another reform process, this time internally generated, is under way.

Even the most clearly articulated policy will prove pointless unless it can be effectively implemented and reviewed. Not only is political will required, but so is the infrastructure of implementation, the civil service. As will be discussed in the following chapters, the appointment of civilians is both a political and management issue. To date, for many CEE states the appointment of civilians in positions of responsibility has worsened, rather than improved, the governance of defence, because these individuals are not professional civil servants, but political appointees, whose allegiance is to their sponsor, not to the state or the institution. If civilians are to be effective contributors in the management of defence then they must be appropriately selected and integrated into the system. This brings to the fore issues concerning the formulation of clear plans and objectives; of organizing resources, including people; of organizational design and authority; information sharing, change management and performance measurement, issues discussed in the latter half of this book.

Traditionally, public sector organizations have been administered rather than managed (Hood 1995), so that even with changes in the political and economic environment, management related skills and knowledge are not necessarily widespread. Effective management is, however, particularly important for three reasons. First, public sector activities consume vast resources that must be financed through public funds (taxation) and which must, therefore, be used to maximum effect. Second, in serving the interests of the whole community (rather than a relatively small group of owners, workers and customers), policy makers and managers have to consider a wide and diverse set of interests, which makes their work complex. As a result, and third, activities within the public sector have a high profile (especially through the mass media), which means that the work of public sector managers is probably more closely scrutinized than that of managers working in commercial companies. If the purpose of the defence sector is not properly defined through doctrine and policy, managerial work becomes even more complicated, as the sector may be used to further other political aims such as reducing unemployment or improving education.

This is particularly so in the defence arena which is capable of consuming massive resources. Defence is a little like an umbrella which is not needed unless it is raining but is a necessity as soon as the rain comes. Defence spending during peacetime is contentious because it diverts attention and resources from other important functions but, if international relations break down, people and equipment must be ready. The task of defence managers, then, is to ensure that all necessary resources are ready for an event that no-one wants to happen. This means that: equipment must be acquired, maintained and stored; that people are recruited and trained, that structures and procedures are in place, and that all are fit for their purpose and kept at readiness. Such activities do not normally happen within the battlespace where, arguably, leadership is more important. Most defence management occurs during peacetime or away from the battlefields, in what may be described as business-space, where defence managers must interact with the rest of the public sector and with private enterprise.

Management is as old as civilization itself. It is an important function that is carried out by most people, to some degree, for much of the time. This does not mean, though, that management is an inborn ability. Effective management requires specialist skills and knowledge that have to be, and can be, learned (Mintzberg 2004), often through experience and for some by more formal education. Where skills can be learned, they can be transferred between people and places (they are *portable*). The blending of specialist management knowledge with the professional, or technical, skills of defence experts can make a powerful combination for ensuring that the defence sector performs effectively and efficiently.

Management is about making plans and getting things done through the appropriate use of resources, people as well as materials. It is relevant in all spheres of human activity and in all organizations, but must adapt to varying needs and circumstances. The knowledge set that underpins management practices is a mixture of both art and science that are brought into focus by experience (Mintzberg 2004). Probably as a result of world events during the first half of the twentieth century, defence issues were a primary influence on management education, as was the legacy of military careers. Principles such as 'unity of command' and *esprit de corps* were taken up by early classical theorists. Later, the word, strategy, also entered managers' vocabularies but, like many other familiar terms, the basic idea was taken up and altered subtly to meet the needs of commerce and the private sector. Hence, military people can easily overestimate their understanding of management thinking. However, the transferability (or portability) of knowledge and skills is particularly important for public sector organizations, as it means that they can learn from the private, or commercial, sphere and apply that knowledge to their own work.

It is not sufficient, though, to pick up one of the thousands of 'How To Do Management' books that are available in bookshops, railway stations and airports around the world. Simply reading another's thoughts is neither professional nor useful; it simply leads to organizations following the latest trend or fad. There is no panacea for organizational problems, neither is there a single best way to do management. Similarly, systems, procedures or processes that are implemented to manage defence in the United Kingdom or United States may not be the best solution for, say African or

South Asian states, which operate within different cultures or have another view of the defence task. What is helpful is to know that there are various means to manage defence and, through the *critical* application of knowledge and experience, to devise methods for the particular situation that needs managing.

Public sector organizations are vast, complex entities that are easily able to consume more resources than are available to them. The traditional view was that they should be well-administered, following policy directives from government, in order to deliver what politicians asked of them. But administration only maintains systems; it does not allow adjustment to meet changing demands nor initiatives to improve performance.

Managing defence in a democracy: an overview

Jeff Haynes discusses the eight major principles of governance, adherence to which will improve the likelihood that policy directives are appropriate and can be followed. He argues, in Chapter 2, that public institutions have three functions: (1) to conduct public affairs; (2) to manage public resources; and, (3) to guarantee the realization of a range of human rights. His treatment of this subject establishes the framework for the discussions in subsequent chapters. Laura Cleary, *et al.*, in chapters three through seven, concentrate on the ways in which the principles of good governance can be operationalized. As noted above, good governance requires vigilance and action, which goes beyond policy pronouncements and empty rhetoric. As Sadako Ogata and Roméo Dallaire have poignantly argued in their respective writings on the genocide in Rwanda, good intentions are frequently undermined by an inability or failure to commit resources. A complaint frequently heard in developing democracies concerns the quality or absence of leadership. This may well be the case in some countries; more frequently, however, it is the absence of management which is the real problem.

The theme of leadership is one which pervades this book. Laura Cleary first raises it in Chapter 3, which concerns the political direction of defence. Alex Alexandrou and Roger Darby, and Derrick Neal give it further consideration in their chapter on Human Resource Management. Within Chapter 3, Dr Cleary builds upon the principles of participation and consensus identified by Haynes as crucial factors in good governance, arguing that if the armed forces are to truly serve the national interest then the nation must be engaged in determining that interest and the best means of achieving it.

Defining the national interest is a precursor to devising a defence policy. As David Chuter argues in Chapter 4, defence policy should provide top level guidance to public servants as to the purpose, structure and deployment of the armed forces. That policy provides a benchmark against which subsequent policies and actions can be made and against which individuals and institutions can be held to account.

The issues of transparency and accountability are the focal point of Chapter 5. Cleary argues that in many political systems it is difficult, if not impossible, to achieve accountability at all levels of government at all times. One significant reason is that the methods of ensuring accountability may have exceedingly high transaction costs which reduce the efficiency and effectiveness of individuals and directorates. In many transitional democracies this situation is compounded by a number of factors pertaining to organizational structures and procedures, and systems of information sharing.

Chapter 6 focuses on that group of individuals with the greatest potential to act as the 'switchmen of history' (Quaglia 2005: 545). The destiny of a nation can take significantly different courses depending upon whether civil servants are for or against particular policies. Despite their significance for policy formation and implementation, the role of the civil servant is generally ignored in the literature on defence reform. Chuter and Cleary examine the ideal role for the civil servant in the governance and management of defence as well as the constraints under which they normally operate.

Trevor Taylor, in Chapter 7, examines the institution in which civilian and military personnel may coalesce in the governance and management of defence: the ministry of defence. As he points out, ministries of defence vary in size, staffing and organization; nevertheless they generally perform the same essential functions.

In many ways, drawing any sort of distinction between governance and management is artificial for they are each part of the same process. However, readers will notice a shift of emphasis in the second part of the book which turns to the practicalities of management, emphasizing how these might be applied within the defence sector. The various authors offer a series of guidelines and make reference to examples of good practice from around the world. Even in the twenty-first century, however, the knowledge base that underpins management thinking is largely a product of industrialization and manufacture; a fact which limits the scope to be truly international in those examples.

Teri McConville (Chapter 8) uses the five basic functions of management: planning, organizing, commanding, co-ordinating and controlling; as a basis for exploring the range of issues with which managers must deal on a daily basis. She sets these within the context of what is (still) known as New Public Management – a concept which emphasizes the portability of management knowledge and the need to concentrate managerial efforts on outputs, and which presents a series of challenges for the proper use of resources.

The first of these challenges, as they are presented here, is for careful and realistic planning, in the form of strategy. In Chapter 9 Derrick Neal shows how this military idea has been transformed to provide a systematic approach that can guide organizational activities. He demonstrates techniques for analyzing the environment, both within and beyond an organization, and suggests that plans need to identify factors that will indicate the success, or otherwise of plans. The implementation of plans comes later (Chapter 15), for that is a matter of managing change.

The best plans start with good information and, as Annie Maddison argues in Chapter 10, that has always been an important resource but is becoming increasingly more so. Information needs to be managed because it is expensive to collect and needs careful preparation if people are not to be overloaded with unnecessary information, which is a real possibility with advances in communications technology. Of course, advances in network-enabled (or network-centric) capability makes information management especially pertinent to the military but that is not the concern here. Rather, Maddison shows the management of information as a process. She guides the reader through the various stages in that process, to ensure that people have the information that they need, in the format that they require, in a timely fashion.

Possibly the most important resource for any organization, in defence or elsewhere, is the people within it. Alex Alexandrou and Roger Darby (Chapter 11) introduce some of the key ideas that have, in recent years, transformed the ways that people are managed in the workplace. They argue that labour is not simply an unavoidable expense; rather that people, as the primary resource for quality, innovation and value, need to be managed in a way that is coherent with organizational strategy and culture. In accordance with the theme of good governance Alexandrou and Darby also explore the human side of enterprise in terms of leadership, values and empowerment.

All public sector services are resource-intensive. Defence is no different, and the drive for value for money means that looking after the finances, and other resources, is imperative. Managing finances is, for many, a daunting task, possibly due to a lack of understanding of the terminology and the ways in which financial reporting can yield so much useful information. Len Nockles and Teri McConville offer a gentle introduction to the topic in Chapter 12. Theirs is not an academic account of theories of financial management. Rather, it is a familiarization with the terminology, used by finance specialists, and some of the key topics that need to be understood for careful management of money, or for communicating with others over financial matters.

Trevor Taylor approaches the challenge of acquisition, in Chapter 13, by taking the reader through the overall concept and outlining the most important tasks. He gives four basic messages. First, is the need to link defence acquisition with capability. Second, from the beginning of the cycle the whole process, which includes final disposal, must be thought through. Acquisition involves multiple agenda, so third, close teamwork is needed. Finally, Taylor notes that the acquisition of defence equipment is, too often, linked with corrupt practices. It is transparency, diligence and courage that can overcome that, to deliver the military capability that a state needs.

As we move from careful administration into professional management, another new challenge for the defence sector, aligning with the value for money concept, is that of performance management. In Chapter 14, Sylvie Jackson makes the case for careful measuring, reporting and management of organizational performance. In particular, Jackson introduces the versatile Balanced Scorecard which has been used to good effect in both the US Department of Defense and the UK Ministry of Defence (MoD). This is a tool to align targets with strategy, and to monitor, report and predict progress. Its strength lies in an adaptability that transcends the normal managerial barriers of cultures and systems

The defence environment of the twenty-first century is characterized by uncertainty and turbulence. Perhaps, then, the greatest challenge to defence managers is to enable and lead the process(es) of change. Building upon his earlier chapter, Derrick Neal, presents some of the most widely accepted ideas and techniques in Chapter 15. In particular he notes how managers have a tendency to concentrate on systems and structures and to overlook the softer, people-related, issues; which can doom any plan to failure. Managing change effectively needs strong leadership to capture peoples' values and enthusiasm – something that holds true whether it is an organization, or entire country, that needs to be guided forward.

Throughout this volume, our intention is to address the most pressing concerns for the democratic development and effective management of the defence sector. We appreciate that our readers are experts in their own fields but realize that they may not have been exposed previously to the breadth of ideas within the spheres of international relations or management. The various authors, also experts in their own fields, have tried to present a range of possible solutions and examples in a manner which is clear but not over-simplified, and which is relevant in multiple circumstances. (We are bound to point out that any views expressed are the authors' own and do not represent the stance of any government, university or other institution.) If you, the reader, were to take but one lesson form this book, we hope that it will be that, in the words of one defence advisor, 'there is another way of doing things'.

Notes

1 Throughout this text the term security services will be understood to encompass the police, gendarmerie, border guards and custom officials; essentially all those responsible for domestic security.
2 The security sector is said to encompass all those institutions and agencies noted above, plus the armed forces, and the judicial and penal services. It also incorporates those elements of the public sector responsible for the exercise of the state monopoly of coercive power, which include the elected and duly appointed civil authorities responsible for the management and control of the security forces,

such as the executive government, the relevant ministries, the parliament and its specialized committees. Security Sector Reform is aimed at the efficient and effective provision of state and human security within a framework of democratic governance. (Heiner Hängii 2004: 2–3).

3 Security is generally a contested concept (Buzan 1991) and the concept of human security is no different. In its broadest sense it can be understood to encompass all aspects of human development such as economic, food, health and environmental insecurity. Other issues frequently incorporated under the heading of human security include the use of anti-personnel landmines, small arms and light weapons, child soldiers, and the trafficking in women (Hängii 2004: 2).

4 Samuel Finer argued that in certain political cultures, in which there is some doubt as to who and what constitutes the legal and moral authority that ought to be obeyed, there is an increased likelihood that the military will meddle in politics (Finer 1976; Sundhaussen 1998: 335).

Bibliography

Bulgaria (1998), *The National Security Concept of the Republic of Bulgaria*, Sofia: Ministry of Defence of the Republic of Bulgaria. www.mod.bg/en/koncepcii/national_security_concept.html (accessed 12 November 2005).

Buzan, Barry (1991), *Peoples, States and Fear*, Boulder, CO: Lynne Rienner.

Chuter, David (2000), *Defence Transformations*, Pretoria, RSA: Institute for Security Studies.

Colombia (2003), *The Defence Policy of Colombia*, Bogotá, Colombia: Ministerio de Defensa, www.mindefensa.gov.co (accessed 15 November 2005)

Dallaire, Roméo (2004), *Shake Hands with the Devil: The Failure of Humanity in Rwanda*, New York: Carroll & Graf Publishers.

Dandeker, Christopher and Freedman, Lawrence (2002), 'The British Armed Services', *The Political Quarterly*, 73 (4): 465–75.

de Tocqueville, Alexis (2000), *Democracy in America*, Chicago, IL: University of Chicago Press.

Finer, Samuel E. (1976), *The Man on Horseback: The Role of the Military in Politics*, 2nd edn., Harmondsworth, Middlesex: Penguin.

Giddens, Anthony (1994), *Beyond Left and Right. The Future of Radical Politics*, Cambridge, MA: Polity Press.

Hängii, Heiner (2004), 'Conceptualising security sector reform and reconstruction', in Alan Bryden and Heiner Hängii (eds), *Reform and Reconstruction of the Security Sector*, Geneva: DCAF. www.dcaf.ch/publications/bm_ssr_yearbook2004.cfm (accessed 29 October 2005).

Henley, Jon (2005), 'Chirac admits riots reveal French malaise', *The Guardian* 15 November 2005, p. 17.

Hood, C. (1995), 'The "New Public Management" in the 1980s: variations on a theme', *Accounting, Organisations and Society* 20 (2/3): 93–109.

Huntington, Samuel (1957), *The Soldier and the State: The Theory and Politics of Civil-Military Relations*, Cambridge, MA: The Belknap Press of Harvard University Press.

Janowitz, Morris (1961), *The Professional Soldier: A Social and Political Portrait*, Glencoe, IL: The Free Press.

Kemp, K. W. and Hudlin, C. (1992), 'Civil supremacy over the military: its nature and limits', *Armed Forces and Society*, 19 (1): 6–27.

Luckham, Robin (1996), 'Faustian Bargains: democratic control over military and security establishments', in R Luckham and G White (eds), *Democratization in the South: The Jagged Wave*, Manchester: Manchester University Press.

Mintzberg, H. (2004), *Managers not MBAs*, London: Financial Times Prentice Hall.

Ogata, Sadako (2005), *The Turbulent Decade: Confronting the Refugee Crisis of the 1990s*, New York & London: W W Norton & Company, Inc.

Quaglia, Lucia (2005), 'Civil servants, economic ideas, and economic policies: Lessons from Italy', *Governance: An International Journal of Policy, Administration and Institutions*, 18 (4): 545–66.

Rose, Charlie (1994), 'Democratic control of the armed forces: a parliamentary role in Partnership for Peace', *NATO Review*, 5 (42): 13–19.

Schiff, Rebecca L. (1995), 'Civil-military relations reconsidered: a theory of concordance', *Armed Forces and Society*, 22 (1): 7–24.

Sherr, James (2001), *Security, Democracy and 'Civil Democratic Control' of Armed Forces in Ukraine* (G90), Sandhurst: Conflict Studies Research Centre.

Sundhaussen, Ulf (1998), 'The military: a threat to democracy?', *Australian Journal of Politics and History*, 4 (3): 329–49.

Tedesco, Laura (2000), 'La ñata contra el vidrio [nose against the window]: Urban violence and democratic governability in Argentina', *Bulletin of Latin American Research*, 19 (4): 527–45.

Weber, Max (1946/1958), *From Max Weber* (Translated and edited by H. H. Gerth and C. Wright Mills), New York: Galaxy.

Wren, D. A. (1994), *The Evolution of Management Thought*, New York: John Wiley & Sons.

2 The principles of good governance

Jeff Haynes

Good governance is important for countries at all stages of development. Our approach is to concentrate on those aspects of good governance that are most closely related to our surveillance over macroeconomic policies – namely, the transparency of government accounts, the effectiveness of public resource management, and the stability and transparency of the economic and regulatory environment for private sector activity.

(Michael Camdessus, IMF Managing Director, Address to the United Nations, 2 July 1997)

Introduction

The terms 'governance' and 'good governance' have become increasingly common in the development literature (Haynes 2005). As a concept, 'governance' has two key aspects: It (1) describes the process of governmental decision-making and (2) the manner by which decisions are put into practice (or, in some cases not put into practice). Theoretically, whatever the precise nature of the political system within which they function, public institutions have three functions: (1) conduct public affairs (2) manage public resources, and (3) guarantee the realization of a range of human rights. 'Good governance' succeeds in delivering these objectives in a manner and context that is (mostly) free of abuse and corruption and with due regard for the rule of law. Note, however, that 'good governance' is an ideal – difficult to achieve and to implement in its totality. There are two key dimensions to its implementation. On the one hand, good governance should be a primary internal goal of (preferably, democratically elected) governments. In addition, virtually all developing countries are dependent on various external actors for developmental inputs and, increasingly, such actors demand proof of the implementation of 'good governance' factors in order to begin or to continue to disburse developmental assistance.

Principles and practice of good governance: external factors

The impact of globalization implies that all governments – especially those in the developing world – must necessarily take into account what happens beyond the borders of their specific polity. Major donors and international financial institutions (IFIs), such as the European Union, World Bank and International Monetary Fund now fundamentally base aid and loan decisions on a key condition: recipient states must implement and be seen to implement political and social reforms informed by 'good governance' concerns.

The main factors in this regard included the International Monetary Fund, the World Bank and other leading international financial institutions' lending for economic structural adjustment, global resurgence of economic neo-liberalism, collapse of Eastern European communist regimes (which for decades offered an alternative development model), and, finally, the global rise of pro-democracy movements. Problematically, however, western actors' 'pushing for democracy as a component of good governance' seemed 'oblivious to how few of the conditions for democratic endurance exist[ed] in the 'Third World' . . . and what their implications for democracy might be' (Leftwich 1993: 607). As Leftwich notes, the World Bank's analysis in the 1990s that 'good governance' was an essential development for successful economic reforms in the countries of the developing world seemed to ignore the fact 'that good governance is not simply available on order, but requires a particular kind of politics both to institute and sustain it' (Leftwich 1993: 612).

To try to encourage the development of good governance, the IFIs sought to impose *conditionality*. This refers to overarching policy imperatives that demanded significant economic and political changes in a large number of developing countries in order to start or develop the characteristics of good governance. It is worth noting that principles of political conditionality were introduced into the development assistance of the Netherlands as early as 1979 (Sørensen 1993: 2), and incorporated by Canada and Scandinavian countries in the 1980s. Large-scale conditionality in development co-operation was launched in the economic realm when the structural adjustment programmes of the IFIs linked financial support to developing countries with demands to liberalize the economy, conduct a sound fiscal policy, and encourage free enterprise. Other actors not only adopted this approach but also applied conditionality to their requests for democratization and respect for human rights. In response to these policies the World Bank proclaimed that 'good governance' was a prerequisite for development (World Bank 2004). As a means to spread liberal democracy to the developing world, however, the imperatives of political conditionality were often treated with scepticism, seen largely in terms of potential or actual risks and pitfalls (Sørensen 1993: 5). It is necessary to tailor the approaches of conditionality to the political situation of individual countries – in order to optimize its impact. Even the earlier austerity programmes of the IFIs shook many authoritarian systems, as they now lacked resources to buy acquiescence from key actors in state and society. Hence these programmes can be seen as paving the way for subsequent liberalization movements, which should not obscure the fact that the very same programmes often inflicted much suffering on the poor in such countries.

For its part, the International Monetary Fund (IMF) has long provided advice and technical assistance with the goal of seeking to foster and develop characteristics of good governance, including the promotion of public sector transparency and accountability. Traditionally, the IMF's main focus has been to encourage developing countries to adopt policies designed to correct macroeconomic imbalances, reduce inflation, and undertake key trade, exchange, and other market reforms that the Fund judged were essential in order to improve governmental efficiency and lead to sustained economic growth. These goals are still highly important to the Fund, yet increasingly the IMF has found that a much broader range of primarily domestic institutional reforms would be needed if countries are to establish the conditions necessary for good governance, inspire and maintain private sector confidence and provide a sound basis for sustained economic growth and development.

Principles and practice of good governance: internal factors

When good governance is achieved, there are three outcomes:

- Corruption is minimalized;
- Decision makers listen to and take into account minority views;
- Decision-making processes and structures take into account the views and opinions of society's weakest and most vulnerable people.

Although an imprecise concept, principles and practices of good governance can be grouped in eight major characteristics:

- Participation
- Rule of law
- Transparency
- Responsiveness
- Consensus-orientated
- Equity and inclusiveness
- Effectiveness and efficiency
- Accountability.

Participation

- Participation involves both women and men;
- Participation can either be direct or through legitimate intermediate institutions or representatives;

- Participation also implies, on the one hand, the existence of an unfragmented civil society and, on the other, more general freedoms of association and expression.

Participation involves consultation in the development of policies and decision-making, elections and other democratic processes. It gives governments access to important information about the needs and priorities of individuals, communities and private businesses. Governments that involve the public will be in a better position to make good decisions, and decisions will enjoy more support once taken. While there may not be direct links between participation and every aspect of good governance, accountability, transparency and participation are reinforced by developing fully democratic political systems.

Recognized forms of participation include those available via *political society* and *civil society*. Stepan defines political society as the 'arena in which the polity specifically arranges itself for political contestation to gain control over public power and the state apparatus', notably parliament and political parties (Stepan 1988: 3). Linz and Stepan (1996) regard a strong and independent political society as crucial for the development of good governance. The situation is characterized by certain types of interaction among political actors, competing legitimately to exercise the right to control power and the state apparatus.

To develop and embed good governance, it is necessary to construct – or reconstruct if there has been a previous democratic experience – core political institutions: elections, electoral rules, political parties, political leadership, inter-party alliances, and legislatures. In the developing world, some recent democratic transitions have taken place in circumstances where previous democracy institutions had been demolished, while in other cases, some appropriately democratic institutions had been maintained during a period of authoritarian rule. Karl (1991), in arguing that the second scenario should offer a better outlook for the development of good governance than the first, emphasizes the advantages for a country that has retained some democratic mechanisms against one that introduces them *de novo*. Some observers suggest that only countries – for example, most Latin American nations had democratic regimes at some time in the past – that previously experienced democratic rule would be capable of developing the structures and processes of good governance now. This is because democratically relevant intermediate structures and democratic routines can crucially aid the re-emergence of earlier alliances among political parties and civil society organizations, as well as aid the return to the political scene of interest groups, unions and other important organizations whose involvement in the development of good governance institutions is crucial. In addition, a prior democratic experience may encourage the mass of ordinary people to believe that, once democracy is (re)instituted, then future political decisions would broadly be in accord with democratic norms. However, such a view would condemn polities that have not experienced democracy to an unremitting undemocratic future, one where good governance is very unlikely to develop.

Political parties

The chances of developing good governance structures and processes, Sartori (1991) argues, are bolstered when there are relatively few, not ideologically polarized, parties. In addition, autonomous, democratically organized, political parties can help to keep the personal power aspirations of political leaders in check – a crucial component of the conditions for good governance. Morlino (1998) argues that such political parties are a crucial key to good governance in the developing world, especially when a pervasive sense of legitimacy does not prevail during democratic transition from authoritarian rule. Morlino also contends that the more rapidly the party spectrum forms during transition, then the more likely is eventual democratic consolidation and good governance. When party systems become institutionalized in this way, parties typically orient themselves towards the goal of winning elections through choate appeals to voters. But when the party structure is only slowly or indeterminently established, then citizens may respond better to personalistic appeals from populist leaders rather than to those of parties. This scenario tends to favour the former who may attempt to govern without bothering to establish and develop solid institutions underpinning their rule. The point is that institutionalizing party systems matters a great deal as they are much more likely to help sustain democracy and to promote effective – and good – governance than the alternative: amorphous party systems dominated by populist leaders. An institutionalized party system can help engender confidence in the democratic process in four main ways. First, it can help moderate and channel societal demands into an institutionalized environment of conflict resolution. For example, in both India and Costa Rica, the party system helped, over time, to prevent the 'landed upper class[es] from using the state to repress protests' (Rueschemeyer, *et al.* 1992: 281). Second, it can serve to lengthen the time horizons of actors because it provides electoral losers with the means periodically to mobilize resources for later rounds of political competition. Third, an effective party system can help prevent disenchanted groups' grievances from spilling over into mass street protests, likely to antagonize elites and their military allies and help facilitate a return to authoritarian rule ('the need for strong government'). Finally, an effective party system, linked to a capable state, can be important in helping imbue the mass of ordinary people with the idea that the political system is democratically accountable.

Civil society

It is often suggested that a robust civil society is crucial for the development of political systems characterized by good governance. Although now a very common term in the relevant literature, in fact the expression, 'civil society', crept largely unexamined into the literature on democracy and good governance in the 1980s, influencing the discourses of many leaders of movements for political reform. While there are many conceptions of civil society and its relationship with the state, Stepan's (1988) is useful. He defines civil society as the arena where social groups and movements – including, community associations, women's groups, religious bodies, and various professional organizations (lawyers, journalists, trade unions, entrepreneurs and so on) – express themselves and seek to advance their interests vis-à-vis the state, challenging the latter's tendency to seek ever greater amounts of power. In short, according to Stepan, civil society, comprising organizations that both limit and legitimate state power, functions as the citizen's curb on the power of the state and its tendency to try to dominate. When institutions and supporting bodies comprising civil society are strong enough to keep the state within substantive and procedural confinement then the chances of good governance developing are more likely to be enhanced than in their absence. Strong civil societies nearly always stem from strong societies. Risse-Kappen argues that 'strong societies' are characterized by a comparative lack of ideological and class cleavages, by rather 'politicized' civil societies which can be easily mobilized for political causes, and by centralized social organizations such as business, labor or churches' (Risse-Kappen 1995: 22).

On the other hand, when civil society organizations are collectively weak it will be easy for the state to incarcerate, co-opt or buy off troublesome leaders and activists opponents. Under such circumstances, the state will 'shape, define, create or suppress civil society and popular reactions hereto' (Manor 1991: 5); while the chances of developing good governance are significantly reduced.

In sum, the political effectiveness of civil society is linked to: (1) its cohesiveness, a factor that depends on the nature and extent of extant class, ideological, ethnic, and/or religious divisions; (2) a country's level of economic development (it is likely that, *ceteris paribus*, the more modernized a country, then the more likely it is to have a strong civil society); and (3) how long a country has been independent. This is said to be important because it takes time to build up the power and organizational capacity of civil society. For example, civil societies tend to be more robust in Latin America than in Africa. States in the former region tend to be comparatively more modernized, richer and less societally polarized than in the latter.

Rule of law

- Good governance requires fair legal frameworks that are impartially enforced.
- Human rights are given full protection, including those of religious and ethnic minorities.

- It is crucial to have both an independent judiciary and an impartial police force, with a minimal role for corruption.

The rule of law refers to the institutional process of setting, interpreting and implementing laws and other regulations. It means that decisions taken by government must be founded in law and that private firms and individuals are protected from arbitrary decisions. For the rule of law to be present also requires a form of governance that is free from distortionary incentives – through corruption, nepotism, patronage or capture by narrow private interest groups; guarantees property and personal rights; and achieves some sort of social stability. This provides a degree of reliability and predictability that is essential for firms and individuals to take good decisions.

The rule of law does not imply that the more specific the regulations are the better. This is because excessive specification can lead to rigidities and risk of selective application of laws and regulations. Interpretation and effective implementation of individual laws will require an informed degree of discretion. This discretion can be counterbalanced by administrative procedure, legislation and external reviews of decisions (appeal mechanisms, judicial review, ombudsmen, and so on).

Reliability and predictability require a certain degree of political stability. Governments need to be able to make credible commitments and persuade the private sector that decisions will not ultimately be reversed due to political uncertainty. While this is not necessarily related to a particular political system in the short term, over the longer term democracy enhances stability by giving a voice to citizens to express their preferences through an open competition.

The rule of law is intimately connected to protection of all citizens' human rights. Emerson suggested 30 years ago that most governments in the developing world then routinely abused large numbers of their citizens' human rights. He noted that the

> intricate set of provisions outlawing arbitrary arrest or detention, asserting the right of anyone arrested or detained to take proceedings before a court, and seeking to guarantee humane treatment, presumption of innocence till proved guilty, and fair and speedy trial are remote from a world in which...preventive detention without right of access to any court is a standard part of the procedure. In much of the Third World...recourse to torture is so common as to attract little attention.
>
> (1975: 207)

Writing more recently, Jackson portrayed a similarly bleak picture of widespread human rights abuses in the developing world, with many governments posing a serious threat to their citizens' well-being (Jackson 1990: 139).

Underlining such accounts, independent non-governmental organizations (NGOs) devoted to human rights, such as Amnesty International and Human Rights Watch, have long catalogued myriad examples of human rights abuses in every developing region. In their annual reports, they typically note: political prisoners, abductions, arbitrary detentions, beatings, torture, political killings, massacres, terror, disappearances, refugees, death squads and wanton destruction of people's livelihood.

Good governance necessarily implies an appropriate human rights regime. Like many other aspects of the development of good governance in the developing world, international developments have interacted with domestic factors in relation to improved human rights regimes in many countries. For years, millions of people in developing countries were forced to live under unelected governments, often characterized by brutal and wholesale violations of human rights, said by the governments to be justified in the name of national security and the collective good. Over time, however, democratic and economic struggles in many countries, especially in some Latin American and Asian countries, not only encouraged the growth of stronger civil societies but also provided focus for demands for wider change, including better human rights and, by extension, better governance structures and processes.

Regarding external factors, we can note the importance of various external factors encouraging better human rights regimes in developing countries. The end of the Cold War in 1989 and associated international changes significantly altered the global picture in this regard. What was the specific impact upon human rights observance in the developing world? Given the current importance attached to concepts like 'democracy' and 'good governance', it might be expected that there would be a new set of conditions more favourable to increased respect for human rights after the Cold War. At this time, two of the most pressing issues for many people in the developing world were a lack of democracy and insufficient economic growth. Each is associated with a basic human right: the right to choose one's government and the right to have a sufficiency to live on ('freedom from want'). In the 1980s and 1990s, these two issues became central to political debates and economic struggles throughout the developing world. Important in this regard was the fact that increasing numbers of governments were democratically elected, while both domestic groups in civil society, as well as international human rights NGOs focused their considerable attention on what governments around the world were doing in relation to protecting and enhancing their citizens' human rights. As Bealey put it: 'Any country's claim that the way it treats its subjects is no one else's business has now become a relic of a past age' (Bealey 1999: 141). The overall result was that it became less easy than before for many governments routinely to deprive their citizens of basic human rights and, thus, it was possible to see progress in a key indicator of good governance.

Transparency

- Accepted and implemented rules and regulations govern how decisions are taken, put into practice and enforced.
- Information is freely available to all, especially those who will be affected by such decisions and their enforcement.

Transparency is an important aspect of good governance. This is because transparent decision-making is critical for the development of a sense that what government does is rooted in the preferences of its citizens. Moreover, accountability and the rule of law require openness and good information so that higher levels of administration, external reviewers and the general public can verify performance and governmental compliance to the dictates of law (see Chapter 5). In addition, governments have access to a vast amount of important information and the dissemination of this information through transparent and open information systems can provide specific and significant information that private sector firms and individuals need to have to be able to make good decisions. For example, capital markets depend on information openness.

Linz and Stepan (1996) argue that good governance does not depend on electoral results *per se*; but rather requires a particular, institutionalized form of democracy with popularly accepted and implemented rules and regulations that govern how decisions are taken, put into practice and enforced. This situation is characterized by a procedural system with open political competition, freely competing multi-parties, and an impressive array of civil and political rights – guaranteed by law. Political accountability is crucial, and operates primarily via the electoral relationship between voters and their representatives. For Linz and Stepan, a regime characterized by popularly accepted and implemented rules and regulations comprises *behavioural, attitudinal* and *constitutional* aspects. First, *behaviourally*, such a situation is said to be in place when 'no significant national, social, economic, political, or institutional actors spend significant resources attempting to achieve their objectives by creating a nondemocratic regime or turning to violence or foreign intervention to secede from the state'. Second, *attitudinally*, when most citizens believe that democratic procedures and institutions are the best means 'to govern [their] collective life'; and where support for 'antisystem alternatives is quite small or more or less isolated from the pro-democratic forces'. Third, *constitutionally*, 'governmental and non-governmental forces become subjected to, and habituated to, the resolution of conflict within the specific laws, procedures, and institutions sanctioned by the new democratic process' (Linz and Stepan 1996: 6). In sum, for Linz and Stepan, good governance amounts to the institutionalization of democratic practices and processes, characterized by a robust regime of appropriate rules, regulations, and opportunities for private citizens and organizations alike. It is in place when the great majority of political actors and citizens concur that such an arrangement is the only acceptable way to resolve societal conflicts.

Responsiveness

- Institutions and processes try to serve all stakeholders within a reasonable timeframe.

Good governance requires appropriate institutional mechanisms – that is, established procedures and organizations – to promote a good level of government responsiveness. First, there are formal political institutions – that is, permanent edifices of public life, such as, laws, organizations, public offices, elections, and so on – found in virtually all countries. Second, there are various informal institutions that also affect outcomes, including the 'dynamics of interests and identities, domination and resistance, compromise and accommodation' that may run parallel or counter to formal democratic ones (Bratton and van de Walle 1997: 276). It is the interaction of these various institutions that help determine the outcome of democratic consolidation in a polity. The relative weight of these factors, as well as the factors themselves, will differ from country to country.

Consensus orientation, equity and inclusiveness

- Ensuring that all members of society feel that they have a stake in governance; no one is excluded.
- It requires that all groups, especially the most vulnerable, have clear opportunities to try to maintain or improve their societal and developmental positions.
- Need of mediation of the different interests in society to reach a broad consensus in society regarding what is in the best interest of the whole community and how this can be achieved.
- It also requires a long-term perspective for sustainable human development and how to achieve it.

When a privileged elite minority is perceived to consume an inappropriate proportion of available resources then popular satisfaction with governance may fall or fail to develop satisfactorily. To avert this, it helps if governments preside over sustained economic growth and convince the mass of people that it is shared with *relative* equity. Przeworsjki *et al*'s (1996) comprehensive survey of evidence – covering 1950–90 – suggests that chances of good governance developing increase when a government: (1) manages to develop its country's economy in a sustained fashion; and (2) gradually, yet consistently, manages to reduce socio-economic inequalities via effective welfare policies.

Linz and Stepan (1996) argue that increasing welfare expenditures played a central role, from the mid-1970s, in the process of development of good governance in three Southern European then – democratizing countries: Spain, Portugal and Greece. Their governments increased tax revenues that, in part, were used to expand social policies and enhance societal welfare. Przeworski (1986) claims that the maintenance of an adequate system of public assistance has a positive influence on good governance as it both reduces the inequalities among different social groups (a factor said to promote democratic collapse) and can help curb social unrest. However, many recent democratic transitions in Latin America, Asia and Africa were informed by economic crisis. It was often difficult under circumstances of societally painful economic reforms to introduce or maintain effective social policies to protect those whose subsistence was threatened.

Evidence for the political efficacy of sustained policies to reduce economic inequality come from India and Botswana. India, a democracy for nearly 60 years, is said to have certain complex conditions facilitating the survival of 'the institutional legacy of post-colonial democracy' (Rueschemeyer, Stephens and Stephens 1992: 24–5). Mitra suggests that of particular importance in helping maintain support for the democratic system was the 'steady and substantial improvements in the physical quality of life' for most Indians (Mitra 1992: 10–11). India's example suggests that the chances of good governance developing are enhanced when there is a conscious attempt to share out national wealth with a concern for ameliorating the plight of the poor via welfare and taxation policies. In addition, in Botswana, a rare example of an African consolidated democracy, 'the egalitarian impact of government expenditure [was] a means of consolidating support for the political system' (Thomas 1994: 76).

In sum, chances of good governance appear to be linked to: (1) sustained economic growth, relatively equitably spread, even if it starts from a low base and (2) governmental focus, via welfare policies, to ameliorate the plight of the poor and underprivileged and, as a result, develop a broad consensus in society regarding what is in the best interest of the whole community and how this can be achieved.

Effectiveness and efficiency

- Processes and institutions produce results that meet the needs of society while making the best use of resources at their disposal.
- It also means sustainable use of natural resources and the protection of the environment.

Environmental problems first emerged as a contentious global issue in the 1970s, becoming a focus of societal concerns in many countries. The first formal awareness of the international dimension of environmental issues was the United Nations Conference on the Human Environment held in

Stockholm in 1972 (Vogler 2001: 192). The conference, attended by 113 countries, drew up 26 principles calling upon all governments to co-operate in protecting and improving the natural environment. During the 1980s Stockholm's message was reinforced by a series of developments, including the 1984 Bhopal (India) disaster, when an explosion at a factory producing toxic chemicals killed more than 4 000 people; a near-meltdown of the nuclear reactor at Chernobyl, Ukraine, in 1986; the destruction of forests in Europe due to acid rain; an expanding hole in the ozone layer and consequential skin cancers; pollution of the seas and over-fishing; and global warming, threatening the existence of many low-lying countries and islands. The overall result was that the 1980s became known as the 'decade of the discovery of the environment'.

Consequently, the relationship between people's social and economic demands and the natural environment began, for the first time, to be discussed in a serious and scientific way. The 1992 United Nations-sponsored 'Earth Summit' held in Rio de Janeiro, Brazil, was a tangible sign of growing global concern. More than 100 heads of state and 30 000 bureaucrats and representatives of non-governmental organizations attended. They discussed 24 *million* pages of preparatory documents and sought to make wide-ranging decisions regarding the future of the global environment. The Earth Summit was called specifically to confront two pressing, inter-linked problems: environmental degradation and poverty and underdevelopment. Coming just after the end of the Cold War, there was expectation that relaxation of international tensions would facilitate progress on these issues. The Earth Summit produced Agenda 21, trumpeted as a plan of action to save the planet, and endorsed by representatives of all countries present. Agenda 21 was a compromise between, on the one hand, most Western states (claimed or actual promoters of environmental conservation) and, on the other, many developing countries (advocates of growth, sometimes with apparently scant regard for environmental protection).

Many developing country governments seemed ambivalent about the very principle of environmental protection, perhaps irritated by Western attempts to prescribe universal environmental standards and goals. Many governments claimed that the West's industrial development was the long-term result of often thoughtless environmental exploitation, both at home and in colonial possessions. As the West's development was the result of thorough environmental exploitation, why should that of the developing world be different? The West stood charged with hypocrisy on two counts: (1) concern with environmental protection was seen by many developing countries as a blatant attempt to prevent them from catching up developmentally by adopting the West's own tactics; and (2) while the West professed to deplore environmentally harmful policies, it strongly urged dozens of developing countries to open up their economies to foreign investment and increase exports of agricultural products and timber leading to more environmental damage.

Accountability

- Governmental institutions, as well as private sector and civil society organizations, must be accountable to the public and to their institutional stakeholders.
- In general organizations and institutions are accountable to those who will be affected by decisions or actions.

Accountability can be both an end in itself – representing democratic values – and a means towards the development of more efficient and effective organizations in the context of the development of good governance. Politicians and public servants are given enormous power through the laws and regulations they implement, resources they control and the organizations they manage. Accountability is a key way to ensure that this power is used appropriately and in accordance with the public interest. But accountability requires that there is: (1) clarity about who is accountable to whom for what and (2) a situation where civil servants, organizations and politicians are held accountable for their decisions and performance.

Accountability can be strengthened through formal reporting requirements and external scrutiny (such as an independent Audit Office, Ombudsmen, and so on). Democratic accountability, as represented by accountability of ministers to parliament and the parliament to voters, can be seen as an objective in itself, but it also strengthens accountability in general. Many countries are now seeking to strengthen accountability structures and processes through more focus on accountability for performance as opposed to limiting accountability to regularity of decisions (see Chapter 5).

Conclusion: relations between different aspects of good governance

It should be evident from the preceding discussion that there are complex relations between the different aspects of good governance. In many ways some factors can be seen as preconditions of others (e.g., technical and managerial competence is one precondition of organizational capacity, and organizational capacity is one precondition of maintaining the rule of law). But there are also important effects in the other direction (e.g., organizational capacity reinforces technical and managerial competence, accountability reinforces the rule of law). For these reasons, improving the quality of governance can often be viewed as a frustrating activity.

There is evidence to suggest that, despite the frustrations, a growing number of countries are trying to ensure improved governance across a range of public sector activities. Politicians in many developing states, however, remain loathe to apply the principles outlined above to the defence sector. There are a range of reasons for this attitude, but the two most common are as follows. First, in a time of radical political and economic change, elites may desire tranquillity in certain sectors in order to ensure the overall stability of the system. The military and police may be called upon to ensure stability, therefore they are made exempt from initial reforms. A second, alternative reason, is that the military establishment may have been an entity separate from the broader body politic. Therefore, new politicians and civilian administrators may lack the technical and managerial competence to broach the defence issue. A failure to address defence issues and to incorporate the military into wider reform and governance programmes can destabilize those efforts over the longer term. As will be argued in the following chapters, the principles of good governance outlined above can be applied, indeed need to be applied, within the defence context if the government of the day is to provide for the security of the people.

Questions to consider

1   What are the main characteristics of a regime characterized by good governance?
2   What are the main drawbacks to the implementation of good governance?
3   What is the balance between external and internal factors when trying to put into practice good governance?
4   Which are the key external actors in relation to good governance in the developing world?
5   How important is human rights observance to good governance?
6   How can religious and ethnic minorities ensure that they benefit from good governance?
7   What is accountability and why is it necessary for good governance?
8   What is the relationship between democracy and good governance?
9   Identify and compare two countries in the developing word that have achieved good governance in recent years.
10   Why have some countries made no progress in recent years in terms of improving governance?

Suggested reading

UNESCAP (2005) 'What is good governance', *United Nations Social Commission for Asia and the Pacific*, www.unescap.organisation/huset/gg/governance.htm, accessed on 1 August 2005.

United Nations Development and Governance Division 'Corruption and Good Governance', *Discussion Paper 3*, United Nation Development and Governance Division, www.magnet.undp.org/Docs/efa/corruption3/corruption3.pdf, accessed on 1 August 2005.

World Bank (2004) *Governance Research Indicator Country Snapshot (GRICS)*, info.worldbank.org/governance/kkz2004/sc_chart.asp, accessed on 1 August 2005.

Bibliography

Bealey, F. (1999) *The Blackwell Dictionary of Political Science*, Oxford: Blackwell.

Bratton, M. and van de Walle, N. (1997) *Democratic Experiments in Africa*, Cambridge: Cambridge University Press.

Emerson, R. (1975) 'The fate of human rights in the Third World', *World Politics*, 27 (2): 205–20.

Haynes, J. (ed.) (2005) *Palgrave Advances in Development Studies*, Houndmills: Palgrave Macmillan.

Jackson, R. (1990) *Quasi-states: Sovereignty, International Relations and the Third World*, Cambridge: Cambridge University Press.

Karl, T. (1991) 'El Salvador's negotiated revolution', *Foreign Affairs*, 70 (2): 147–64.

Leftwich, A. (1993) 'Governance, democracy and development in the Third World', *Third World Quarterly*, 14 (3): 605–24.

Linz, J. and A. Stepan (1996) *Problems of Democratic Transition and Consolidation. Southern Europe, South America, and Post-Communist Europe*, Baltimore and London: The Johns Hopkins University Press.

Mason, J. (1991) 'Introduction' in Manor, J. (ed.), *Rethinking Third World Politics*, Harlow: Longman, pp. 1–11.

Mitra, S. (1992) 'Democracy and political change in India', *The Journal of Commonwealth and Comparative Politics*, 30 (1): 9–38.

Morlino, L. (1998) *Democracy between Consolidation and Crisis. Parties, Groups, and Citizens in Southern Europe*, New York: Oxford University Press.

Przeworski, A., Alvarez, M., Cheibib, J. A. and Limongi, F. (1996) 'What makes democracies endure?' *Journal of Democracy*, 7 (1): 39–55.

Risse-Kappen, T. (1995) 'Bringing transnational relations back in: introduction', in T. Risse-Kappen (ed.), *Bringing Transnational Relations Back In*, Cambridge: Cambridge University Press, pp. 3–33.

Rueschemeyer, D., Stephens, E. and Stephens, J. (1992) *Capitalist Development and Democracy*, Cambridge: Polity.

Sartori, G. (1991) 'Rethinking democracy: bad policy and bad politics', *International Social Science Journal*, 129: 437–50.

Sørensen, G. (1993) *Democracy and Democratization*, Boulder, CO: Westview.

Stepan, A. (1988) *Rethinking Military Politics Brazil and the Southern Cone*, Princeton, NJ: Princeton University Press.

Thomas, A. (1994) *Third World Atlas*, 2nd ed., Buckingham: Open University Press.

Vogler, J. (2001) 'Environment', in B. White, R. Little and M. Smith (eds), *Issues in World Politics*, 2nd edn, Basingstoke: Palgrave, pp. 191–211.

3 Political direction

The essence of democratic, civil and civilian control

Laura R. Cleary

Introduction

Before a defence policy is formulated or resources allocated, two questions should be addressed:

- What is it that we seek to defend?
- Why do we wish to defend it?

The answers to these questions will be derived from a strategic analysis of the security environment, and they will inform decisions on force size, structure, mission and deployment. The answers to these questions, however, are also dependent upon there being a clear and shared understanding of the national interest.

The concept of the 'national interest' is vaguely defined within academic literature, and perhaps more vaguely articulated by political elites. British Prime Minister, Lord Palmerston (1856) once said,

> When people ask me...for what is called a policy, the only answer is that we mean to do what may seem to be best, upon each occasion as it arises, making the Interests of Our Country one's guiding principle.
> (Cited in Kissinger 1994: 95)

Some countries, like Ghana and Ethiopia, have attempted to fix their interest within a particular place and time by incorporating declarations of national interest within their constitutions, while others, like Bulgaria, have articulated that interest within the more flexible framework of organic law, such as the National Security Concept.

Although perceptions and methods of declaring the national interest may vary, they can generally be said to encompass what a state needs – security, economic well-being, and so forth – and what it aspires to become – a developed country, a regional power, the promoter of ideological preferences and so forth.

As David Chuter argues in the following chapter, the establishment of a national policy, that is, the national interest, should be a precursor to the articulation of foreign, security and defence policies. When a state does not have a clear understanding of the national interest then the actions it takes on the world stage can be viewed as *ad hoc* and may result in an increase in insecurity (Kissinger 1994: 170). Many developing democracies find it difficult to achieve consensus on the national interest. This may be because the state is involved in post-conflict reconstruction and is having to contend with broader issues of the reintegration of combatants. The immediate concern is to achieve consensus on what the state should be today; setting objectives for the future is deemed a longer-term priority. Alternatively, the state may be in transition from a form of authoritarianism. Such cases are generally marked by an explosion in the number of political movements and parties, which are typified by the promotion of single issues or the advancement of a politician's personal ambition. As we have seen in Central and Eastern Europe and in some of the republics of the former Soviet Union, it is impossible to achieve consensus on the national interest and defence issues until the number of political parties declines from hundreds to a handful, and those remaining begin to coalesce around broader national concerns. So long as a consensus on issues pertaining to the national interest does not exist, however, radical alterations in policy will be more likely when governments change. The tendency is for political parties to overturn the policies of their predecessors and thus assert their own authority, rather than pursue the public good. The determination of the national interest requires a degree of political leadership, where leadership is in part defined by the ability to encourage participation and achieve consensus; those same attributes of good governance identified by Jeff Haynes in Chapter 2.

A criticism frequently made by military officers in developing democracies pertains to the absence of quality leaders in the political realm, and thus to the lack of direction they receive in the formulation and implementation of foreign and defence policies. Within the remainder of this chapter characteristics of political leadership will be addressed as they relate to the political direction of defence.

Political leadership

At military academies and staff colleges around the world, officers learn their craft by studying the exploits and campaigns of past generals. Politicians do not receive the same kind of designated training and, even if they were to do so, there are few texts available to instruct them on how to become a good leader. There are, of course, classic texts such as Thucydides' *History of the Peloponnesian War* (1998) and Niccolò Machiavelli's *The Prince* (1961), but there are varying interpretations of the true significance of leadership in the former and Machiavelli has been castigated throughout the ages for his supposedly immoral prescriptions. Studies have been conducted of political leaders during war, and

Eliot Cohen's *Supreme Command* (2004) is a fine example of this type, but there are few works on what constitutes good political leadership of the defence sector during a period of peace.[1]

Increasingly, those interested in the subject are turning towards management texts for a definition of leadership, and while these have some utility, the management of a corporation and the leadership of a country pose rather different challenges. This is particularly true in the case of democratic states where there is an inherent tension when it comes to leaders. Voters may think that they are electing a 'leader' of their country when they cast a ballot for president or prime minister, but democracies based on the rule of law and consisting of a series of checks and balances are in fact designed to curb executive authority and thus the scope for leadership (Ruscio 2004).

Given their organizational design, what many democracies require are managers who have the *potential* to become leaders. It has been argued that, while the roles and functions of the manager and leader overlap, a distinction between the two can and should be drawn.

> *[M]anager* implies that authority has been formally granted to an individual by an organization. Management involves power (usually formal authority) bestowed on the occupant of a position by a higher organizational authority. With the power of management comes responsibility and accountability for the use of organizational resources. In contrast, *leader* implies effective use of influence that is rather independent of the authority granted to one because of position. Leadership cannot be bestowed upon a person by a higher authority. Effective managers also must be leaders, and many leaders become managers, but the two sets of rules and functions differ.
>
> (Ott *et al.* 2003: 30)

In the case of a democratic state, power is bestowed upon the occupant of an office, for example the president, by a higher organizational authority, the people in whom sovereignty resides. The office holder is thus responsible and accountable to the people for the use of organizational resources (see Chapter 5).

Developing democracies can be categorized as being in either a state of crisis or a state of reform. The leadership qualities required to deal with these conditions are vastly different and, as Boin and 't Hart (2003) argue, often incompatible. When a state is in crisis, whether that is because of economic failure, environmental disaster or inter or intra-state conflict, citizens demand that their leaders 'do something'. Note, for example, the criticism of the US President George W. Bush for his delayed response to the destruction of the city of New Orleans and the humanitarian disaster caused by Hurricane Katrina in 2005. Boin and 't Hart argue that public expectations of political leaders during a crisis generally exceed individual or institutional capacity to respond adequately to crisis. The best way in which to mitigate against the effects of future crises is to reform political institutions, making them more effective and efficient. This, however, requires 'reform leadership'.

Boin and 't Hart suggest that reform leaders need to articulate that the status quo is untenable, propose a coherent set of radical and politically sanctioned reforms, and guard their integrity during reform implementation. Reform leadership requires the embracing of novel policy ideas, the skills to sell them to diverse audiences, and the wielding of power to see them enacted (Boin and 't Hart 2003: 549).

This suggested model of behaviour is broadly in line with earlier writings on the subject of leadership within a democracy. For example, J. Roland Pennock (1979: 485–7) identified four tasks or functions of modern leadership:

> aiding the thoughts of others by identifying and pointing out problems for which political action is appropriate;
> enabling opinions to be effective once they are formed; providing goals and sets of ideals which people can support;
> obtaining the agreement of an effective coalition on any policy and establishing priorities;
> translating the area of agreement into action.

This is in accord with what Noel Tichy and David Ulrich have described as transformational leadership (1984: 59), and it is also a central attribute of James McGregor Burns (1978) theory of leadership. Burns suggests that leadership should facilitate the process of discerning the points on which we can agree in the midst of turmoil. Reform, whether it is of political or economic structures, is more likely to take root when it is based on a clearly envisioned need and an agenda upon which there is broad agreement. As Burns argues, if leaders take action by force without addressing the motivations and attitudes of followers, they cease by definition to be leaders and become mere wielders of force (Burns 1978: 439).

Nelson Mandela provides an excellent example of a transformational leader. Mandela and the African National Congress (ANC) proved able to articulate a vision of South Africa, which South Africans of all races could share. By means of open debate within the legislature, the establishment of truth and reconciliation commissions and through the media, greater awareness of opposing perspectives of past and present policies was promoted and eventual compromise achieved. As a result of both political approach and organizational design, the predicted racial conflagration post-apartheid was avoided, and indeed never seemed to be a viable option.

Contrast this with the situation in Russia during and after the collapse of the Soviet Union. During the August 1991 coup Boris Yeltsin displayed the attributes of a leader in a crisis by marshalling the support of the people, other politicians and elements of the security forces. The image of Yeltsin astride a tank delivering his message to the leaders of the coup is an abiding one of that period. Yeltsin subsequently proved unable to build the types of political coalitions necessary to advance democratic reforms in Russia. Instead of working with the Duma, the Russian parliament, he ended up bombing it in 1993 when agreement on a new constitution could not be reached. Having come to power as the result of crisis, he proceeded to define many subsequent political events as emergency situations, resorting to rule by decree. The establishment of democracy and democratic procedures was significantly delayed as a result.

Political leadership of the defence sector during peacetime often requires a form of reform or transformational leadership. This is particularly true of societies undergoing defence and/or security sector reform, where the establishment of new systems and procedures must be seen to make a significant contribution to stability and security. For this reason, two additional concepts, participation and consensus, also deserve discussion.

Participation and consensus

If political leadership is in part defined by the ability to identify common problems and potential solutions and then obtain agreement on the implementation of policy, that implies a receptivity to the views of others, or the willingness to encourage participation. As Jeff Haynes notes in Chapter 2 (p. 20), 'participation involves consultation in the development of policies and decision making, elections and other democratic processes'.

Frequently within developing democracies the willingness or ability to engage in a process of consultation is limited. This is especially true with regards to defence and security issues, which many may feel need to be shrouded in secrecy. There may be wide-scale distrust of opposition parties, of civil society organizations and the people themselves, whose security the state is meant to guarantee. Incorporation of wider view points, however, can make for more robust defence policies. Recent events in both Britain and Slovenia are illustrative of this point.

In 1997 the newly elected Labour government conducted a Strategic Defence Review (SDR). The Minister of Defence, George Robertson, encouraged the MoD to work closely with other government departments (OGDs) in order to ensure that future defence policy was in support of national and foreign policies. It was also imperative that proposals for future military missions and tasks were accurately costed; thus the MoD also worked with the Treasury to ensure that policy prescriptions were within Treasury guidelines. The Defence Minister was also willing to solicit the opinions of non-governmental organizations, university academics and civil society. This he did by holding public fora around the country, participating in radio phone-ins and writing a number of articles and responding to feedback from the public. Policy proposals were also debated in the Parliament.[2] The resulting policy was one which the military, OGDs, other political parties and the public supported. This method of consultative or participatory policy formation has continued, and *SDR: New Chapter* (2001) and the *Defence White Paper* (2003) are products of it.

Slovenia also has employed this participatory method in defence restructuring. Despite the victory achieved in the 10 Day War of Independence from the Federal Republic of Yugoslavia, there was a general recognition amongst the political elite and the public that the armed forces would not be able to ensure the territorial integrity of Slovenia. The government conducted a series of public opinion surveys and tailored their foreign and defence policies accordingly. The result was a stated ambition to join NATO, now realized, and the structuring of the armed forces such that their principle functions would be to provide niche capabilities for NATO and aid to the civil community in case of environmental disasters.

What both of these cases highlight is the need for trust. Ideally government departments should work together, rather than in competition, to ensure the provision of the public good. Furthermore, in a representative democracy all political parties should have an input into the formulation of policy, whether this is on the floor of the parliament or in committee. Individual citizens, and the organizations they choose to represent their opinions, should be viewed as partners in the development and implementation of appropriate policies. Regrettably, there are countries in which the people are viewed as obstacles to, rather than the subjects of, political agendas, and Zimbabwe is a case in point.

Political direction of defence

The preceding discussion has concentrated on attributes of political leadership, but how, specifically, can that leadership be felt within the defence realm? If democratic, civil and civilian control of the armed forces is to be achieved, then there are five defence related questions that should

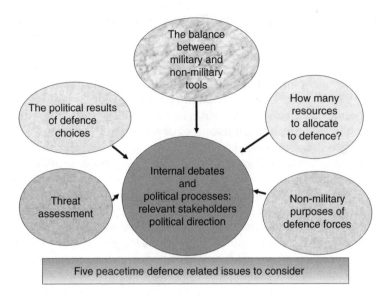

Figure 3.1 Peacetime questions for defence.

be addressed during peacetime if the state is to deliver effective and efficient forces in time of war.

It should be clear from the preceding discussions that the role of the state should be to serve the national and public interest. Defence is but one of many elements within that interest. It is the area, however, most likely to consume the lion's share of resources, and the area most susceptible to corruption (see, for example, Transparency International's *Corruption Perceptions Index 2005*). In cases in which there is little or no political oversight of defence, these conditions are likely to worsen and may, despite the vast sums of money being spent, hollow out the defence capability.

It is important to understand that the significance and role of the armed forces will vary between countries and over time. If state survival is threatened by external military forces and state survival is seen as very important, the expertise of the professional military officer will be greatly influential. Generally, however, states are not threatened in this manner and wish to avoid such circumstances. A range of issues need to be considered if states are to avoid precipitous foreign and defence policies (see Figure 3.1).

Threat assessment

Threat can be very simply understood as *capability* × *intention*. The military will often lead on capability and may well stress the hostility or danger from another entity in order to justify its budget. Take, for example, the case of the Soviet Union when Mikhail Gorbachev became General Secretary of the Communist Party of the Soviet Union, and effective Head of State, in March 1985. At the time the United States, under the presidency of Ronald Reagan, was engaged in a massive arms build up targeted at the Soviet Union. Gorbachev was advised by his military to counter this perceived threat by investing more in procurement. At the same time, however, Gorbachev was also receiving reports from the Ministry of Foreign Affairs that Soviet domination of Central and Eastern Europe was increasingly untenable, from the Ministry of Finance on the perilous state of the economy, and from the Ministry of Interior about growing social unrest, in part the result of economic collapse, but also the result of the Soviet Union's war in Afghanistan (Cleary 1998). There were clearly multiple and various threats to the stability and security of the Soviet Union and it was Gorbachev's responsibility to assess the probability of risk and respond accordingly. The armed forces and the MoD are but two of many important stakeholders in threat assessment. The ministries of foreign affairs, interior, environment, finance, employment, health and education will all have perspectives on the threats to the nation's security and the best means of countering them.

In the United Kingdom, the Ministry of Defence, working with other ministries of state, conducts a strategic analysis of its security situation across seven dimensions. These are:

- Physical
- Technological
- Economic
- Social and cultural
- Legal, moral and ethical
- Political
- Military

The aim is to identify challenges, risks and threats, as well as strengths, in each dimension and to determine the extent that national, regional and international factors will influence the security of the state (JDCC 2003). The end result should be one in which politicians are making decisions on the basis of information and prior analysis, rather than ruling by gut instinct. This more holistic approach can appear quite novel in countries in which the military has dominated decision making processes.

Defence choices and political consequences

Carl von Clausewitz declared that war was a continuation of politics by other means. Even when we are not engaged in war, politicians should be aware that the defence choices they make will have political consequences. While the intended result may be to demonstrate resolve, determination or to deter further hostile actions, the consequences of actions can prove far greater than this. A few recent examples serve to highlight this point.

Shortly after assuming office in 2001, US President George W. Bush announced plans to resuscitate the National Missile Defence (NMD) programme begun by Ronald Reagan in the 1980s. This announcement, coupled with a State of the Union address in January 2003 in which the President referred to an 'axis of evil', caused diplomatic ruptures across the world, with Russia and China openly wondering if they were the targets of the new NMD system. While the Secretary of Defense, Donald Rumsfeld, was fully conversant with the plans for NMD, neither he nor the Secretary of State, Colin Powell, were party to the formulation of the phrase 'axis of evil' (Woodward 2004). As a result of this oversight, both men's agendas were overtaken by the need to clarify the President's defence and foreign policy objectives and calm international fears of a new arms race.

In Nepal, King Gyanendra has taken a number of steps to quell the Maoist insurgency. Actions include arming peasants in remote villages so that they can defend themselves, calling upon the armed forces to patrol Kathmandu, and implicitly sanctioning the arbitrary arrests, disappearances, torture and extra judicial killings by the army (Pokharel 2005). The arming of the peasants raises a series of legal questions about rules of engagement and human rights. In condoning the military's actions King Gyanendra has exposed Nepal to harsh criticism. India, the United States and the United Kingdom have halted military assistance to Nepal, and India has opposed its neighbour's participation in the South Asian Association for Regional Cooperation (SAARC). For a nation greatly dependent upon foreign assistance, such sanctions cannot long be endured.

As these two examples demonstrate, defence choices can have significant legal, social, economic, political and diplomatic repercussions. For this reason, foreign ministries and other government departments may want to have a voice in defence strategy formulation.

The balance between non-military and military means of addressing a threat

Governments can address a threat by military and non-military tools. The current global war on terror provides us with examples of two different approaches. As is evidenced by the United States led actions in Afghanistan and Iraq, the American government is pursuing a policy of pre-emption: strike at terrorist strongholds before terrorists can strike the US mainland. The European Union has adopted a different approach, that of prevention, and in doing so seeks to address the root causes of terrorism: poverty, inequality, religious and ethnic divides. It is argued that by engaging with a state, rather than confronting it militarily, tensions can be reduced. This has been the EU's approach to relations with Libya and Iran over the last couple of years.

Determining the balance between the use of military and non-military tools must ultimately be a political judgement. For example, since the end of the Second World War Germany has tended to favour non-military tools of conflict prevention and has been wary of military involvement. Recent deployments to Afghanistan under a NATO flag were a hotly contested issue. Japanese politicians have also faced similar public opposition to plans to increase the size of the armed forces and to deploy them abroad.

Ideally, non-military tools and military strategy should be complementary. Should the state continue with development aid when the recipient misbehaves? This question has arisen frequently over the last ten years with respect to human rights abuses in China and Zimbabwe and the aggressive military posturing of North Korea. The answer is not a simple one to ascertain and it is likely that different ministries may hold rather different views. In the United Kingdom a policy of 'joined up government' has been promoted to reduce the frequency with which ministers and ministries compete on the foreign stage. The establishment of the UK's Global and African Conflict Prevention Pools has been one way of co-ordinating the activities of the Ministry of Defence, Foreign and Commonwealth Office and the Department for International Development in the field of security sector reform.

How many resources for defence and security?

It is generally understood that there exists a complex relationship between economic growth and security. Inadequate security discourages investment, but over-spending on defence damages the economy by raising taxes and depressing consumption. It also has the potential to absorb scarce skilled labour and R & D resources, thus in turn stimulating inflation. Very few countries can afford to incur large deficits in order to fund defence. The United States is the exception, but the vast majority of states find that their defence expenditure is fixed at a certain percentage of GDP because of alliance commitments or conditions set by international financial institutions. The determination of how much to spend is dependent on answers to a series of related questions:

- How does the state define security?
- How does the state define the role of the defence forces and security services?
- Is spending on defence clearly linked to the government's overall priorities (thus bringing us back to the issue of the national interest) and readiness to raise taxes?
- Is the government willing to endure security risks?

While the military may be predisposed to favour increased spending on defence, a number of other ministries will also be interested in the defence budget. As discussed above, during the Strategic Defence Review of 1997–98, the UK MoD made a point of costing its proposed activities and sharing those estimated costs with the Cabinet Office and other ministries. As a result, the MoD was able to achieve the consent of the other government departments and the Treasury for its spending plans, since all stakeholders were in agreement that the MoD was working in support of the broader national interest.

The non-military uses of armed forces

In order to serve the public and national interest military units are designed to serve a range of military and non-military purposes. In countries across the world the military may be used to construct roads or build bridges, to provide relief during environmental disasters, as the Indian and Pakistani armed forces were asked to do following the earthquake in Kashmir in 2005. Such work is referred to in Britain as providing aid to the civil community, but the armed forces may also be called upon to provide aid to other civil ministries or to the civil power. While this is wholly acceptable, it should be borne in mind that the repeated and continued use of the military in non-military roles can hinder optimum military effectiveness and can also debilitate other services.

In the case of a country in which there is widespread lawlessness and the police are deemed to be corrupt, there is a tendency for politicians to call on the military to step into the breach. While the military may be trained in the lethal use of force, they are not necessarily trained, unless they are military police, in the collection of evidence and the preservation of sites. Their use as law enforcement agents may in fact undermine the rule of law as a whole. This issue has certainly given Argentine and Peruvian army officers cause for concern, and it may well be causing the same effect in Nepal. While a political decision is needed in order to deploy and sustain the armed forces in non-military roles, that decision should be in accordance with both national and international law. As is noted in Chapter 6, the military operates under a code of law which not merely entitles, but actually requires, them to disobey an order which is manifestly illegal. This domestic code has been further underpinned by the bringing into force of the Rome Statute and the creation of the International Criminal Court. It is one thing to bemoan the intervention of the military into politics, it is quite another to address the fact that it is frequently civilians, in contravention of constitutions and domestic law, who pull the military into the arena. If democracy is to be sustained then politicians, civil servants and the military must act in accordance with the law.

Conclusion

To achieve democratic, civil and civilian control of the armed forces all parties within that relationship must understand their own and each other's role and the limits placed upon them. If democratic, civil and civilian control is successfully implemented then the result should be defence forces that,

- are efficient and use resources appropriately;
- enjoy the support of the government and the wider population, including during combat operations;
- understand the purposes of their organization as a support to the government and the state and as a source of particular expertise;
- are not an embarrassment or a threat to the government and the population.

These outcomes are dependent upon political, as well as military, leadership. The political leadership should have a clear understanding of the national interest, but it should also understand the purpose and function of the military in achieving that interest. There is a tendency to assume that because a large sum of money is spent annually on the armed forces they should be able to respond to every situation. This may not, however, always be the best use of resources. Eliot Cohen (2002) has argued that good wartime leaders are individuals who engage in defence issues and are capable of asking appropriate and demanding questions of their commanders. These attributes are also required of peacetime leaders. Whether at war or in peace, leaders need to take an interest in the issues and feel able to ask questions, but equally importantly, they should listen to the answers.

Questions to consider

1   In your national interest:
    a   What do you believe to be the core values of your society?
    b   How would you define the national interest of your country?
    c   Is your view of the national interest one that is widely shared?
    d   Are there any existing policy documents in which a statement of the national interest is clearly articulated?

2   How is the threat of terrorism assessed in your country?
    a   Is the assessment co-ordinated at the level of the office of the President or the Prime Minister?
    b   Does the military or the intelligence services take the lead in conducting the assessment?
    c   To what extent are other ministries engaged in an analysis of the strategic context and are their findings shared amongst other ministries?
    d   To what extent is your prioritization of threats determined by outside actors?

3   How would you define leadership within the context of your culture?
4   Of the international political elite who would you class as a good leader? Why? What qualities have they displayed?
5   Do politicians in your country engage in defence issues? If not, why not?

Notes

1 It is important to note that I am referring here specifically to political leadership of the defence sector. There are in fact a vast number of articles and books on political leadership of the economy at both national and local levels. The subjects of these studies are generally Western democracies, although there are a few works on democratic leadership in India and on leadership in East Africa and South-east Asia.
2 It should be noted that within the United Kingdom there is little divergence between the three main political parties on defence issues. Recent proposals to reduce and restructure the armed forces had the backing of the Conservatives and the Liberal Democrats, who differed only in terms of where the cuts should fall. The exception to this general rule concerns the UK intervention in Iraq in 2003. While the Liberal Democrats opposed the war they remained in support of the British armed forces.

Suggested reading

Chattopadhyay, Raghabendra and Duflo, Esther (2004), 'Women as policy makers: Evidence from a randomised policy experiment in India', *Econometrica*, 72 (5): 1409–43.
Diamint, Rut (2004), 'Security challenges in Latin America', *Bulletin of Latin American Research*, 23 (1): 43–62.
Goldsmith, A. (2004), 'Predatory versus developmental rule in Africa', *Democratization*, 11 (3): 88–110.
Helms, Ludger (2005), 'The presidentialism of political leadership: British Notions and German Observations', *The Political Quarterly*, 430–8.
Shatkin, Gavin (2004), 'Globalization and local leadership: Growth, power and politics in Thailand's eastern seaboard', *International Journal of Urban and Regional Research*, 28 (1): 11–26.
Silva, Patricio (2002), 'Searching for civilian supremacy: the Concertación Governments and the military in Chile', *Bulletin of Latin American Research*, 21 (3): 375–95.

Bibliography

Boin, Arjen and 't Hart, Paul (2003), 'Public leadership in times of crisis: mission impossible?' *Public Administration Review*, 63 (5): 544–53.
Burns, James MacGregor (1978), *Leadership*, New York: Harper & Row.
Clausewitz, Carl von (1976), *On War*, Princeton, NJ: Princeton University Press.
Cleary, Laura R. (1998), *Security Systems in Transition*, Aldershot: Ashgate.
Cohen, Eliot A. (2002), *Supreme Command: Soldiers, Statesmen, and Leadership in Wartime*, New York: Simon and Schuster.

JDCC (2003), *Strategic Trends*, www.jdcc-strategictrends.org, accessed on 12 November 2005.

Kissinger, Henry (1994), *Diplomacy*, New York: Simon and Schuster.

Luthans, Fred, Van Wyk, René, Walumbwa, Fred O. (2004), 'Recognition and development of hope for South African organizational leaders', *Leadership and Organization Development Journal*, 25 (6): 512–27.

Machiavelli, Niccolò (1961), *The Prince*, Harmondsworth: Penguin.

Museveni, Yoweri Kaguta (2005), 'The Power of knowledge', in Bert Hamminga (ed.) *Knowledge Cultures – Comparative Western and African Epistemology*, Poznan Studies in the Philosophy of the Sciences and the Humanities, New York: Rodopi.

Ott, Steven J. Parkes, Sandra J. and Simpson, Richard B. (2003), *Classic Readings in Organizational Behaviour*, Belmont, CA: Wadsworth/Thomson Learning.

Pennock, Roland J. (1979), *Democratic Political Theory*, Princeton, NJ: Princeton University Press.

Pokharel, Tilak P. (2005), 'Choose between "repressive" monarchy and people: Leahy', *Kathmandu Post*, 19 November, www.kantipuronline.com/kolnews.php?&nid=57542

Ruscio, Kenneth P. (2004), *The Leadership Dilemma in Modern Democracy*, Cheltenham: Edward Elgar.

Tichy, Noel and Ulrich, David (1984), 'The leadership challenge – A call for the transformational leader', *Sloan Management Review*, 59–68; reprinted in J. Steven Ott, Sandra J. Parkes and Richard B. Simpson (2003), *Classic Readings in Organizational Behaviour*, Belmont, CA: Wadsworth/Thomson Learning, 77–86.

Transparency International, *Corruption Perceptions Index 2005*, www.transparency.org, accessed on 12 November 2005.

U.K. Ministry of Defence (2001), *Strategic Defence Review: New Chapter*, London: HMSO.

—— (2003), *Delivering Security in a Changing World: the Defence White Paper*, Norwich: TSO.

Woodward, Bob (2004), *Plan of Attack*, London: Simon and Schuster.

4   Policy formulation and execution

David Chuter

Introduction

Governments are elected to do things. Electorates expect them to implement their promised policies, manage continuing problems and react to new circumstances when they arise. This is as true of defence as elsewhere, and suggests the need for a well thought-out and well-organized system for defence policy-making and implementation. There is sometimes a misunderstanding about the nature of defence policy, and it can be confused with statements or publications by government on defence issues. Policy is what governments do, not what they say, and so this chapter is concerned essentially with practical issues. Whilst details of defence management are covered elsewhere, many aspects of the management of the defence forces (position of women and minorities, pay and conditions, use of land for training, closure of bases, purchases of equipment) will have a high political profile, and are policy issues at least as much as technical ones. For that reason, they are also treated here.

Basic principles

To carry out their duties to electors and taxpayers, governments will have a variety of organizations at their disposal. A well-organized state will have, for example, a police service, a prison service, a customs service, a health service, as well as teachers, fire-fighters, and a number of both specialist and generalist civil servants helping to formulate and implement policy in different areas. This is the context in which we view the defence forces of a country:

- They are an *executive* arm of the state, concerned with turning policy into practical action.
- They may therefore *advise* on the making of policy, but they do not make it themselves, any more than teachers make education policy.

The executive nature of defence policy – because it is largely about implementation – means that defence policy cannot be considered in isolation, but as part of a hierarchy of government policies. At the top of this hierarchy is, obviously, the overall direction of government policy. Below this, are the foreign and interior policies of the state. Each of these, depending on the context, may involve the security forces in some way – not just the military, but the intelligence services, paramilitary forces and perhaps a coastguard and customs service. We can isolate the area of *Security Policy* as the one where these various organizations come together. Under Security Policy are included, for example:

- Politico-military relations with neighbours and others.
- Policy towards regional organizations and the UN.
- Intelligence priorities and collection.
- Arms control, non-proliferation and treaty regimes.
- Peacekeeping and participation in multinational operations.

Defence forces have a role to play in most, if not all, security policy subjects, and defence policy is therefore about providing and managing the capabilities required to fulfil the tasks which are given to them. Thus, we have a simple hierarchy:

A defence policy hierarchy

- Government policy
- Foreign and interior policy
- Security policy
- Defence policy

In practice, of course, this hierarchy cannot work quite as simply as it might appear. It is not a hierarchy of action: that is to say, it is not necessary for each level to wait for the level above to finish its work. It would be ridiculous, for example, for those responsible for making defence policy to sit around idly until the newly made security policy arrived in the post. In fact, this hierarchy has two important characteristics:

- The levels are not completely distinct from each other.
- Each level is influenced by those below it.

In particular, the formation of higher policy has to take account of what is actually possible. Thus, what we have here is something scientists call a *tangled hierarchy* which is to say that each level affects the others. An example may make this clearer.

A small, but reasonably stable and prosperous state is frequently criticized by its neighbours because it is reluctant to take part in regional peacekeeping missions. At a regional political summit, the President (accompanied only by the Foreign Minister) is unexpectedly presented with a demand to make a contribution to a forthcoming mission and for wider political reasons, agrees to do so. There is no time to get specialist advice. The Ministry of Defence is very concerned when it hears of this agreement, and the Minister and the Chief of Defence explain that there are no forces trained in peacekeeping skills, and that the military has no experience yet of foreign deployments. In addition, the defence forces are in the middle of a five-year major reorganization. The President accepts that what has been agreed to will be difficult, but the Minister and the CoD accept that higher-level political objectives have to take precedence, and agree to do what they can.

This kind of situation – often encountered in real life – illustrates the need for a flexible hierarchy which accepts advice from below. In this situation, it would have been wise for the President's Office to have anticipated the demands, and asked the Ministry of Defence what might be feasible. That said, it is also clear that defence policy, and the defence forces, ultimately work in the interests of the nation as defined by higher levels of policy.

This brings us conveniently to the question of how we define the contribution of defence forces to the higher objectives of the state and with which defence policy should therefore be concerned. In the past, this was often described in very simplistic terms – for example as 'to fight and win wars' in a work which has unfortunately been influential (Huntington 1957: 90) – and even today most constitutions define the role of defence forces merely as the protection of national territory and the nation's interests. Yet it is doubtful whether the roles of defence forces have ever, in practice, been conceived so simply by those who use them. In particular, definitions of the role of defence forces in terms of military tasks ignore the question of the strategic use of military power: what, in other words, is one fighting and winning wars *for*?

In practice, defence forces, if intelligently used and well-trained, can be a major force multiplier for the wider political objectives of a state. Some simple examples are given below.

International negotiations are like a game of poker: the outcome depends on what you have in your hand and how skilfully you play. Well-trained and expert defence forces give nations options in the international arena, but they also provide them with negotiating capital. This is most noticeable in the case of nuclear-weapon states, but it applies pervasively. In the UN Security Council or in regional debates, possession of defence forces of a reasonable size, provided they are well-trained and deployable, gives a state the ability to influence debates on security issues. Mandates for international missions, for example, will be disproportionately influenced by states with capable forces and with experience of deploying them abroad. Important command positions will tend to be reserved for states with a history of commanding international missions, or at least armies where the higher levels of command are frequently exercised. Outside these international fora, states are often invited to give views or help define international procedures on the basis of their military capabilities. Such capabilities are a necessary condition for influence, but not, of course, a sufficient one. It is also necessary to have a good system by which military advice can quickly be sought and incorporated into political positions – a theme which is covered in more detail below.

Collectively, also, well-trained and led military forces can assist international political processes without taking part in combat, or even threatening to. The obvious example of this type of operation is peacekeeping, where neutral troops can provide reassurance that, for example, demilitarization protocols are being implemented and thus help a political process along. But sometimes the intimidatory presence of forces – which do not have to be used – can overcome political obstacles which were previously insurmountable. An example is Bosnia from 1992 until the time of writing.

A UN force – UNPROFOR II – was deployed in Bosnia from 1992. Its mandate was a limited one, for political reasons, but, with a more extensive mandate, it would not have been capable of imposing its will on the combatants. At its peak, UNPROFOR (United Nations Protection Force) had a strength of some 20 000 personnel, but no more than a handful of its battalions could actually be used operationally. Some national contingents were there only to gain experience, others were earning revenue for their governments from the UN, and many were poorly trained and equipped. Although UNPROFOR fought a number of actions with casualties on both sides, for political reasons it could only mount attacks against Bosnian Serb forces, and even then it did not have the combat power or cohesion of aim to do so consistently. Indeed, it was so inferior in combat power to the various factions that its troops sometimes wound up being taken hostage. American reluctance to risk their own forces meant that the NATO command structure, which could have eased some of these problems, could not be used. After the fighting ended, a NATO-based force was deployed in early 1996. The United States was now willing to deploy its own troops, and it was possible to use the NATO command structure. The armed forces of the various factions were now exhausted by years of war, and the NATO-led forces easily overmatched them in combat power, although they never actually fought an engagement. Such political progress as has been possible since 1996 has been due, in part, to the intimidatory effect of these deployed forces.

Increasingly, in the modern world, the formulation of defence policy has to take these wider objectives into account. It is true, of course, that some countries still have land borders with potential enemies, and that there are many parts of the world which are unstable and where large-scale conflict is still a possibility. (Major engagements with sophisticated weapons were fought in Angola up to the turn of the millennium, for example.) Obviously armed forces must be capable, depending on the environment in the region, of conducting conventional operations and fighting wars, but this does not have to be the only way of addressing security problems. Indeed, it was not always so in the past.

For example, during the Cold War, Norway, Sweden and Finland, although neighbours with many historic and cultural links, chose quite different ways of preserving their independence from their large Soviet neighbour. Norway was a full member of NATO, with its forces integrated under US command. Sweden opted to continue its policy of armed neutrality (although it would in practice have co-operated with NATO in war). Finland chose a policy of accommodation with its large neighbour. In their own ways, all of these policies were successful.

If this discussion seems a little complex, and the range of possible defence tasks very great, it might be worth recalling the words of the great Prussian writer Carl von Clausewitz. There have always been two tendencies in writing about the military; one is concerned primarily with weapons, forces and tactics, the other, in which this current chapter is modestly situated, with the wider questions of the purpose of using military force and the ways of achieving those purposes. Clausewitz, concerned that there had been too much emphasis on the correct employment of military gadgets, wanted to remind people what the purpose of military operations – 'war' in an age which used that term without embarrassment – actually was. It was, he said, as an instrument of state policy, to provide further options for continuing with the policies beyond the usual diplomatic and economic means. Building on Clausewitz, we can therefore say that the purpose of a defence policy is:

To develop and maintain assets, including combat forces, which can be used in the support of the security policy of a state, and to ensure that coherent arrangements exist, agreed across government, for their possible employment.

This formulation reminds us that traditional concepts of defence policy – built around 'threat' are now outdated, if, indeed, they were ever very useful. *Threatism*, as we may call it, is really a relic of an earlier era, when defence policy-making was dominated by the military, and was largely technical in its orientation.

Of course, there are other assets (such as diplomacy and the police and intelligence services), which can also contribute to this purpose. What sets the military apart is that they are trained and equipped to use violence. Indeed, we can say that 'Defence forces exist to underpin the foreign and interior policies of a state with violence or the threat of violence'.

In addition, of course, there is a long tradition of the use of the military in non-violent situations where their organization, discipline, availability and specialist equipment are all of use. The classic example is disaster relief, where the military are active all over the world. But this kind of activity – like support to humanitarian relief operations, maintenance of essential services in a crisis or air-sea rescue – has to be seen firmly as a *secondary function*, and it is wrong to structure and maintain forces especially for it. If you find that your maritime helicopters are spending nearly all their time helping civilian ships in distress, then perhaps what you need is a civilian coastguard. Likewise, it is true that many defence forces have long traditions of assisting with development activities, and even providing education which would not otherwise be available. In addition, military service in a number of nations is important for bringing different ethnic or national groups together and building a sense of national identity. These factors can be very important, but, whilst defence policy has to take account of them, they have to remain secondary functions also.

If it is now clear what functions defence forces serve, and what defence policy-making is, the next question is the mechanics of its formulation. Here, it is useful to make a distinction between groups which have to be *involved* in defence policy making, and those which might be *consulted*, according to circumstances. The first group consists of:

- Those with professional involvement in the subject or whose expertise is needed in particular areas.
- Those who, by law or custom, are normally involved or have to be consulted.
- Those whose views, for one reason or another, cannot be ignored.

The first category is largely self-explanatory, and will be dealt with in more detail below. The second category can include specialist departments of government concerned with, for example, legal issues, social problems or the management of the public services. Thus, a proposal to change the arrangements for the pensions of the military, for example, would have to take into account government policy on pensions in general. The second case is largely a matter of pragmatic political judgement, but obviously major allies, donors or International Financial Institutions could come into this category. As discussed in Chapters 3 and 5, a more inclusive approach to policy formation can make a contribution to enhanced levels of transparency and accountability.

Because, as we have seen, defence policy is really a sub-set of security policy, the community of actors involved in making policy (we can call it the *Security Community*) will be quite large. It will generally include the following:

- *The President's or Prime Minister's Office.* Major decisions about defence and security will have to be approved at this level anyway, and their staffs should therefore be involved at an early stage. In some government systems, these staffs will have a general co-ordination function for government policy anyway, and perhaps chair major committees.
- *The Foreign Ministry* will be continuously involved, often at quite a detailed level. Regional departments will have views on subjects as disparate as ship visits, attendance on foreign training courses, the management of attachés and joint exercises. Functional departments will be heavily involved in regional security arrangements, arms control and treaty regimes which affect the defence forces and international legal questions.
- *The Interior Ministry* may well have a substantial interest. In some nations, support for the police is a major role of the defence forces, and may even be the principal role when an insurgency is in progress. In any event, there will need to be close co-operation between the two ministries – the issue of how and when operational control passes from the police to the military is a sensitive one in any nation.
- *The Finance Ministry* will be involved since everything costs money. As well as the discussions about the overall size of the defence budget, it is normal for the finance ministry to be consulted about major items of expenditure as they arise.
- *The Intelligence Services* (in addition to the intelligence staffs of the defence ministry) will be major providers of information and advice, and may also have operational links with the defence forces.
- *The Trade and Economics Ministries* will be involved when purchases from overseas are made or when there are major domestic economic implications of defence decisions. In addition, they will be interested in such potential military tasks as protection of trade and natural resources.

This list is not exclusive – other agencies could also be involved – but at the same time it should not be seen as rigid: not all of the agencies above will be involved in every subject, and the key to the efficient functioning of a security community is the involvement of these agencies to the right extent at the appropriate time.

The agencies listed above are all *involved with* the making and execution of defence policy, as a result of their specialist knowledge and their legal status. But of course defence is a subject of wider interest as well, and other interest groups will want to be *consulted,* or will offer unsolicited advice. How do defence policy-makers deal with them?

Outside central government, there will often be *local or regional government* organizations, or *semi-official bodies* concerned with more detailed and technical issues. Local government in particular will want to be consulted about anything which affects the local economy or the local environment, and indeed there may be laws which require this to be done. It is usually wise to consult such bodies at an early stage. Their reactions to policy proposals will naturally be conditioned by their limited viewpoints, but policy-making will be easier in the end if efforts are made to consult them and respond to their concerns.

There is then the question of relations with *Parliament.* This is a complex issue, and depends very much on the political structure of the country itself. Where Parliament is strong (often because governments are coalitions of several parties) specialist committees can be quite powerful, at least in the negative sense that they can obstruct and delay. In many nations, major procurement decisions and programme laws have to be approved by parliament as well. The degree to which Parliament plays a useful role depends upon the power to which it is entitled under the constitution and which it is willing to exercise. There are some countries where parliamentarians may be genuinely unaware of the extent of their powers, or nervous about involving themselves in traditionally sensitive issues. A well-informed parliament, however, which conducts serious debates and has expert specialist committees can make a real contribution to the formulation of defence policy and can help to ensure that issues are thoroughly debated and receive wide public support. In addition, defence, because of its long-term nature, benefits particularly from a stable consensus among political groupings. On the other hand, a legislature like that of the United States, which tries to be an alternative government and whose members overtly pursue their own political and financial interests in the defence area, tends to have an adversarial and negative relationship with government, which in turn makes policy formulation and implementation more difficult than it need be.

A related question is of relations with the *Media.* An honest and conscientious media is important if defence issues are to be properly debated and the public is to be well-informed: it is a shame that in most countries such a media does not exist. Even in an ideal situation, however, policy-makers have to recognize that the interests of good government and the interests of the media are basically different. Journalism flourishes on conflict, scandal and failure: good news, as the old proverb has it, is no news at all. Even the most responsible media will look for exciting stories, and will sometimes invent them if they are not readily available. Talking to the media, and explaining the position of government is important, and is a democratic obligation, but policy-makers should understand that their chances of a fair hearing will never be very good. The opposite situation – a media that is too dependent on government – may be more convenient for policy-makers, but is hardly good for the level of debate or accountability.

Finally, there are a large number of groups active in the defence and security area which have no formal status but may seek to influence policy and will offer unsolicited advice. Some are described as *non-governmental organizations* (NGOs) and some as *Civil Society Groups* (see Chapter 2), although these categories often overlap, and there are no generally accepted definitions of either. Certain groups can play a helpful role. In particular, academic experts and think tanks may have useful ideas and even specialist knowledge of use to governments. In transitional environments, informal groups from outside government have often played a valuable role in bringing the military and opposition political groups together. In a number of cases – especially in Africa in recent years – these relationships have proved fruitful and mutually beneficial, because the two sides have seen their relationship as essentially co-operative. In most societies, however, there will be a profusion of other groups, often funded by foreign governments, asserting that they defend human rights or represent the interests of various sections of society. Some such groups do good work, or are at least well meaning. But from the practical perspective – given that no-one elects such groups – they have to be treated essentially as political lobbyists are treated.

In discussing these external actors, we have to remember that we are dealing with politics, not with an academic discussion. Groups currently out of power will seek to extend their influence, where they can. They may adopt fashionable slogans and seek to ally themselves with foreign agencies. Likewise, many groups, inside and outside formal politics, see themselves as primarily opposing the government, whatever it may be doing at the time, and so will always criticize the government's policies in public, even if they privately agree with them. As a result, policy-makers have to recognize that a true consensus may often not be possible, and would, indeed, probably be meaningless even if it could somehow be reached. It is generally better to stick with a policy in which you have confidence, recognizing that there will always be opposition, and that such opposition (just like support) may owe much more to the dynamics of the political process than to the merits of the argument.

Limitations

The model sketched out above is an ideal one, which is to say that it is a description of how defence policy should be made in a perfect world. In practice, of course, there are a number of factors which are peculiar to specific countries and which will affect how policy is made and the influence of the various actors.

The most important set of such factors are those to do with *History*. A country may have a long history of war, occupation and furious defence of its national territory. The names of famous battles and great commanders will be widely known. Another state may have a glorious past, where it was pre-eminent in the region and a military superpower. A third may have had an overseas empire and a professional army and navy, but few or no battles on its own territory. Still a fourth may be a young state with no military tradition, struggling to find a role. In each case, the relative strength of each member of the security community will be different, as will political issues surrounding the use of the military.

An important component of history is the *Position of the Armed Forces*. In many countries, from, say, Indonesia to Namibia, the military are seen as the founders of the nation itself, fighting successfully for independence from a colonial power. In other cases – in parts of Africa for example – the colonial transition was peaceful, and armies inherited their organization and traditions from the colonial power. This was often an ambiguous legacy: many colonial states used the military as an internal security force, and deliberately recruited from minority ethnic groups to ensure political reliability. Some militaries have been involved in politics, and some have mounted coups, others have conducted domestic campaigns of violence against political opponents. Yet the historical legacies of military interventions are often complex. In certain cases (Pakistan is an example) the military is seen as honest and efficient, and its interventions in politics have been generally welcomed. In some Latin American countries, military intervention, even if brutal, was still supported by some parts of society because of their fears of disorder and political extremism. In a number of countries, including some in Africa, the military are discredited by their evident appetite for power and the wealth which comes from control of the resources of the state. Finally in a country like Japan, in spite of the impeccable behaviour of the Self-Defence Forces today, they remain victims of a widespread pacifism caused by war and occupation in the past.

All these factors contribute to the *National Culture* as it affects the military. So in some countries overseas deployments may be a matter of routine, perhaps notified to Parliament, but not considered controversial. In others, there may be no tradition of foreign deployments (or a tradition of unhappy ones) and such deployments may be bitterly controversial and lead to long public and parliamentary debates. The military may be seen everywhere on the streets in uniforms and may be popular with ordinary people. They may equally be resented or feared for their past behaviour, or indeed the position of the military itself may be a divisive political issue. Anniversaries of famous battles may be an occasion for collective celebration or bitter controversy. The military may be seen as a national unifying force, a school of the nation, or it may be a resented symbol of the dominance of one group, and so on.

Many of these problems result from social and political tensions between different groups. Even in a benign environment, there may be practical difficulties in making the defence forces broadly representative of society as a whole. Some groups may have a tradition of military service and others not, just as some groups may be traditionally hostile to, or suspicious of, the state and its institutions. In many countries, professional soldiers may be drawn mainly from poor rural areas where few other jobs are available and so groups which live mainly in towns and cities will not be so well represented. In some cases, ensuring a proper ethnic or linguistic balance in the defence forces and making sure that defence spending is seen to be fairly distributed, are major issues in defence policy-making.

There are also issues external to the Defence Department, but which have an influence on how policy is made and implemented. Most political systems can be placed on a continuum from, in terms used by Max Weber (1968), the *Charismatic*, where an elected or self-appointed leader with a large personal staff holds sway, to the purely *Bureaucratic*, where power is decentralized and depersonalized into committees and hierarchies, and decisions are taken by consensus. Political systems which are nearer to the charismatic model often result in a close connection between the leader (elected or otherwise) and the armed forces: indeed, such leaders sometimes have a military background. This is not surprising when we recall that war was the main business of the traditional leader: from the best hunter in the tribe, to the hereditary leader in war and diplomacy, to the strong man taking power in a time of national crisis, there has always been a connection between personal leadership and military forces. In such a situation, important decisions about defence and security are often taken by the President personally, and the role of the Defence Department and its civilian and military professionals is substantially reduced. In some African states, the President is the effective Defence Minister as well, and in Sierra Leone, for example, that status is official. Most republics have a constitutional provision making the President the Chief of the Armed Forces. Where the President is appointed by Parliament, this generally has little practical impact, but where the President is directly elected, it may determine the functioning of the entire system. In extreme cases (such as that of France) there can be a personal relationship between the President and the Chief of Defence from which the Minister is excluded.

Similarly, much depends on how government as a whole is structured. If government is very personalized, with new Ministers bringing in their own advisers in the form of a *Cabinet*, then ultimately policy-making suffers because permanent officials do not have a chance to develop their skills consistently and at a high level, and outsiders, often with little expertise, will be put into the most important jobs. But if this reflects how government in general operates, or the special problems of transition, where a new government might not trust career officials, then the situation will simply have to be managed.

Finally, questions of general political culture will also be important. More than most subjects, defence requires a sizeable community of individuals co-operating to produce and implement policy. Ideally, this should be done at a fairly low level, and through contacts which are as informal as possible. Defence policy-making therefore works best in a political system which encourages these working methods. But many political cultures are not like this: rigid hierarchies, lack of informal consultation, disputes about responsibilities and top-down management, common in many governments, make the process of formulating and implementing defence policy much more difficult.

Something has already been said about the need to ensure that policy can be turned into actuality: otherwise, all the policy-making in the world is pointless. Any policy has to be based on what can be achieved and what can be afforded. There are two specific things to bear in mind when making this linkage:

- All the implications of a policy have to be thought through. A role in regional peacekeeping, for example, requires, at a minimum, a review of training needs and implementation of any recommendations, exercises at various levels, including multinational ones, the training and preparation of commanders and staffs, provision of logistic support and transport arrangements, adequate communications, and welfare and medical support. Such mundane problems as lack of suitable clothing, or problems in supplying vehicle spares, can completely undermine a mission.

- It follows that the defence programme as a whole, including force structures and equipment, and the procurement programme to sustain it, have to support the policy which has been agreed, and in turn that policy must be feasible given programme and procurement constraints. What this implies is that the three Ps – policy, programme and procurement – have to be taken together, and have to be co-ordinated in the same place, by the same people, with policy considerations leading.

Conclusion

As is evident from the preceding discussion, there are a number of variables which impact both the formulation and implementation of defence policy. Some of these issues will be explored more fully in the following chapters. It is important to remember that defence policy provides both guidance and a benchmark for subsequent policies and actions. The existence of a defence policy which is widely and clearly communicated to those who will be effected by it, politicians, the military, civil servants and the public, makes the governance and management of defence that much easier.

Questions to consider

1   This chapter suggests that defence policy should be subordinate to other government policies. Is this just a normative principle, or does it matter in real life? Can you think of examples where defence policy has

been allowed to dominate foreign policy rather than the reverse? What happened?

2   Clausewitz said 'war is an act of force to compel an enemy to do our will'. Is this principle still relevant in the modern world?

3   How do defence arrangements in your own country differ from the ideal pattern described here? Can you think of any improvements?

Suggested reading

Cawthra, Gavin (2003), 'Security transformation in post-apartheid South Africa' in Gavin Cawthra and Robin Luckham (eds), *Governing Insecurity: Democratic Control of Military and Security Establishments in Transitional Democracies*, London: Zed Books.

Chuter, David (1997), 'Triumph of the will? or, why surrender is not always inevitable' in *Review of International Studies*, 23, pp. 381–400.

Cohen, Eliot (2002), *Supreme Command: Soldiers, Statesmen and Leadership in Wartime*, New York: The Free Press.

Heuser, Beatrice (2002), *Reading Clausewitz*, London: Pimlico.

Bibliography

Clausewitz, Carl von (1976), *On War*, Princeton, NJ: Princeton University Press.

Huntington, Samuel (1957), *The Soldier and the State: The Theory and Politics of Civil-Military Relations*, Cambridge, MA: The Belknap Press of Harvard University Press.

Weber, Max (1968), *On Charisma and Institution Building* (ed.) S. N. Eisenstadt, Chicago, IL: Chicago University Press.

5 Transparency and accountability

Laura R. Cleary

Introduction

Transparency and accountability are focal points in the promotion of good governance and security sector reform. Much of the literature equates an increase in accountability with increased levels of prosperity and stability. While there is undoubtedly a correlation between the two, those trying to improve their systems need to understand not only the benefits of doing so, but the challenges they may face. Overcoming those challenges may require a transformation of individual attitudes and working practices, organizational design and legal and procedural frameworks. The skills of the political leader and the bureaucratic manager will both be required if greater accountability is to be achieved. This chapter will address these issues by looking at the role that the legislature can play in ensuring transparency and accountability of defence.

Principal tasks

Democratic systems vary from country to country. In some cases, like the United States, a clear separation of powers is evident in the system of checks and balances that has been established. Alternatively, as in Britain, it is a fusion, rather than a separation, of powers which prevails. In between these two types are a number of countries that have mixed presidential and parliamentary systems to varying degrees and with variable effect.

Ideally, a legislature should perform four principal tasks:

- Ensure accountability
- Exercise influence
- Contribute to transparency
- Bridging

The subjects of transparency and accountability will be discussed in full within this chapter, but before doing so it is necessary to briefly examine the concepts of influence and bridging.

Potentially, one of the greatest powers any legislature has is the 'power of the purse'. A legislature can exert a good deal of influence through budget appropriations. Providing full financial backing to a programme or policy is evidence of approval. Failure to complete financial deliberations in time or in full can seriously undermine policy implementation. In both Bulgaria and the Czech Republic, the failure of politicians to come to terms with the financial management of defence delayed and hindered the development of new civil–military relations and accession to NATO (Cleary 2003; Dimitrov 2001; Zipfel 2001).

Bridging refers to the role that the legislature can play as a link between the military and the society which it is meant to serve. Viewing the soldier as citizen first, the legislature should ensure that the military is properly legislated for, and that the rights and freedoms of the soldier are catered for and guaranteed. Traditionally, legislatures have been viewed as a means to check executive power and prevent tyranny. Through control of the budget and oversight of policy formulation and implementation, they seek to prevent the abuse of the military as an institution and as individuals, and to ensure that the military is in service to the people, not a ruling faction.

These are clearly ideal scenarios, and as will become evident from the following discussion, not all legislatures are equal. It is rare in a developing democracy to see an overly strong legislature; more often it is the executive which holds sway. The United States Constitution (1789), under Article I, Section 8 grants the Congress a range of powers related to the governance and management of defence. There is only one article, Article II, Section 2, which refers to the power of the President, and that is only to state that the office holder shall be Commander-in-Chief. Compare this to the constitutions of Turkmenistan or Uzbekistan which enumerate a range of executive powers, but grant the legislature the power to simply approve or ratify the decisions of the executive. In other cases, such as that of Ghana, the legislature is granted numerous powers with respect to the oversight of defence and security, yet discussions with members of parliament reveal that they are either unaware of the scope of that power or are frustrated by procedural rules in the execution of it. Understanding constitutional and procedural frameworks is critical to the exercise of political power.

On accountability

Understanding what accountability means poses one of the first, and sometimes the most formidable, obstacles to achieving it. In Russian and in Serbo-Croat there is no separate word for accountability, and its meaning is either subsumed within that of responsibility (*otvetstvennost'*) or circumscribed by use of the term public finance accountability (*publichnaya finansovaya podotchetnost'*). Lack of clarity in terminology can have an impact on the systems established and the actions taken to achieve accountability. It should be understood that in English a distinction is drawn between responsibility and accountability. Responsibility can refer to the duties or tasks that one undertakes and to be responsible implies that the individual has some control or authority over the performance of those duties. Accountability advances the concept of responsibility and infers that an individual should be able to explain and answer for their actions and may be legally obliged to do so.

As Jeff Haynes notes in Chapter 2, 'accountability can be both an end in itself – representing democratic values – and a means towards the development of more efficient and effective organizations in the context of the development of good governance'. Such a description is inherently based on both ethical and legal considerations. This becomes evident in Joy Moncrieffe's (2001) theory of accountability, which encompasses two forms of accountability: *ex-post facto* and *ex-ante* (positive) accountability.

Ex-post facto accountability

Ex-post facto accountability refers to holding public officials accountable through the law, other monitoring and sanctioning mechanisms and ultimately through elections. The methods of achieving it are various and, at times, interdependent.

Direct citizen assessment

Within a system of representative democracy the citizens are given periodic opportunities to express their approval or disapproval of their representatives and the policies implemented in their name. The legislative framework of the state, beginning with the constitution, should establish the frequency with which this activity takes place, qualifications for, and terms of, office. Hundreds of years ago, as the first democratic states were being established, little thought was given to the need to systematize elections or to limit terms of office. It became apparent, however, that unregulated elections gave rise to corrupt and unaccountable electoral procedures and government. Countries engaged in the third and fourth waves of democratization during the twentieth and twenty-first centuries have explicitly sought to limit terms of office and ensure that free and fair elections are regularly held. There are a number of international bodies that monitor elections to ensure that the democratic process is upheld, and any state that seeks to subvert their constitutional guidelines concerning terms of office is guaranteed both domestic and international criticism, as Uganda's President Museveni recently discovered when he announced that he would run for a third term.

Within an election the voter is expressing their approval for the implementation of past policies and support for future policy promises, or they are if they are well informed. Ideally, voter choices are made not on the basis of how people look, although demeanour and charisma will always be factors, but on the policies being advocated. In order to make that judgement the citizen requires information, which may be forthcoming from the government and the competing parties, NGOs and the media.

An informed media

> There are three estates in Parliament but the reporters' gallery yonder, there sat a fourth estate more powerful than them all.
>
> (Macaulay 1828)

Journalism has always received a mixed press. At one end of the spectrum journalists are lauded as a great safeguard to liberty, at the other they are denigrated for scandalous and irresponsible reporting which is deemed to put democracy at risk (Marr 2005). Woodward and Bernstein are venerated as journalistic heroes for their uncovering of the Watergate scandal which brought down the presidency of Richard M. Nixon, while the radio journalists in Rwanda are publicly condemned for the part they played in the incitement to genocide in 1994. Journalists are not all heroes or villains; but they are a necessary part of the democratic landscape, if that democracy truly values freedom of speech and the right to information.

Most citizens rely on the media, in one form or another, to provide them with information on government activities. In an ideal world two conditions would be met: first, that a citizen would counter whatever he or she learned through the media with other sources of information and, second, that the media would report in an objective, impartial and balanced fashion. Unfortunately, these two conditions are infrequently met, in the first instance because average citizens have other demands on their time, which prevent them from spending a life engaged in research of government activities, and in the second instance because the very nature of media ownership, editorial control and the writing process means that all reports have some form of bias. If government is to get its message across it will need to be proactive and court the media, bearing in mind that unless it owns the media outlets it will not be able to control journalistic output.

A frequent complaint is that the media does not understand defence and security issues, and misreporting may put lives at risk. The question that is not generally asked is what is government doing to rectify that situation? If government completely closes the media out and keeps journalists in the dark about issues, then the media is more likely to 'create' stories. If, however, the government is willing to brief journalists on a regular basis; allow officials to speak to journalists 'off-the-record', so that they are allowed to gain a perspective of the issues; educate journalists, by running seminars on defence terminology and concepts; and provide pre-deployment sessions prior to major operations, then the likelihood is that the reporting will be more balanced and certainly more informed.

An officer from Trinidad and Tobago, who was previously responsible for media affairs, said that she cultivated relationships with journalists in order to encourage them to specialize in defence. Although she could not prevent the publication of negative articles, she was at least given the opportunity to respond, so that both sides of the story would appear. A working relationship had been established. This sentiment has also been expressed by Brigadier Ratnayake of the Sri Lankan Army. Responsible for media affairs during the Tsunami crisis of December 2004, Brigadier Ratnayake claimed that by adopting a co-operative, rather than a confrontational, approach towards the media meant that reporting of the situation was more favourable and balanced (Ratnayake 2005). As a result, the citizens had a better sense of what the government was doing, and could subsequently use that information to form political judgements.

Elected representatives

The issue of defence receives varying levels of interest from elected representatives. In the United States it is viewed as significant, and ambitious politicians are keen to gain a seat on either the Senate Armed Services Committee or the Foreign Affairs Committee. In the United Kingdom, given the geographical distribution of air stations and the fact that army regiments historically have been linked to specific localities, defence is of concern to almost all Members of Parliament (MPs); service personnel are their constituents. In many developing countries the priorities are different. In Hungary, for example, defence has not impinged significantly on the calculations of the politicians (Dunay 2005).

MPs, potentially, can hold the executive to account by raising parliamentary questions. In the United Kingdom, ministry staff are under a legal obligation to respond to parliamentary questions within a designated time frame. Regardless of the political affiliation of the MP the question must be answered. In other countries, parliamentary procedures actually hinder, rather than facilitate, the raising of questions by opposition party members. As a result, the ability of the legislature, as a whole, to ensure accountability suffers.

Although parliamentary questions are a means to expose government policy, most oversight activities are conducted within select or special committees. Again, the powers of such committees will vary. Congressional committees in the United States are deemed to have much greater power to hold the executive to account than their British equivalents. Rt Hon Bruce George MP, the former chair of the House of Commons Defence Committee, has commented on a number of occasions that parliamentary committees in the United Kingdom are very good at conducting civilian oversight, but have limited power to hold the government to account. By means of reports and publications the Defence Committee can make public its findings on the expenditure, administration and policy of the Ministry of Defence. It can also make recommendations in order to improve government practice. The government is under no obligation, however, to accept those recommendations.

Congressional and parliamentary representatives in the United States and in the United Kingdom are very much aware of the constitutional and procedural framework in which they operate, and frequently vie with the executive to increase their power. The history of the legislative/executive relationship in the United States is one of constant struggle for supremacy over defence and security matters. In some developing democracies parliamentarians may well be ignorant of their rights. In at least one African country the constitution empowers the Defence and Interior Committee to demand annual reports from the respective ministries. Those annual reports have been submitted only twice in the last 30 years. When MPs were questioned on this point they were unaware that they had the right to demand those reports. Again, without evidence it is difficult, if not impossible, to hold government to account.

Civil servants

The business of politics is a time consuming one, and it is a foolish politician who believes that they can undertake that business alone. An effective politician is one who can rely on, and delegate to, a competent and professional staff. As will be discussed in Chapter 6, civil servants can play a potentially critical role in the formation and implementation of policy. That potential can only be realized if the civil service has not been politicized, marginalized and fragmented.

Western democracies tend to take the professionalism of the civil service for granted, but such an assumption cannot be made in all developing democracies. Given the nature of the transition to democracy in Central and Eastern Europe (CEE) there was a tendency on the part of the incoming politicians to presume that civil servants were supporters of the old regime and would thus actively obstruct the implementation of reform. Attempts are being made to replace the *politbürokratie* (Josza 1988, 1989 cited in Verheijen 1999: 1–2) with a professional and impartial civil service capable of serving a democratically elected government, but the task is a difficult one. The transformation is occurring during the period of radical political and economic change and must address the lack of specific civil service employment conditions, the prior and continued politicization of the service, and rampant corruption (Verheijen 1999: 2–3). Clearly new human resource management systems will need to be designed and implemented if the proposed civil service reforms are to prove successful (see Chapters 11 and 15). If a newly professional civil service is to make a contribution to improved levels of accountability and good governance, it will need, at its heart, a code of ethics. George Hanbury has made reference to a series of obligations that could serve as instruments to guide the civil servant through the ethical problems with which they might be confronted. They include:

- Obligation to the Constitution
- Obligation to Law
- Obligation to Nation
- Obligation to Profession and Professionalism
- Obligation to Family and Friends
- Obligation to Self
- Obligation to Middle-range Collectivities (interest groups, churches, unions, etcetera)
- Obligation to the Public Interest or General Welfare
- Obligation to Humanity
- Obligation to Religion or to God

(Hanbury 2004: 191)

For Hanbury, bureaucratic ideals should epitomize 'objectivity, fairness, and actions that can be easily anticipated by citizens' (2004: 197). If civil servants were to operate on the basis of such a code their actions might temper those of politicians and contribute to better governance.

Independent monitoring agencies and institutions

Two Lies: An auditor walks into a business and says 'I'm from the auditor's office. I'm here to help.' The businessman says, 'I'm so glad you have arrived.'

One of the principal means of ensuring accountability, and one of the least appreciated, is by audit. There is a tendency to view auditors with suspicion and hostility, and those subject to audit believe that the auditors are only there to find fault. If, however, the purpose of accountability is to develop more efficient and effective organizations, then an audit, depending on how it is conducted, can make a significant contribution to that end.

All states have some form of audit mechanism in place, and in the majority of cases the National Audit Office, or Office of the Auditor General, claims some level of independence from government. This may mean that while the Audit Office reports its findings to the parliament it is not under direct ministerial supervision, as is the case in the Republic of South Africa. Alternatively, as in Burkina Faso, the State Audit Office remains under Prime Ministerial authority, but it is independent in terms of its relation to the administrations, services and other entities that it audits.

Depending on legal culture and historical and contemporary political influences, audit offices will only undertake reviews of public expenditure, thus adhering to the Russian definition of accountability noted above, or they will review expenditure, operations and management. The latter approach is the one that has been adopted in the United Kingdom, Canada, and South Africa.

> The Office of the Auditor General in South Africa has undergone significant change over the last fifteen years. The purpose of the reform was twofold: (1) to enhance the ability of the Office to support constitutional democracy and, (2) to increase the professionalism of the Office, thereby building trust and confidence amongst its clients. By means of a change management programme and through the assistance of a network of auditing agencies it has achieved its goals.

There is a great deal of information and support on offer to those agencies interested in improving their practices. The National Audit Office of Lithuania, for example, has worked closely with the British, Swedish and Danish NAOs to improve its procedures. Bulgaria has had a similar relationship with the British NAO, and now finds itself in the privileged position of being one of five states represented on the International Board of Auditors for NATO (Bulgarian National Audit Office 2005).

At the heart of many attempts to improve professionalism is the establishment of a code of ethics. The Canadian Office of the Auditor General has established such a code based on the principles of professionalism, objectivity, honesty and integrity. The Code of Ethics outlines employee responsibilities to Parliament, audit entities, the public and the Office. In many respects it mirrors the obligations advocated by Hanbury. Papua New Guinea is also keen to professionalize its Audit Agency and has established a similar code of ethics, which is in accordance with international standards (Wani 2004).

All of the methods outlined above have as their principal focus the assurance of democratic values. If, however, the desire is to ensure not only that those values are upheld, but that the process of government is improved then we need to consider a different form of accountability.

Ex-ante accountability

Moncrieffe (2001) suggests that ex-ante, or positive, accountability allows for a continual check on policies. It aims to enhance the responsiveness of agents to those whom they are expected to serve, and by these mechanisms improve the quality of representation. It is far more difficult to achieve for the simple reason that it is trying to ensure accountability during the process of decision-making, rather than after the fact.

Moncrieffe identifies four ways in which this form of accountability can be achieved. The first method is by taking account of, but not necessarily accepting, sectionalized or partial interests. To understand this method let us consider a hypothetical situation. A ministry of defence has been told that it will have to close a base and that it must prepare a series of options. A working group is assigned with that task. With whom do they confer and how should they prioritize their response? Ideally, the working group would seek input from outside of the ministry and the general headquarters. They might receive guidance from the ministries of Finance, Foreign Affairs, Interior, Environment and Employment, as well as from local and regional politicians. The more widely the group consults the more likely it will achieve consensus on its final decision. In many developing democracies, however, this participatory form of decision-making would not be advocated. There are a variety of reasons for this. There might not be any tradition of delegated decision-making, in which case the president alone would make the decision. Defence issues may have been shrouded in secrecy and there is residual suspicion about exposing such deliberations, in which case the decision-making process would remain confined to the general headquarters and maybe the ministry of defence. Alternatively, although other ministries might be consulted, little consideration would be given to political representatives, especially if they represented the opposition party.

The second method is to subject policy choices to deliberation and consultation. This refers to discussions amongst ruling and opposition party members within the legislature. As discussed in Chapter 3, during the Strategic Defence Review the Labour Government made a point of outlining its proposals for defence to the House of Commons. The Shadow Cabinet was also briefed by civil servants on those proposals. As a result it was possible to develop a shared vision for defence reform. Frequently in developing democracies, however, and especially when it comes to defence and security issues, the ruling party does not trust the opposition parties sufficiently to divulge and debate its proposals. This lack of trust is one of the greatest obstacles to achieving any form of accountability, and it is an issue which will be discussed in more detail below.

The third way of achieving ex-ante accountability is by means of referenda. This is not to infer that a referendum should be staged for every policy issue, simply for those that may have constitutional implications. Note here the approach adopted by many states of the European Union with regards to the implementation of a constitution for that organization. Were that constitution to come into force it would have serious repercussions for national constitutions, and thus it was deemed appropriate to hold referenda. The timing and phrasing of referenda should be chosen carefully. In the Baltic States approximately a dozen referenda were held within the space of a decade on various issues pertaining to the respective constitutions, and NATO and EU membership. The result was voter fatigue which then had an impact on turnouts for general elections. Although referenda should not necessarily be viewed as a tool of last resort, they should, perhaps, be used sparingly.

The final element of ex-ante accountability is not a method, but a principle. Government must understand that it has a duty to explain and justify its actions. This may seem a simplistic and naïve prescription but it goes to the heart of 'government for the people, by the people'. Ensuring accountability is not simply about establishing certain institutional structures and procedures, but about altering patterns of behaviour. In order to remain vigilant we need to have a clear aim to which we can work, as in the case of the South African OAG noted above, and we also need to understand that structures have consequences for ethical behaviour (Hanbury 2004: 191).

On transparency

The success of much of what has been proposed above is dependent upon transparency. Individuals need to understand what is going on within their own departments, in other ministries, across government and within society if they are to be effective decision-makers and to manage change (see Chapter 15). When discussing the issue of transparency as it relates to accountability it is possible to refer to two types: domestic and international transparency.

Domestic transparency relates to the ease or difficulty with which a country's own legislature plus the media, interest groups, civil society and the public at large can see what is going on. Ideally, the aim should be to achieve transparency in decision-making, allocation of budgetary resources and administration of the rule of law. The publication of parliamentary reports and the findings of the National Audit Office enhance accountability and transparency simultaneously. How the media, the public and MPs interpret and use those reports, however, can be deemed an expression of democratic freedom. For example, a United States' General Accountability Office (GAO) Report suggested that

> Substantial weaknesses in DOD business operations adversely affect its ability to provide timely, reliable management information for DOD and Congress to use in making informed decisions. Further, the lack of adequate transparency and appropriate accountability across all of DOD's major business areas results in billions of dollars annually in wasted resources in a time of increasing fiscal challenges.
>
> (2004: 1)

In the preface to that report it was indicated that similar findings had been presented to Congress in previous years, but that no action had been taken. Transparency is an important pre-condition for accountability, but accountability is meaningless unless follow up actions are taken.

The other type of transparency, international transparency, refers to the ease or difficulty with which other countries can observe that state's affairs. Generally, countries that are good at domestic transparency will be good at international transparency; however, the reverse is not always true. During the period of NATO expansion in the 1990s applicant states were very good at informing the Alliance of their budgetary allocations, their force strength and their progress on implementing the Conventional Forces in Europe Treaty agreements. The same information was not available to the general public, who did not understand why large sums of money continued to be spent on the military during a period of economic decline. As those states intensified their efforts to join the Alliance they had to focus much more on carrying the public with them. Public information campaigns, and thus increased domestic transparency, became crucial to success.

Overcoming the obstacles to accountability

The obstacles to accountability can be grouped under the following headings:

- Lack of professionalism
- Lack of trust
- Inappropriate systems and procedures
- Lack of transparency
- High transaction costs

The methods of overcoming these individual obstacles are generally inter-related. Gains in one area will need to be supported by changes or reforms in other areas. Thus a holistic, rather than a piecemeal, approach is required.

Lack of professionalism

As noted in Chapter 3, military officers in developing democracies frequently complain about the quality of political leadership, about a general lack of professionalism. When asked to explain what they mean by this accusation they refer to politicians' ignorance of defence and security issues, an unwillingness to address those issues, engagement in corrupt practices, and a concern solely with electoral, rather than public, interest.

Ignorance of defence and security issues may be the result of a past political culture – authoritarian and secretive – which made it difficult for anyone to acquaint themselves with security related matters. It is not necessarily the intention of the politician to be wilfully ignorant, but they may not have the means available to them to address their shortcomings. If politicians are to perform their civic responsibilities they require education and information.

The recommendation being made here is not that politicians must have a degree in International Relations or Security Studies in order to legislate for

70 Laura R. Cleary

and oversee defence, but that they do require on-the-job training in order to sensitize them to the relevant issues. In the United Kingdom an Armed Forces Parliamentary Scheme (AFPS) has been established. MPs who participate in the scheme are attached to one of the single services and receive a series of briefings, both technical and policy oriented, as well as participating in military exercises. Periodically, they also receive joint service briefings so that they acquire a better understanding of how the single service to which they are attached makes a contribution to defence overall. AFPS has been well-received by politicians and military personnel. In a society where only a handful of politicians have served in the Armed Forces it is viewed as a means to close the civil-military gap.

Similar schemes are being piloted elsewhere. In Ghana a Security Sector Governance and Management Course (SSGM) has been established, which seeks to enhance security literacy amongst military and civilian practioners at senior grades. In 2004, the first year of the course, a one day parliamentary workshop was held to introduce MPs to the issues of policy formation and implementation, oversight and accountability, and financial management for defence. In 2005 two MPs joined military personnel and civil servants for the three week course. The plan for 2006 is to increase the number of participating MPs, and to also hold briefings on defence and security as part of the induction for new parliamentarians. It is argued that if Ghana is to truly put its history of military coups behind it then the political class must take responsibility for all aspects of the public and national interest.

The establishment of the SSGM was financially supported by the British government, but the British are not alone in sponsoring such activities. The Geneva Center for Democratic Control of the Armed Forces has been actively engaged in holding workshops and courses for those involved in the implementation of defence reform in CEE, and now in Africa. Another organization which is gaining increasing prominence is the Club of Madrid. Comprised of 57 former heads of state and government, the Club of Madrid acts as a consultative body for governments, democratic leaders and institutions involved in the process of democratic transition. Political elites may not be willing to expose their ignorance or concerns to those who serve them, and if that is the case they can turn to others who have been in similar positions for strategic support and technical advice.

Ideally, however politicians should be able to obtain technical information within their state. In many developing democracies, however, politicians have inadequate relations with the expert community. As discussed earlier, a primary support should be provided by the civil service, but in many cases that service has been politicized and is thus deemed suspect. An alternative source of information might be NGOs and think tanks, but they exist in limited numbers, if at all, in newly post-authoritarian regimes. If they do exist they tend to have a narrow focus. They are experts on specific issues, such as human rights or small arms proliferation, but they do not necessarily have the expertise to contend with the myriad issues pertaining to the management of defence. NGOs may also be viewed with a certain amount of suspicion by the defence and security services, and a politician who relies too heavily on information from such a source is subsequently tainted by association. As with political parties, NGOs will tend to proliferate given time and supportive legislation. For many democratic theorists an increase in the number of independent research institutes is seen as a measurement of the strength and diversity of civil society (Kaldor 2003). Certainly in CEE this has been the case as political systems have stabilized and politicians who have left office, but retained an interest in the issues, have established their own think tanks. There is an increasing flow of information and personnel between civil society organizations and government. For example, before becoming Bulgaria's Foreign Minister, Solomon Passy headed the Atlantic Club of Bulgaria, an NGO which advocated NATO membership before that became popular. In Chile, Michele Bachelet, former Defence Minister and presidential candidate, was a human rights activist before joining the government. Recall, as well, that the membership of the Club of Madrid is made up of former heads of state and government. Thus NGOs can act as sources of information, as advocates and as fora for debate (Kuenzi 2005). They have the potential to enhance the vibrancy of democracy.

Ultimately, however, the desire to become knowledgeable on defence and security related issues and to engage fully in those subject areas is dependent upon feeling comfortable about doing so. It is about overcoming fear and increasing trust. Depending upon the nature of the previous regime, however, fear and a lack of trust may be the dominant characteristics of the early phases of transition.

Lack of trust

Within the context of defence governance, trust can be broadly understood to mean a mutual respect for the competence and professionalism of civilian planners, parliamentarians and military planners. If even a basic level of trust exists then the partnership between politicians, civil servants and the military, which Rebecca Schiff (1995) advocates, is more likely to occur.

In the initial stages of transition, however, it is more likely that these three groups will be working in isolation than in partnership. A frequent refrain from the military is that while they respect the political office (of president, prime minister or defence minister), they do not trust the individual who holds that office. Transforming this attitude is a question of approach and design. In their study of trust within corporations, Robert Galford and Anne Seibold Drapeau (2003) suggest that trust has three components:

- *Strategic Trust*: the trust that employees have in the people running the operation to make the right strategic decisions.
- *Personal Trust*: the trust that employees have in their own managers.
- *Organizational Trust*: the trust people have in a company/institution. This relates to the extent that people consider the processes to be well designed, consistent and fair.

Although this typology was designed to describe trust within a corporate setting, it still has relevance for a discussion on government. Strategic trust can be equated with the trust that citizens have in politicians to run the country effectively. Personal trust relates to the way in which civil servants and military personnel view their political masters, while organizational trust pertains to the degree of trust individuals have in ministries and government.

Many government institutions desirous to make a contribution to good governance and accountability recognize that they need to improve their credibility and enhance the level of trust within their working practices. If we look again at the example of the OAG in South Africa, its leadership sought to build trust and confidence in its clients. Galford and Drapeau suggest that the building blocks of trust are consistency, clear communication and a willingness to tackle awkward questions. Within the context of government, the first two of these can be achieved, in part, through the establishment and publication of a code of ethics. Fernando (2005) has argued that the establishment of a high standard of ethical conduct among public officials is central to the maintenance of public trust and confidence in the process of government. Fernando suggests that Sri Lanka, for instance, should learn a lesson from post-war Japan and seek to establish the concept of the four-Ds: *Diligence*, *Dexterity*, *Discipline* and *Dedication*. George Hanbury would prescribe an ethics check:

1   Is the action legal?
2   Is the policy balanced and fair?
3   How will it make me feel about myself? How will it look the next day on the front page of the paper?

Political direction and leadership (see Chapter 3) is required if behaviour is to become consistent and clear communication is to become the norm. Ideally, politicians should also perform the ethics check. It could provide a means of determining balance between the electoral and public interest. All politicians are at risk of succumbing to the pursuit of electoral interest over public interest, as this quote from US Senator John Danforth illustrates:

> [We] have hurt America – quite intentionally we have hurt America, for the purposes of getting ourselves elected. We have told Americans that they should feel sorry for themselves. We have told them we can give them something for nothing. We have told them we can reduce taxes and we can increase benefits, and the numbers do not add up, and people want to believe that this is not a problem.
>
> (Danforth cited in Ruscio 2004: 8)

Political leadership manifests itself in the willingness of the individual to lead by example. A call for this type of leadership has been made in Sri Lanka. It has been argued that the country needs to recover from more than just the 2004 Tsunami; it must also recover from years of insurgency and poor governance. If Sri Lanka is to recover from these misfortunes then 'values and attitudes have to change, the sense of right and wrong has to be restored and accountability and responsibility have to be zealously ensured at all levels' (Fernando 2005: 9). The key is the formulation of effective strategies to build values and promote ethical behaviour.

Inappropriate systems and procedures

Those strategies may also need to address institutional arrangements. Some common defects within developing democracies include the following:

- The executive has the power to take decisions on a wide range of issues which are not subject to parliamentary oversight.
- A failure to profess interests.
- A lack of awareness of, and adherence to, the law (domestic and international).
- An inability to exchange information because there are questions over how to provide that information and to whom (see Chapter 10).

These problems may be corrected either by means of constitutional amendments or an evolutionary approach to the establishment of procedural framework. Amending a constitution should always be approached with caution and with care, lest amendments further undermine the constitutional framework. Within the first five years of independence, Russia amended its constitution some 300 times, thus raising serious questions about its validity and relevance. In Kenya attempts to draft a new constitution have proven fraught, and an inability to approve the constitution is now destabilizing the electoral system.

For democratizing states allowing time to take its course and procedures to evolve slowly can seem unacceptable in the face of public demands for immediate action and external pressures to demonstrate marked improvements in terms of governance. Governments may feel at a loss when they compare themselves to the 'established democracies', but it is worth bearing in mind that the United Kingdom and United States systems have taken hundreds of years to evolve and they are still not perfect. The aim should be better governance, not perfect governance.

Lack of transparency

Transparency, or the lack of it, is at the heart of many of the problems listed in the preceding section. Governments find it difficult to operate in an information vacuum; good governance is impossible to achieve in such a climate. The difficulty is that in many developing democracies information is viewed as power. To share that information is to dilute one's personal power. If politicians are to make not just decisions, but the right decisions then they will need access to a range of information sources: NGOs, the media, government ministries and the military itself. Greater transparency is ultimately dependent upon political policies and managerial approaches. The following example illustrates the point.

The United Kingdom passed the Freedom of Information Act in 2000. Previously, the working premise was that everything was secret, unless otherwise stated. Under the new legislation everything is deemed to be public unless it falls into specified excepted cases, such as when the release of information compromises the privacy of the individual or the security of the state. The Freedom of Information Act has had a direct effect on the way in which ministries, including the ministry of defence, handle information. The Act is deemed a significant step forwards in terms of promoting greater transparency and accountability, because the government is being transparent about why it is not being transparent.

Transaction costs

To assert that government is accountable is to provide assurances that gains have been achieved in the following areas:

- Public accountability
- Ministerial accountability
- Parliamentary accountability
- Bureaucratic accountability
- Accountability from professional groups
- Intra-institutional accountability
- Inter-institutional accountability

- Financial accountability
- Managerial accountability

It is difficult, however, to ensure equal degrees of accountability across all of those areas simultaneously. The reason is due to the fact that formal systems of monitoring and accountability either entail very high transaction costs or are simply impossible because of the lack of specificity of the underlying activity. As Sylvie Jackson discusses in Chapter 14, before you can measure something you need to know what it is you are measuring. The same principle applies to accountability. Individuals and institutions need to know what they are accountable for and to whom. Even when these criteria are met, attempts to demonstrate accountability may prevent an individual from performing the specific task. Public sector workers in the United Kingdom frequently complain that they spend more time completing paperwork then in doing their jobs, for example, teaching or nursing patients. A decision needs to be made as to the balance between ensuring accountability and efficiency and effectiveness.

Conclusion

Accountability is not simply about uncovering wrong doing, it is about improving the individual and collective behaviour and the process of government. This is why the preceding discussion has touched upon issues of vision, ethics and procedures. Accountability requires more than a statement that we will do better in the future, it requires action to turn those promises into reality. If an officer is found to be selling guns and ammunition designated for his unit is he punished, perhaps discharged, or is he moved to a new unit where he can continue his activities? If a politician has taken bribes does he lose his seat on the cabinet or is he given a slightly more discrete position of responsibility? In these cases actions should speak louder than words.

Ultimately, accountability will be enhanced by overcoming secrecy and developing trust. A component of that is the recognition that internal actors (the media, opposition parties and the public) are not the enemy. The recognition that politicians, civil servants and military personnel can work in partnership will also be integral to success.

Questions to consider

1   Does a code of ethics exist for the legislature and the civil service in your country? If yes, how strictly is it applied? If no, what values would you like to see such a code incorporate?
2   Do the laws on secrecy in your country support or hinder efforts to ensure accountability?
3   How would you define parliament's role in the processes of developing, decision-making, implementing and evaluating the national security policy?

Suggested reading

DCAF (2003), *Parliamentary Oversight of the Security Sector: Principles, mechanisms and practices*, Geneva: DCA, www.dcaf.ch, accessed on 20 November 2005.

Eekelen, Willem F. (2002), *Democratic Control of Armed Forces: the National and International Parliamentary Dimension*, Geneva: DCAF.

—— (2005), *The Parliamentary Dimension of Defence Procurement: Requirements, Production, Cooperation and Acquisition*, Geneva: DCAF.

Saldanha, Cedric (2004), 'Strategies for good governance in the Pacific', *Asian–Pacific Economic Literature*, 18 (2): 30–43.

Bibliography

Bulgarian National Audit Office (2005), 'Chairman of the International Board of Auditors for NATO visited Bulgaria', *Press Statement*, //www.bulnao.government. bg/en/document.html?docID=320, accessed on 20 November 2005.

Cleary, Laura R. (2002), 'The changing nature of civil-military relations in post-totalitarian Bulgaria', In Andrew Cottey, Timothy Edmunds and Anthony Forster (eds), *Democratic Control of the Military in Postcommunist Europe – Guarding the Guards*, Houndmills: Palgrave, pp. 140–58.

Constitution of Turkmenistan, www.uta.edu/cpsees/ TURKCON.html, accessed on 18 November 2005.

Constitution of the Republic of Uzbekistan, www.uta.edu/cpsees/UZBEKCON.htm, accessed on 18 November 2005.

Constitution of the United States, www.archives.gov/ national_archives_experience/charters/constitution.html, accessed on 18 November 2005.

Dimitrov, D. (2001), 'Military reform and budgeting for defence in Bulgaria (1989–2000), *The Journal of Communist Studies and Transition Politics*, 17 (1): 113–28.

Dunay, Pál (2005), 'The half-hearted transformation of the Hungarian military', *European Security*, 14 (1): 17–32.

Fernando, J. T. Rex Sqn. Ldr. SLAF (Ret), 'Accountability of politicians, bureaucrats, and NGOs', *Sri Lanka Daily News* (7 February 2005), p. 9.

Galford, Robert and Drapeau, Anne Seibold (2003), 'The enemies of trust', *Harvard Business Review* (February), pp. 14–19.

GAO (2004), *Department of Defense: Further Actions are Needed to Effectively Address Business Management Problems and Overcome Key Business Transformation Challenges*, GAO-05-140T, Washington, DC: GAO.

Hanbury, George L. (2004), 'A "pracademic's" perspective of ethics and honor: Imperatives for public service in the 21st century!', *Public Organization Review: a Global Journal*, 4: 187–204.

Kaldor, Mary (2003), *Global Civil Society*, Oxford: Polity Press.

Kuenzi, Michele (2005), 'The role of non-formal education in promoting democratic attitudes: Findings from Senegal', *Democratization*, 12 (2): 223–43.

Marr, Andrew (2005), *My Trade: A Short History of British Journalism*, Basingstoke and Oxford: Pan Macmillan.

Moncrieffe, Joy M. (2001), 'Accountability: Idea, ideals, constraints', *Democratization*, 8 (3): 26–50.

Ratnayake, R M D Brig, (2005) Comments made during an address to the Defence Governance and Management Course in Sri Lanka, February 2005.

Ruscio, Kenneth P. (2004), *The Leadership Dilemma in Modern Democracy*, Cheltenham: Edward Elgar.

Schiff, Rebecca L. (1995), 'Civil-military relations reconsidered: A theory of concordance', *Armed Forces and Society*, 22 (1): 7–24.

Verheijen, Tony (1999), *Civil Service Systems in Central and Eastern Europe*, Cheltenham: Edward Elgar.

Wani, Mark (2004), 'Audit profile: AuditorGeneral's office of Papua New Guinea', *International Journal of Government Auditing*, www.findarticles.com/p/articles/mi_qa3662?is_2000401?ai_n9375092/print, accessed on 20 November 2005.

Zipfel, T (2001), 'The politics and finance of civil-military reform in the Czech Republic', *The Journal of Communist Studies and Transition Politics*, 17 (1): 96–122.

6   Civilians in defence

David Chuter and Laura R. Cleary

Introduction

The role of civilians in defence has been the cause of a great deal of confusion and controversy, most of it quite unnecessary. This chapter explains what that role normally consists of, why it is important and how to perform it better. The chapter covers both the practical benefits of a civilian role in defence policy-making and implementation and the political arguments of principle, in a democratic environment, for such involvement. In this sense, 'civilian' includes a civilian political leadership as well as permanent and temporary civilian officials.

General principles

Governments conduct policies across a wide range of subjects. To do this they need assistance from permanent officials of different kinds. Some of these will be technical experts on subjects such as health, transport or the environment.

Others will assist with the formulation and presentation of policy, relations with parliament and the media, financial and legal issues or international relations. The English name for such a cadre of permanent officials is the *Civil Service*. The organization of states, and definition of Civil Servants, varies from country to country, and it is common for some of the technical advice to be provided by non-career personnel from outside. Examples might include policemen (especially where the police are organized regionally), scientists from research establishments or universities, and medical experts.

Defence should not be an exception to these principles. Whilst some of the technical advisers will be military officers, defence is a deeply political subject, and a minister of defence needs advice on policy formulation, on handling parliament and the media, on dealing with other departments and other countries and on wider policy and legal issues, financial management and international matters at least as much as, say, the minister of education.

Confusion has arisen because, unlike doctors or teachers, the military have had their own national organizational and executive structures for some time. From the nineteenth century, and especially after the military successes of

Prussia against Austria and France in 1866 and 1870, European nations began to organize and train large standing armies in peacetime, and to develop staff organizations to manage them and to plan their use. This tendency – which spread rapidly throughout the world – led to the creation of large military staffs organized into recognized divisions: organization, intelligence, operations, logistics, etcetera. Clearly, such an organization of career professionals was in principle capable of providing military advice to a government on issues such as mobilization plans, capabilities of potential enemies and military manpower requirements. Where one service (usually the Army) was dominant, this tended to produce a kind of embryonic defence ministry. A century ago, when life was simpler, and defence had less political sensitivity, such a system could work reasonably well. But these days, political, technical and managerial complexities are such that military staff divisions, no matter how competent, cannot be expected to cope alone.

In principle, therefore, the military in a ministry of defence today have a function analogous to doctors in a ministry of health, and, as with health, in the defence area there are structures (armies rather than hospitals) which exist outside the central government apparatus. But unlike doctors, the military conduct operations at national level, sometimes outside the country, and in large disciplined groups. The military therefore fulfil two basic functions for the government, which together go rather beyond the roles of other specialist advisers:

- They are *technical advisers* to the government on military issues, in conjunction with civilian colleagues.
- They are responsible for the *training and administration* of forces and for *planning and conducting operations*.

These are two distinct functions, and only the first of them really belongs to a ministry of defence. However, arrangements for carrying them out vary greatly, and it is not unusual to see the military headquarters function and the ministry of defence function performed in the same place and even by the same people. This can make sense, especially in a small country where the defence forces have a limited number of tasks, so long as the two functions are understood to be different. It also proves to be the case in countries in which it has proven difficult, or been deemed inappropriate, to integrate civilian and military personnel within the MoD (note the example given later).

An African country, which has succumbed to a number of coups since attaining independence, finds it difficult to recruit civilians to work within the Ministry of Defence. The ministry itself is situated within a large military camp, alongside the military headquarters. Officers working within the headquarters tend to perform many of the tasks that should be undertaken by the ministry, such as financial planning and procurement. There is generally a poor level of communication between the personnel working within the headquarters and the ministry. Although the civil service as a whole is well staffed and well trained the minister and his permanent secretary are finding it difficult to meet their recruitment targets, because the general sense amongst the civilian population is that if you walk onto a military base you are unlikely to leave it again.

If you were the Minister or the Permanent Secretary what would you do to rectify this situation? Think about this not just in terms of the political decisions that may be required but also in terms of the arrangements that could be made with respect to the recruitment and training of personnel, and the organization, administration and location of the ministry of defence.

The complexity of modern defence issues has produced two broad models, both of which are described informally as a 'ministry of defence':

- In the first, military staffs provide all the technical input as part of their normal duties. The minister will have a personal staff for policy issues and relationships with parliament, which may, in some countries, be quite large. Financial and legal issues may be dealt with by other departments or by specialists brought in from outside.
- In the second, a department of government is created providing both military and civilian advice to ministers, whose own personal staffs will generally be much smaller. The military headquarters function may, for convenience, be carried out at the same place, but will be functionally distinct.

A more extreme version of the first option existed in a number of countries up until about the end of the Cold War, although it has since become much less common. Here, the defence function was completely militarized, and the minister was a serving or retired officer; not the civilian head of a department, but rather the representative of the military to the government. This was the system employed in the Soviet Union and its satellite states, and variants of it also existed in countries, ranging from Angola to the Republic of Korea, which were at war or in a permanent state of preparedness. But such a system is hard to reconcile with the norms of a democratic society, and is now being progressively abandoned. Its legacy does, nonetheless, pose special problems for the introduction of civilian staff, and these are treated in more detail later.

With either of these models, pragmatic decisions have to be made about the employment of civilians in different functions. Practical problems, discussed below, can limit the use of civilians in certain cases, but as a general principle, we can say that:

> The military should be employed in jobs where recent military experience is required. Civilians should be employed in jobs where continuity and broad experience are needed, as well as in specialist non-military areas.

A few examples may make this clearer.

- Advice on the planning and conduct of operations, and what is militarily feasible, is best given by those with recent practical experience in operations. The political dimensions of operations, involving liaison with other government departments and other governments, handling the media and perhaps dealing with parliament, are issues where long experience and knowledge of the workings of government are required.
- Getting things done in the defence area can often involve long, exhausting and technical negotiations with the finance ministry. The mechanics of getting the money are probably best left to civilians familiar with inter-departmental negotiations.
- Specifying equipment, and understanding how it will be used (e.g. what happens when you drop an expensive radio in water) is a job for those with recent operational experience. Negotiating contracts and managing the actual programme, by contrast, may be better left to civilian specialists.
- Specialists such as economists, statisticians, psychologists, accountants, and research and development personnel will generally be civilians. It is usually not worth the substantial extra training needed to turn a military officer into one of these specialists.

Obviously, there are no absolutely rigid distinctions: a military officer who is an electronics engineer may also have the personal skills to manage a programme, for example. In addition, civilians and military officers cannot work in isolation from each other: the military will need to have political guidance for their planning; the civilians will need technical guidance to help them prepare advice for the political leadership.

There are also some issues of principle, even in an established democracy, which influence how civilians should be employed. In a democracy, it is desirable that a government can give an account of what it is doing in every area, to parliament and the public (see Chapters 2 and 5). This implies, in the defence area, an elected political head of a department. But, in turn, such an elected head requires the kind of expert support which the military is not usually in a position to give, to carry out these functions. Moreover, especially in peacetime, it is wrong for such advice to be given entirely by an organized and disciplined group that is not part of the career central government machinery: rather as though all political decisions on health-care were based entirely on the advice of doctors, for example.

In addition, the military are, quite properly, technocratic in nature. It is their job to be professionals in the use of force, and, within that, to specialize in particular areas during their career. But this background can produce an overly technocratic approach to problems, looking for military solutions in circumstances where perhaps non-military solutions are better. Civilians can represent the wider picture, because they also stand as surrogates for the voter, the taxpayer and the citizen, as well as trying to interpret the desires of the elected political leadership. Civilians can bring to bear a range of 'intangible assets', which Quaglia has defined as:

> *information*, including access to empirical data; *technical knowledge*, which can take the form of specific policy paradigms; and *organizational culture*, especially a strong civil service ethos that also affects the perception of a given bureaucracy as an apolitical body.
>
> (2005: 547)

This is especially important in countries where the civilian head of the department, rather than its political leader, is responsible to Parliament for the way the money is spent.

As a consequence, if civilians are properly trained (on which more below) they act as an important buffer and reality check for the military. There can easily be a disconnect between a technocratic military, accustomed to detailed and complex presentations of technical issues, and a political leadership which thinks in headline terms and tends not to read documents more than a few pages in length. This can easily produce a situation where the political leadership is frustrated at the complexity and formality of the advice they are receiving, where even a routine briefing of a minister takes hours of rehearsal; and the military in turn feel that a lot of the work they do is ignored or unappreciated. A properly organized cadre of civilian experts can help here by assisting the military to produce what the political leadership wants, as well as explaining in simple terms to that leadership what the military can do and what the problems are.

Finally, in the absence of a strong civilian cadre, there will be a tendency for senior military officers to become politicized in a way which is potentially unhelpful in a democracy. If the senior military are continually asked for advice on issues which are, bound to be very sensitive politically, there is a risk that they will compromise their professional integrity as a result. In turn, the route to promotion to the highest levels may then be by pleasing ministers, or just being the kind of person ministers find it easy to talk to. In a polarized political system, or one in which different political parties control different ministries, this can produce relationships between politicians and serving military officers which are unhealthy for a democracy.

Beyond these broad principles, the issue of exactly how and where civilians should be involved in defence is a complicated one, and the answer will vary greatly depending on circumstances. But there are four general considerations worth bearing in mind in all situations:

- Civil servants should be politically neutral and job security should not be subject to political whim or patronage. For the sake of policy continuity there should be a career civil service. In the United States, in Chile and in Bulgaria, to name only three, senior administrative offices are filled by political appointees, or functionaries. While these individuals may be more than capable, policy continuity and institutional memory are both severely disrupted when political administrations change. During the 1990s in Bulgaria political parties found it difficult to retain power for more than 13 months at a time. As a result, the top posts within the civil service changed hands just as frequently and there were long hiatuses in policy development.
- Separate hierarchies should be avoided as far as possible, since their creation will simply institutionalize conflict. The military will see a new civilian hierarchy as a threat, and seek to destroy or circumvent it. The civilians will see the existing military hierarchy as a challenge to their access to ministers. Attempts to set up such parallel structures (as in South Africa after 1994) have generally not worked well and have usually been abandoned or modified. There will be a tendency for quite trivial disputes between lower levels of the hierarchies to escalate to a level at which egos and careers are involved. It is essential to avoid a situation where the political leadership is continually being forced to choose between advice from civilians and advice from the military. This destroys working relationships and turns every issue into a question of who wins and who loses.
- This is achieved by ensuring a *differentiation of roles*. Civilians and military staffs may well do different *parts* of the same job, but if they are actually doing the same job, then there is something wrong with the system. In (say) the case of flying training, the military would set the syllabus and training levels, carry out the actual task and specify the equipment needed. The civilians would look after the finance of the training and equipment, handle the media in the event of an accident, and deal with complaints about low flying.
- Notwithstanding the above, the working culture of a ministry of defence is much more important than its formal structure. As anyone who has worked in a large organization knows, there is a formal structure, in diagrams and hierarchies, and there is the way the organization works in practice. Civilians (and the same applies to military in reverse) have to approach their work in a cooperative spirit, seeing the military

as colleagues and not adversaries; to be persuaded, perhaps, but not fought. This is the essence of Rebecca Schiff's Concordance Theory (1995), discussed in Chapter 1. All too frequently, however, a very different approach is adopted. For example, the generation of Japanese Defence Agency personnel who entered in the 1960s and 1970s often thought (and would tell you) that their job was 'to keep the military down'. Similar attitudes appear to be prevalent in parts of South-Eastern Europe today. A confrontational culture of this kind will always prevent an organization from working well, irrespective of how good it looks on paper.

The reasons of principle and expediency for a state to have a defence ministry, organized like any other ministry with a strong civilian component, should now be reasonably clear. But a civilian component has to be properly trained and adequately experienced if it is to be effective, and even more if it is to be credible. Civilians possess no special skills or credibility just by virtue of being civilians: both have to be gained over a period of time.

As with other departments of government, civilians should first have the basic skills and attitudes needed for government work. Some of these are intellectual, including the ability to write and speak clearly, to analyse complex problems and to find solutions which are politically feasible. The ability to manage oneself and others is also critical. Some of the skills are appropriate to working in a political environment – primarily the sixth sense that one has to acquire for the nature of political problems and their resolution. Depending on the political culture of the country, some formal legal training may also be needed.

Personal qualities are also important, and the main one, of course, is integrity. Those who join government should already have committed themselves to work in the public interest and not to expect the kind of material rewards they could anticipate elsewhere. This is more difficult in a society where government jobs may be prized because they offer regular and secured salaries, and governments always themselves have an obligation to look after the morale and welfare of their staff to ensure that this commitment remains strong.

As with all government work, civilians in defence need to become familiar with the technical subject matter of their job. In defence, this is a particular problem because of the vast range of the subject matter and the highly specialized nature of much of it. Some of this familiarity will be general; other elements will be gained 'on the job'.

Some kind of initial induction training is a good idea; usually a mixture of theory and practice. At the most basic level, it is advisable to know the difference between a major and a major general, to have some idea of the structure of one's armed forces and to recognize some of the principal equipment in service. Beyond that, the experience of being with the military in the field is priceless not only for educational purposes, but also for credibility with the military themselves. An awareness of just how much noise even quite small weapons make when they are fired, or what it feels like to be on a naval vessel in a gale or in a helicopter during a difficult landing, helps civilians not only to do their jobs better but to establish some points of common experience with the military. Much practical understanding is also gained by normal social interaction; few military officers will need much encouragement to tell you about their job and their experiences. By contrast, previous military service is not especially useful as a preparation. Either it will be too brief (e.g. military service) to have any relevance to management and policy issues, or, if longer, it will result in the individual being too much like a soldier to function easily as a civilian.

There should also be an effort to increase intellectual understanding of defence issues. Civilians attending staff colleges at different levels benefit both sides, and links with outside academic experts can also be valuable. The idea is not to create miniature versions of military officers, which would be pointless, or to challenge their expertise, which would be counter-productive. Rather, it is to create a civilian cadre which is knowledgeable and experienced enough across a range of issues that its members understand broadly what is involved in problems which arise and can ask intelligent questions and make intelligent proposals to help their resolution. One of the most useful functions civilians can perform, in fact, is to act as a reality check, discussing options with the military from an informed perspective and helping to discard those which are not feasible.

As this description implies, civilians can bring to their dealings with the military their own expertise and experience, which the military can find useful. For the military, politics is often a confusing and unattractive world. In contrast to their own organized and disciplined lifestyle, politics appears to be chaotic and irrational, full of compromise, careerism and corruption. Two common reactions are undue politicization of the military on the one hand, and cynical dismissal of politics on the other, neither of which is good for democracy. Civilians are generally better able to navigate these treacherous waters and, more importantly, help the military to achieve things in a political environment. Again, this is dependent upon their neutrality in the political process. As noted above, there is a tendency to politicize the civil service, and in some cases, as in parts of South East Asia, to militarize it. Either method may compromise the individual's ability to provide impartial and objective advice.

Much has already been said about the need to avoid a confrontational relationship between civilians and the military, and this applies at all working levels. Civilians should have the right to veto proposals on financial grounds in systems where the civilian permanent head of the department (often called the Secretary General) is separately responsible to Parliament for expenditure. Civilians should have a *de facto* veto over proposals on political grounds, where they are legitimately sure in advance that the political leadership will reject them. Assuming that relations between the military and the civilians are good, the military are wise to accept this kind of advice rather than press the issue as far as open disagreement. However, this is not the same as a general rule of dominance of civilians over the military, still less a licence for the political leadership and its civilian advisers to give the military any orders they like. The ideal model of instant and unswerving military obedience to the least political command is a fantasy best left in textbooks. The reality is much more complex, for ethical as well as practical reasons. The military generally operate under a code of law which not merely entitles, but actually requires, them to disobey an order which is manifestly illegal. Similarly, international humanitarian law, which is binding on individuals, restricts the activities which the military can be asked to perform, and both domestic and international law will add further limitations on what is possible for governments, as opposed to individuals, to request. In any event, in a sensible working environment, the military have a positive obligation to act as proper interlocutors, pointing out problems and difficulties, and not just dumb machines swinging into action when a button is pushed.

Complications

Implicitly, the above has assumed a relatively stable democracy in which the time and effort is available to set up the kind of ideal arrangements sketched out here. But often there are pressures for the introduction of civilians into the defence system very rapidly, and this, in turn, is often because the role of the military itself is undergoing changes. The rest of this chapter is therefore concerned with the introduction of civilians into a defence system in circumstances that are not ideal. Three broad situations can be distinguished:

- At the conclusion of a war or domestic emergency which may have lasted for some years, and where the military have come to play a major role.
- At the conclusion of a civil war, where the military has either supported one side, or has itself fractured into different parts.
- After the end of an authoritarian political regime where the military have played a major role.

It is important not to confuse these situations, which offer many distinct challenges. However, there are some general comments which can be made first:

- The introduction of civilians into a defence system is no panacea, and it may even make things worse. In many cases, it is another challenge to deal with, and one that might sensibly be left for a later stage – especially after a civil war, for example. Yet donors and foreign governments will generally demand a whole series of changes at the same time after a conflict, and it is normal for 'civilianization' to be one of them, whether the circumstances are suitable or not.

- In periods of political change, there will always be a scramble for power and influence, and control of the defence forces is an attractive objective. It provides a solid power base, and the ability, through the use of intelligence and other assets, to damage your political opponents. Obviously, to insert your political supporters into key positions in a defence ministry, under the guise of 'civilianization' is a way of making this easier.

- As a result, in a transitional situation, relations between 'the civilians' and 'the military' may not really be the issue, because neither may be a cohesive bloc. It is wrong to assume, therefore, that civilianization of defence is all that needs to be done. It may be a necessary condition, but it is never a sufficient one.

Taking the three situations individually:

After a war or a long period of militarized crisis, there is a need to reconfigure the structures of defence for peace. Although, in a properly organized state, the political leadership should never have lost control of the war, history suggests that in war or crisis the position of the military is always strengthened. They will tend to have direct access to the political leadership, and that leadership will find, of course, that much of its daily agenda is military in nature. This is natural, and probably unavoidable, but will need to change with the return of peace and the relative reduction in importance of defence issues. Likewise, these issues themselves will change in nature, and become much more about force reductions and post-war planning. In a stable democracy, this is not really an issue of civilianization or of limiting the power of the military; it is to do with reasserting normal peacetime arrangements. The position is obviously more complicated after, for example, a successful war of liberation or succession, where a politico-military movement may have to change itself quickly into a government with a conventional military, perhaps at the same time as fighting elections. In such a situation, it is clear that there has to be an order of priorities, and that civilianization may have to wait its turn until the wider relationship between government and the military has itself been settled.

After a civil war much depends on whether any political settlement has satisfied all the parties. If so, then the construction of a 'civilian' ministry of defence should begin reasonably soon, because the kind of problems it will have to confront – reduction and unification of military forces, sorting out a coherent budget and programme, conducting a review of defence and security policy etc. – are very much ones where civilian political skills may be required. Yet it is doubtful, even there, whether a cadre of genuinely neutral civilian officials can be developed quickly, and the best that may be pragmatically possible is to ensure that no single group is able to dominate civilian policy-making by putting its people in key positions. The position is much more difficult when – as frequently – one or more of the parties is participating in a peace agreement unwillingly, and is trying to retain the option of going back to war if necessary. In such situations, there will often be a struggle for political control of the defence, police and intelligence services, both to strengthen the position of various groups in negotiations and in case those negotiations fail. Trying to set up a 'civilian' ministry of defence is likely to be a waste of time in such circumstances, and will have to await a final political resolution.

After a period of authoritarian rule some of the same considerations apply. The situation will vary depending on the degree of support which the previous government enjoyed. There are, in practice, very few authoritarian governments without a political constituency of some kind in the general population. In some cases (as in parts of Latin America in the 1970s and 1980s) there can be considerable support from the educated middle classes – exactly the part of society from where civilians might be recruited to work for the defence ministry. There may also be a tradition of the armed forces as the permanent guardians of the national interest, and conversely of the involvement of civilians in defence affairs as part of the problem rather than part of the answer. A new government will often be formed from groups which were at odds with the previous regime, if not actually persecuted by them, and may feel obliged to pack the defence ministry with its political supporters, in order to 'control' the military. The military, in turn, may well have taken over, or supported an authoritarian government, because they believed that the safety of the country was being jeopardized by the very forces that are now in power. The situation is less complex if a military has either discredited itself in power, and has few supporters left, or if it took power in the first place for what were obviously mercenary purposes.

In any event, it is important to ensure that the introduction of civilians into a defence ministry is not presented as punishment of the military, but rather as an attempt to reorient them, and a natural development. In the most literal of senses, of course, some reductions in the role or importance of the military are inevitable if their previous monopoly in policy advice in implementation is diluted by the involvement of civilians. But this is not necessarily a bad thing for the military themselves. Consider the issue of the defence budget for example.

In certain historical cases, the military have been able to effectively decide the level of the defence budget, and give absolute economic priority to defence (as in the former Soviet Union). There have also been many cases (including some in Latin America) where the military were at least able to influence the size of the budget and veto changes. There has been a general move away from these arrangements, and, although this has coincided with greater civilian involvement in defence, it is not really a civilian vs. military issue at all. It is rather to do with the ability of a democratic political leadership to set and enforce financial priorities, and the responsibility of the military (as a component part of the state) to respect these decisions. In addition, now that there is no Soviet Union to fear western aggression, and likewise no authoritarian regimes to fear a communist revolution, it is time for normal peacetime arrangements to be introduced, and ways of reconciling the military to this requirement are described below.

However, in most cases, all that the military have is *responsibility* for budgets and programmes, rather than control. One of the staff branches will be responsible for budget negotiations, another for managing the *programme* and so forth. Observation suggests that this is not a role the military particularly relish, and there is nothing in their training which prepares them for political negotiations with the finance ministry, for example. In addition, military organizations tend to find it more difficult to make judgements about military priorities, given the historic tendency of all militaries to tribalism. In practice, a system where the Secretary General, rather than the Chief of Defence conducts negotiations with the finance ministry and briefs the minister is likely to result in a better outcome for the military themselves. They will continue to offer specialist advice, but they will leave the rough game of politics to those whose speciality it is.

So in general terms, the introduction of civilians into a defence structure is an opportunity to strike a new and better balance between the roles of those with very different training and backgrounds, and to get a better result for all. It should not be presented as a struggle for power.

The question remains of how to reconcile the military to the apparent loss of status which some of the features of the introduction of civilians can give rise to. Part of the answer lies in the wider context.

- The civilians should seek to earn the respect of the military by being themselves professional and well trained, and by demonstrating that they add value by their presence. In turn, they should respect the professional expertise of the military.
- The politicization of the military should be avoided. In particular, promotions (except at the very highest level) should not be influenced by civilians. Likewise too, in order to engender trust and a co-operative working relationship the politicization of the civil service should be avoided. There should be a clear and agreed division of *roles*, together with recognition that civilians and the military share the *responsibility* for making the system work.
- In addition, there is what might be called *normalization therapy*. The military is perhaps the largest and best organized professional association in the world, and its members have a long tradition of seeking bonds across national boundaries. Militaries which emerge from authoritarian rule or political power will find that all sorts of opportunities open up – ship visits, staff courses, invitations to defence

exhibitions – which were denied before. An alert government will therefore emphasize to the military that the process of civilianization carries with it benefits as well as apparent disadvantages.

The discussion so far has set out principles which should be ideally followed, but also identified areas which might prove difficult. As an ideal, a single ministry of state with career civilian and military officials reporting to a minister is probably the best solution. But even in an established democracy there may be issues of political culture which make it difficult, and of course it requires a number of prior conditions if it is to work properly. First, there has to be a stable political environment in which careers can be made on merit without political interference. Then there has to be a supply of suitable individuals and the time and resources to train them. Finally there has to be time: a decade, perhaps, before the system starts to work well; a generation before it is embedded. Usually, this amount of time is not available, so, instead of, or as well as, the recruitment of a permanent cadre, three other options are commonly pursued:

- *Civilianization.* Military officers are retired or reassigned to civilian status. Sometimes this is the only feasible option, but it is not a very good one. Individuals are often confused about what they are supposed to be doing, and rapidly revert to the military attitudes with which they are familiar.
- *Secondment.* Specialists are brought in from outside to handle particular areas – diplomats to do policy, finance ministry experts to do the budget, for example. In principle, interchange of officials is a good idea, but of course the more it happens the more it ultimately obstructs the development of a professional cadre.
- *Outsiders.* Another option is to bring in outside experts. In some cases this can be useful, but the expertise needs to be narrowly focused. Areas such as regional problems, issues of language and culture and technical legal issues can be usefully addressed in this way, but by contrast academic qualifications in economics or political science do not really qualify you to do anything. Additionally, of course, such people have actually to be fitted to work in a political environment.

Conclusion

The difficulties involved in introducing civilians into a defence environment should now be clear; it remains an important objective, but one which has to be pursued sensitively. Indeed, too hasty and superficial an approach can make the underlying situation worse. In the end, the issue is not a statistical one – what proportion of a ministry's staff is civilian – but a political, one. If the military understand and respect the primacy of the elected political leadership, with the safeguards they have been given, then much has been accomplished already, and the introduction of civilian personnel can take place in the confidence that the revised system will actually work.

Questions to consider

1   How is the civil service viewed within your country? How might its reputation be enhanced?
2   Is there a code of ethics which pertains to your civil service? If not, and you were asked to devise one, what might you include?
3   In what way can a ministry of defence be organized to encourage the maximum interaction of civilian and military personnel, so that they develop a more cooperative relationship?
4   It has been suggested that the role of civil servants in changing modes of governance depends on the resources that they master in the system in which they operate. How do civilians distinguish themselves within your bureaucratic system? How can these attributes be brought to bear for the greater benefit of the defence sector?

Suggested reading

Bekke, Hans A. G. M. and van der Meer, Frits M. (2000), *Civil Service Systems in Western Europe*, Cheltenham; Edward Elgar.

Burns, John P. and Bowornwathana, Bidhya (2001), *Civil Service Systems in Asia*, Cheltenham; Edward Elgar.

Halligan, John (2003), *Civil Service Systems in Anglon-American Countries*, Cheltenham; Edward Elgar.

Hanbury, George L. (2004), 'A "pracademic's" perspective of ethics and honor: imperatives for public service in the 21st Century!', *Public Organization Review: A Global Journal*, 4: 187–204.

Quaglia, Lucia (2005), 'Civil servants, economic ideas and economic policies: lessons from Italy', *Governance: An International Journal of Policy, Administration, and Institutions*, 18 (4): 545–66.

Verheijen, Tony (1999), *Civil Service Systems in Central and Eastern Europe*, Cheltenham; Edward Elgar.

Bibliography

Quaglia, Lucia (2005), 'Civil servants, economic ideas and economic policies: lessons from Italy', *Governance: An International Journal of Policy, Administration, and Institutions*, 18 (4): 545–66.

Schiff, Rebecca L (1995), 'Civil-Military relations reconsidered: A theory of concordance', *Armed Forces and Society*, 22 (1): 7–24.

7 The functions of a defence ministry

Trevor Taylor

Introduction

In many countries, the Ministry of Defence (MoD) is either based in an imposing building in the centre of the capital or it is tucked away in a massive military camp. In either case, to the great majority of citizens, however, it is not obvious what tasks are being undertaken by the tens, hundreds or perhaps thousands of people who work there. This author knows from personal experience that most British people who do not have a professional interest in politics have little sense about what happens within a ministry of defence. In a wider picture, governments seeking to establish democracies and militaries that are under effective political direction are often uncertain about precisely what a defence ministry should do. This chapter is an effort to build awareness of the essential and more optional roles that a defence ministry can play. It does not address specifically two related and equally important questions – how a defence ministry should be organized and how it should be staffed, not least with reference to the civil service-military personnel balance (see Chapter 6). Each country needs to establish its own answers to these questions and, even among prominent Western democracies, there is no consensus. In the United Kingdom civil servants are very prominent within the defence ministry whereas in Germany, military officers predominate in the *Verteidigungsministerium*. The United States makes extensive use of political civilian appointments at senior levels in the Department of Defense, a practice not found in Western Europe. This chapter addresses primarily issues of function not structure, although on occasions the reader is invited to ask what sort of person and organisation would best be fitted for particular tasks.

It must also be noted that the functions of a defence ministry are not debated explicitly and intensively in the academic literature. In part this may be because defence ministries are relatively novel institutions, with the Department of Defense in the United States only having been set up in 1947 as a result of experience in the Second World War and the international political prospects at the time. The British MoD grew steadily in scope and weight after the Second World War, with individual service ministries having been predominant before that[1]. An excerpt from the UK MoD's own website illustrates both the relative novelty and scope of the organization.

> That the MoD can seem complex and confusing is partly attributable to the variety of tasks we undertake, but another reason lies in the Department's origins. Today's MoD is a fusion of old ministries: from 1946 to 1964 there were five Departments of State doing what the unified MoD does now: the Admiralty, the War Office, the Air Ministry, the Ministry of Aviation and the Ministry of Defence itself. In 1964 the first three and the MoD were amalgamated, and the defence functions of the Ministry of Aviation Supply (as it had by then become) were absorbed in 1971, when the MoD took over responsibility for supplying military aircraft and guided weapons.
>
> (Ministry of Defence 2005)

Defence writing often devotes great attention to policy but little to the relevant machinery of government, with some exceptions (Dillon 1988; Hopkinson 2000; Murray & Viotti 1994; Smith 1996). This chapter thus relies extensively on the author's own observations and experience in teaching defence and its management in Latin America, Africa, Europe and Asia.

The military headquarters and its limits

To understand the functions of a defence ministry, it is helpful to consider first what goes on within a military headquarters. In broad terms such a headquarters is concerned either with the preparation of defence capability or with the effective conduct of military operations. Preparing defence capability includes the need to recruit suitable people, to train them as individuals and then as collective units, to order, receive, operate and maintain military equipment, to establish information and communication channels, to generate and apply operational doctrine and so on. Executing military operations means building on this range of tasks, with their execution in perhaps a more urgent and dangerous context.

Figure 7.1 provides the main headings under which military headquarters are normally organized within the North Atlantic Treaty countries and many others.

Thus we can recognize that there are many technical and professional aspects to the building of military capability and its use. However, there is also need for sensitivity to the fact that there are many areas of potential disagreement regarding defence, depending on one's values and calculations as to the nature of the world. Consider the questions listed below?

- Which countries or groups will be a country's adversary in the coming decade?

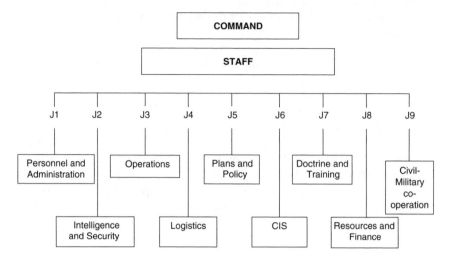

Figure 7.1 Military HQ staff functions.

- How will those groups or countries behave and what sorts of challenges will they issue?
- What mixture of military and non-military methods (such as expanded trade) would be best as a means of dealing with these actual or potential threats?
- Should national armed forces concentrate solely on combat activities or should they also have a natural disaster management role?
- What will be the internal and external political consequences of any defence efforts that a country makes?
- How much money should be devoted to defence and how heavily should defence spending weigh in comparison with other calls on government money?

This bundle of questions and related matters, none of which have a technical military answer, is one reason why a defence ministry is important, as a means of making authoritative judgements and of transmitting the direction of the legitimate political authorities to the armed forces. To aid the discussion, the broad functional areas are depicted in Figure 7.2.

The functions of a defence ministry: policy

It is fundamental that a central function of a defence ministry is to make, monitor and review defence policy. The basics of such policy are closely tied to assessments of a state's external environment and foreign relations, its

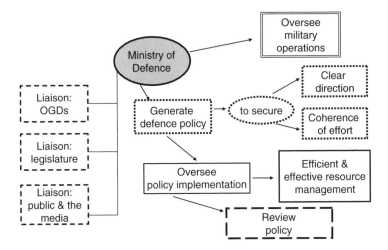

Figure 7.2 The functions of a ministry of defence.

economic prospects and capabilities, as well as the broader internal security situation of a state. Military authorities need guidance as to who a state's adversaries are likely to be, and how the government would like to use its armed forces. There will also be legal and political parameters that the government wishes to set on military preparations. Governments often enter into legal obligations that limit their freedom of action in the defence sphere. For example, many countries have signed the Biological Weapons Convention, the Chemical Weapons Convention, the Nuclear Non-Proliferation Treaty, the Land Mines Convention and other arms control and disarmament measures, all of which have an effect on how operations can be conducted. Chile's Book of the National Defence (2002) actually lists the 17 elements of international humanitarian law to which the country is a party, and clearly the MoD should ensure that the armed forces in all their activities respect these conventions.

Defence policy as a topic is covered elsewhere in this volume (see Chapter 4) but here it is necessary to underline that its formulation is not solely a matter for military personnel, although they clearly must provide extensive information and advice. Stakeholders in many areas of government and society have an interest and it falls to a ministry of defence either to collect their views in an overt way, as was the case with the 1997–98 Strategic Defence Review in the United Kingdom, or to operate in a more discreet fashion, as when rather a small number of people directed the Options for Change exercise in the United Kingdom in 1991.

Through the generation of defence policy, and then overseeing its direction, governments can achieve much of the needed political direction of defence and a defence ministry can be the central enabling institution in this respect. However, if like one African government which the author has encountered, the generation of defence policy as well as its implementation is left largely to the military, the prospects for political direction are poor.

A well-shaped defence policy constrains and directs how resources will be used. As Germany has endorsed the development of a European Common Security and Defence Policy, its defence policy has been modified so as to direct the German armed forces to be able to intervene in external conflicts rather than simply concentrating on the defence of German territory. This capability requires units of deployable forces at high readiness levels, suitable communications and access to transport assets. By committing itself to buy a large number of the collaborative A.400M military transport aircraft, Germany is signalling that it would like to build a specialist role in enabling force projection by European states acting multilaterally.

Below are some instances of government-set policy laying down defence parameters:

- The French Government's decision in the mid-1990s to phase out conscription and to introduce all professional armed forces.
- President Gorbachev's decisions in the late 1980s to reduce the size of Soviet forces and to abandon the USSR's efforts to maintain an invasion capability against Western Europe.
- The decision of the South African Government after the end of apartheid to merge the ANC and other previous warring factions into the new South African Defence Forces.

Political direction and thus policy is rarely concerned just with national strategy and can reach down into the detail of military preparations. In the United Kingdom the Government is pressing the armed forces to introduce equal opportunities to the maximum extent possible and is directing the armed forces to recruit more people from racial minorities and to make more posts open to women. The issue of gender in particular is generating a defence debate on the relationship between equal opportunities and operational effectiveness. The British Strategic Defence Review in 1998 and subsequent Defence Policy documents illustrated the menu of defence policy concerns in the contemporary United Kingdom.

It would be imprudent of government not to obtain professional military advice when considering policy initiatives and the armed forces should be organized so as to be able to provide such advice on an authoritative and coherent basis. The government, however, will sometimes wish to reject the predominant professional military advice, as was the case when the United

Kingdom abolished conscription after 1957. Policy is such a central concern of most defence ministries that, like the Japanese Self-defense Agency (Japan 2005), they devote a separate section to its generation, monitoring and implementation.

The functions of a defence ministry: cohesion

Closely tied to the role of a defence ministry in providing direction to the armed forces is its potential to provide a cohesive and integrated effort by the various armed services. Both the United States and the United Kingdom built defence ministries as a means of limiting the inclinations of their armies, navies, air forces and, in the United States case, marines, to go their own ways. Even when there is a relatively clear defence policy, insular behaviour by the services can generate unnecessarily duplicated capabilities as well as gaps. Harvey Sapolsky (2003) has summarized the experience of the United States in the Second World War, before the creation of a central ministry:

> It was usually difficult, at times impossible, to gain cooperation among the various branches of the military. In the European theatre, the Navy and Army Air Forces argued over control of long-range aircraft importance in the fight against U-boats. In the Pacific theatre, three separate commands were established to accommodate the conflicting plans and ambitions of the services. Priorities for allocating scarce resources such as manpower and shipping were never fully reconciled. The governmental authority for ascribing production priorities was in near constant flux. The national strategy for fighting the war, although clearly stated, was often contradicted by implementing agencies.
>
> (2003: 16–17)

One of the central tasks of a defence ministry is thus to decide on the scope and depth of single service discretion, with the United Kingdom having gone much further than any of its major allies in generating joint organizations responsible for procurement, logistics, support helicopters and so on (Greenwood 1994; House of Commons Library 2004; MoD 1998; Taylor 2003). Moreover these issues need periodic review as technology advances, new operational demands become prominent and cost pressures evolve. As a minimum, defence machines need to arrange the effective sharing of information and collection among different branches of the armed forces, which means that the defence centre should have a C4/ISTAR (Command, Control, Computers and Communication/Information, Surveillance, Target Acquisition and Reconnaissance) element. As noted in Chapter 13, NATO, the US and the UK are among those that treat this as a specific area of capability. In the business space where defence capability is prepared, the German government followed the United Kingdom example at the end of the 1990s in establishing a tri-service body to provide many logistics and support functions. There are, for instance, economies of scale to be achieved in areas such as white fleet vehicle provision and support, storage and movement, and the supply of uniforms and clothing. This moves us from the role of the ministry of defence in assuring a coherent defence effort to its responsibilities for making the defence effort both efficient and effective.

The functions of a defence ministry: effectiveness and efficiency

Cohesion of defence effort is part of the wider picture of defence management under which defence ministries have a responsibility to ensure that the armed services (the military headquarters and below) use the taxpayers' resources that they receive as effectively and efficiently as possible. All ministries have this role in their specified sphere but in defence it can be seen as particularly significant given that appropriate defence outputs, let alone outcomes, are not easy to define. Very often defence spending is to provide capabilities that hopefully will not be used, that require significant funds and only indirectly support growth in national income. Certainly governments normally do not want to spend more than is necessary on defence. Moreover, if wasted expenditure in the defence sector is noted by the public, it may well reduce the readiness of public opinion to support funds for this sector in the future.

In this managerial role ministries can lay down processes and procedures, prescribe organizations, recommend and publicise good practice, specify outputs and monitor performance. They can and usually do establish audit mechanisms under which they assess the legality and good sense of how defence monies have been spent, but audit essentially looks backwards. Defence ministries should also be prescribing sound behaviour for the future.

In their management role, defence ministries often need to take account of wider government standards, rules and behaviours. For instance, there was a UK government decision in the mid-1990s to adopt something close to a commercial accounting system within government as a whole. Called Resource Accounting & Budgeting, it was meant to enable the government better to understand the costs of activities and to understand which resources had been consumed within a single year. When capital purchases are made, resources consumed are very different to cash spent: if a new building with a 50-year life is bought for £5 million, the government must hand over that figure in cash to the vendor. However, in any given year the government will use only one fiftieth of that building's life, which should be valued as £100,000. The introduction of RAB into the governmental defence sector was a major MoD activity well into the twenty-first century, requiring accounting rather than military knowledge but having a significant impact within the armed forces' own financial systems.

A significant element in management is control and defence ministries have a particular responsibility to ensure that defence spending does not exceed the limits of the monies provided by the legislature. Defence ministries, hence, have a constant obligation to ensure that military units have their expenditure under control and that government limits are not exceeded.

From a western perspective, financial control is an element of the government's management of the defence sector but in many states, where there is little civilian capability or readiness to understand the detail of defence, power over money is a way of assuming some political control over the defence sector. Through its lead of financial management, a defence ministry can go a considerable way to ensuring that there is a strong link between the policy direction that it is providing for the armed forces and the ways in which the armed forces are actually directing their efforts. Especially because few military officers see financial management (the planning, approval and monitoring of expenditure) as a desirable specialism, in many states the ministry of defence with civilian officials plays a large role in the area.

Another area of management worth noting is that of risk and here again the ministry of defence should set central standards and approaches that can be applied across the governmental defence sector, including the armed forces. A sub-field of note concerns a system for the security classification of documents and information and for the clearance of individuals (see Chapter 10). Many developing countries lack such a system, which hinders appropriate information flows because of the caution that the absence of a clear system induces.

Defence management is a complex business, in part because so many elements have to be brought together for sustainable defence capability to be generated. Recruitment, multiple forms of training, new equipment, doctrine, medical and other forms of support, command, organization and many other factors need to be put together in the right order. Moreover, the governmental defence sector needs to address a wide range of time scales so that it can successfully execute the tasks of today, be ready to undertake tasks that may arise tomorrow, and be confident that it will be ready for the challenges that may lie ahead in the more extended future. It thus has to balance spending on a new piece of equipment, which might not bring improved capability for five years or much more, against spending on training that should have a much quicker effect. The defence ministry may provide the frameworks that can help the military to manage their resources effectively, but it should certainly monitor to ensure that resources are not being abused. Interestingly not all defence ministries have a clear element in their structure that is devoted explicitly to improved management, although it is common for defence ministries to have important finance sections where civilians are prominent; Uganda is a case in point.

The functions of a defence ministry: liaison with other government departments

The need for defence ministries to be in contact with other government departments (OGDs) has already been noted with regard to the generation, monitoring and review of defence policy and with regard to the application of central government policy, for instance on financial management, to the defence sector.

More generally, the defence ministry should be the main route for contact between all government departments and indeed the legislature, on the one hand, and the governmental defence sector on the other. If the army is to undertake an exercise in an Arab Gulf state, there needs to be contact with appropriate parts of the foreign ministry. If a major procurement is imminent that could change the employment situation in a region, the economics ministry will be particularly interested. If biological or chemical warfare issues are prominent, there needs to be good links between the defence and health ministries. This illustrative list could be much extended. Generally defence cuts across the concerns of many government departments and the defence ministry should lead in dealing with them. Moreover, since such OGDs are staffed by civil servants, a defence ministry might wish to have its own civil servants on hand to talk to them in their own language.

The functions of a defence ministry: links to the legislature

In a democracy, the legislature should have oversight of the Executive. It can ask questions of the Executive and scrutinize its activities to see if they have been wasteful or ineffective. A function of the defence ministry is to provide a machine that will answer the questions of the legislature on defence matters. It is also rarely a military core competence to research the answers to defence questions posed by a legislature. This is not to say that the armed forces will never have direct contact with a legislature, but that they will do so under the direction and lead of the defence ministry. In cases where individual branches of the armed forces can have direct contact with the legislature, dangers arise, particularly that the armed forces may try to use those links to evade direction coming from the ministry of defence.

In terms of its function of overseeing the implementation of policy and directives, a defence ministry needs to ensure that the policy guidance and priorities that the legislative authorities have provided for defence are reflected in the plans and budgets for the use of defence money. Countries vary in the extent to which their legislatures specify the detail of defence spending. Most countries have a separate area of the budget for new equipment but the US Congress also specifies what can be spent on individual weapons systems. In terms of its oversight role, the defence ministry should monitor that the specified requirements of the legislature are met.

The functions of a defence ministry: links with the media

As well as dealing with other government departments and the legislature, the governmental defence sector must interact with the rest of society and here links with the media are of particular significance. Since the funds of taxpayers are being spent on defence, the government has an obligation to explain to the public how the funds are being used. To build awareness of the armed forces and their needs, it is essential that the forces have a capacity to communicate directly with the public, not least through recruitment exercises and so on. But the ministry of defence should have overall oversight of such activities and should do much media activity itself in order to ensure that defence messages are conveyed accurately, effectively and coherently. Their activities in this area may be directed by a Freedom of Information Act (FOI), and they will certainly be linked to larger government initiatives to ensure greater transparency (see Chapter 5). Through the world-wide web, defence ministries have an important opportunity to communicate directly with the wider public and in many states the development and maintenance of an MoD website has become an ongoing and important challenge. The extent of information available by means of this resource varies from country to country; with some simply providing a history of the armed forces while others make available current policy documents, information on the organization and structure of the armed forces, and current career opportunities within the services and the MoD itself. Information provided must of course be co-ordinated with policy on risk and security, while bearing in mind that people in general have limits regarding the extent to which they will be happy to pay for things that they do not even know about, let alone understand. The ministry of defence thus has a public affairs role, and must deal with both the media and the public.

The functions of a defence ministry: military operations

Military operations pose particular problems for governments. On the one hand the military are likely to want maximum freedom of action in order to achieve the aim that the government has set and to minimise the dangers to their material and human assets. On the other hand, military actions have political and other consequences that may not be salient or even visible to the military mind, but may be very important for the political leadership.

Particularly through the careful specification and issue of rules of engagement, reflecting ethical, legal and political considerations, a ministry of defence can do much to shape and constrain military operations so that they remain under political direction.

However, in a fast-moving and sensitive situation, it may not be possible to write rules for every contingency and so a military headquarters will often need to consult a senior political authority for direction. Such a political authority is most obviously a ministry of defence, consulting other government departments as appropriate.

However, it must be recognized that major military operations often have such political salience that, for many of their aspects, *de facto* political responsibility rises from the defence minister to the head of government. History is full of political leaders who assembled war cabinets made up of a small number of valued advisers to give top level direction to a military campaign.

Oversight of a military operation by a defence ministry or the government as a whole depends simply on the political sensitivity of the stakes and the issues. Once operations have become largely routine, there is usually and properly a defence ministry lead. The 1999 Allied bombing campaign against Serbia over Kosovo, on the other hand, involved many difficult choices regarding targets and senior politicians were involved. The political reality is, of course, that heads of government are extremely busy people who must delegate if timely decisions are to be taken. They want direct involvement in only the most pressing and sensitive issues. Sometimes military operations have this status, and at other times they do not.

Securing recognition of this by armed forces in peace and on operations is not always straightforward. In Indonesia the armed forces have been reluctant since 1998 to submit to the direction of a (civilian) defence minister because they like to think that they work directly for their commander-in-chief, the President. In other cases, such as in the states of Central and Eastern Europe and the former Soviet Union, there has been constitutional ambiguity as to who has overall responsibility for the armed forces, the President or Prime Minister, the Defence Minister or the Chief of Defence Staff. This has resulted in unclear lines of communication and chains of command, which in turn has hindered overall reform efforts.

The government should also want to regulate particularly closely any domestic operations which involve violence against a state's own citizens. Government military forces can so easily alienate a population by abuse of their powers of violence. The United States is so concerned by this issue that it has a constitutional provision forbidding the use of the American armed forces to uphold domestic law, although this is coming under review in the light of terrorist threats. In the United Kingdom the formal answer is to define armed forces as giving 'aid to the civil power' and under the direction of civilian authorities. In many developing countries, however, the armed forces answer only to their own authorities, if anyone at all.

The functions of a defence ministry: procurement

Defence procurement (the purchase of equipment and services to support capability and operations) requires a range of purchasing skills including contracting, negotiation and relationships management. In most countries, therefore, a specialist body is set up away from military headquarters to perform these tasks, although in some governments all government purchasing, (civil and military) is done by a single purchasing body. Purchasing is not technically an MoD centre function but, especially in industrialized states, the purchasing body is often very close to the MoD. This is for several reasons.

- As already observed, the MoD is the major link between the military and other ministries.
- Defence purchases often have macro-economic, political and techno-logical consequences that are of great interest to other government departments.
- Purchasing skills are not easy to acquire and sustain. Therefore, except in the United States, where buying is on a large scale, the procurement function is normally executed by a joint-service organization which, like the ministry of defence, works with all the armed services.
- A state's choices of equipment and suppliers reflect its overall defence and security policies. Therefore the policy sections of defence ministries are often interested in the equipment programme since that programme can reinforce or undermine the broader terms of a government's defence policy.

Defence purchasers buy largely what others have specified and it is normally appropriate that military authorities should have the lead in the specification and even prioritisation of military requirements. Arranging an acceptable management system for acquisition as a whole is an MoD responsibility under its role of ensuring the efficient and effective generation of capability that supports endorsed defence policy.

The functions of a defence ministry: other functions

The roles outlined above are not comprehensive. For instance, an MoD that employs civil servants (and many do, although predominantly in low level functions) needs to provide policy and a machine to look after their careers. What should be the normal length of their job tours? Should they be encour-aged to seek postings outside the defence ministry? What grading system should operate and what should be the basis for recruitment and promotion? All these and other issues must be addressed by an MoD personnel system. Similarly a government must decide if it wants a defence ministry to have access to its own intelligence organization and for what areas, or should it rely on either single service-military intelligence units or other government intelligence bodies. As indicated at several points, a defence ministry needs access to legal expertise and it may either employ its own or use outside lawyers. Outlined above are core tasks that present the MoD as having central responsibility for shaping and managing the defence effort.

Conclusion

By way of summary, the parallels between a health ministry and a hospital and the defence ministry and a military headquarters can be noted. A health ministry may wish to issue policy direction, for instance to focus resources on the eradication of a particular disease or on a particular age group of the population. This will influence the funds available to different sorts of doctors. The health ministry will also wish to check that its direction is being followed and will monitor the use of funds. The role of a defence ministry is also to set directions and priorities so that funds can be allocated consistently and coherently.

More broadly, the health ministry should seek to monitor how well its operational forces, doctors and hospitals, are performing. It can do this by collecting data and requiring the submission of reports. Similarly a defence ministry has a quality management role and should collect the information to check that its armed forces are as ready and capable as they should be. Such reports can clearly, in turn, influence policy: if a unit is not achieving the readiness rates that are needed, it may be necessary to move resources from one area into a budget heading (perhaps training funds) that directly supports the required readiness rate. The military headquarters will wish to understand how well forces are performing, but the ministry of defence in turn needs data if it is to manage the national defence effort as a whole.

Overall a defence ministry can only carry out its tasks effectively if it has a capacity to listen to others, and the armed forces clearly should have a voice to be heard with care and hopefully respect. No healthy system for the political direction of defence can work if armed forces feel that their views are not at least taken seriously. As Jeff Haynes argued in Chapter 2, consensus is an important element in achieving good governance. In terms of policy continuity, and the long-term stability of the state, consensus amongst civilian and military personnel responsible for the delivery of defence is vital. A well structured ministry of defence is one institution in which that consensus can be developed.

Questions to consider

1 How would you analyse the question of whether defence policy is best made within the context of a ministry of defence or a military headquarters?
2 Could you explain how the functions associated with a defence ministry are executed in a country with which you are familiar?
3 Why should effective management be an important concern of a ministry of defence?
4 What parallels can you see between the functions of a defence ministry and those of a health ministry?

5 Which groups within government would you identify as major stakeholders in defence and how should the ministry of defence link with them?

6 In a state with which you are familiar, what would you estimate to be the consequences of a ministry of defence neglecting the role of liaising with the media?

Note

1 A British Minister for the Coordination of Defence was established in 1936 and operated until 1939 when other arrangements for the direction of the war effort were set up (Smith 1996).

Suggested reading

As noted, few analysts have considered explicitly what functions defence ministries should and do undertake. However, reference to white papers and official websites giving details of the organization of defence ministries can provide indirect evidence of what governments see as significant tasks. The UK Ministry of Defence site includes links to the official sites of around 50 countries, see www.mod.uk/links/ministries.htm#africa

A particularly interesting structure is the Japanese Self-Defense Agency. Details for this are online, available www.jda.go.jp (use the various tabs to explore the site and to find other links).

Chuter, David (2000), *Defence Transformation: A Short Guide to the Issues*, Pretoria, RSA: Institute for Security Studies.

Civil-Military Relations section on the Global Facilitation Network website, www.gfn-ssr.org/good_practice.cfm

Hopkinson W. (2000), *The Making of British Defence Policy*, London, The Stationery Office.

Ministry of Defence (undated), *The Organisation & Management of Defence in the United Kingdom*, London: Ministry of Defence, www.mod.uk/aboutus/omd, accessed on 24 April 2006.

Bibliography

Chilean Ministry of Defense (2002), *Book of the National Defense of Chile*, Santiago: Ministry of Defense.

Dillon, G. M. (ed.) (1988), *Defence Policy Making: A Comparative Analysis*, Leicester: Leicester University Press.

Greenwood, D. (1994), 'The United Kingdom', in D. J. Murray and P. R. Viotti (eds), *The Defense Policies of Nations*, London: Johns Hopkins University.

Hopkinson, W. (2000), *The Making of British Defence Policy*, London: Stationery Office.

House of Commons Library, *The Defence White Paper*, Research paper 04/71, 17 September, 2004), www.parliament.uk/commons/lib/research/rp2004/rp04-071.pdf, accessed on 24 April 2006.

Japan (undated) *Outline of Organization of Defense Agency and SDF*, www.jda.go.jp, accessed on 24 April 2006.

Ministry of Defence (1994), *Front Line First: the Defence Costs Study*, London: The Stationery Office.

—— (1998), *The Strategic Defence Review*, London: Stationery Office.

—— (2005), www.mod.uk/aboutus/history/mod.htm, accessed on 4 October 2005.

Sapolsky, H. M. (2003), 'Inventing systems integration', in Prencipe, A, Davies, A. and Hobday, M. (eds), *The Business of Systems Integration*, Oxford: Oxford University Press.

Smith, P. (ed.) (1996), *Government and the Armed Forces in Britain 1856–1990*, London: Hambledon Press.

Taylor, T. (2003) 'Jointery as management' in McConville, T. and Holmes, R. (eds), *Defence Management in Uncertain Times*, London: Frank Cass, pp. 70–89.

Part II
Defence management

8 The principles of management applied to the defence sector

Teri McConville

Introduction

A notable difficulty for those who need to manage within the defence sector (and for those that try to teach them) is that many words seem familiar. However, just as the word *pitch* might mean different things depending on whether you are playing cricket or flying an aeroplane, a term such as *strategy* does not convey exactly the same idea for a military commander and an organizational manager. Many ideas that managers now use do have their origins in the defence sector (Sun Tzu's *The Art of War* is as popular in business school libraries as in defence colleges) but the basic notions have been adapted for use in a competitive world. Derrick Neal will explain the notion of management strategy more thoroughly in Chapter 9 but, for now, in order to set a context for what is to come, it is best to consider some of the fundamental principles that underpin management knowledge.

The nature of management

Management has been described as: getting things done through people, which is a useful idea as it shows that managerial activity is purposeful and emphasizes that organizations are made up of the people within them. However, it overlooks the needs for planning and for the husbanding of resources, which would include human resources. A more useful definition would, then, be 'Deciding what to do and then getting it done through the effective use of resources' (Armstrong and Stephens 2005: 3). Although brief, this definition is sufficiently broad to transcend the barriers of nationality, culture or business sector. The meaning it conveys is as apt for the Balkans as for South America (or, indeed, anywhere else) and within voluntary and public sector organizations as in the most aggressively profit-seeking businesses. It is, then, just as applicable for national or international defence activities. If the role of the defence sector is to support the government's objectives and to optimize military capability, then the task of managers in defence is to produce military capability through careful planning and the efficient and effective use of all available resources.

At first glance such a task seems immense and, indeed, many of the early industrialists struggled to bring together various activities, such as getting problems under control, allocating resources and mustering the talents and motivation of assorted workers. The defence sector presents an equally enormous challenge as it brings together diverse organizations: the military, the civil service in various departments of government, defence agencies and private sector industries. However, with the rapid expansion of manufacturing industry during the nineteenth century came the growth of knowledge and theory about how to manage. Drawing on past wisdom and new research we, living in the early twenty-first century, are able to utilize a rich body of learning to help us to understand the task better and learn the skills of effective management.

The management task

We could begin in ancient history by examining the massive managerial task that underpinned the construction of the pyramids at Giza, or the hanging gardens of Babylon. The issues faced by our ancestors would have been strikingly similar but, alas, we do not have sufficient evidence to really learn from those projects. Instead, our starting place is the work of Frenchman Henri Fayol (1916) who was among the first people who really tried to capture the essence of management, and is credited as being a founder of what is now called the classical school of management (Crainer 1996; Parker and Ritson 2005). While they lack the flexibility that many present-day organizations require, on the whole, classical theories have stood the test of time and from one important strand of Fayol's work we can identify a set of management functions that are as relevant today as they were a century ago; and that can apply regardless of whether management is happening in the public sphere or in the private sector. These functions are the planning, organizing, commanding (or leading), co-ordinating and controlling of activities within an organization. There are specific activities within each of these individual functions that will impact upon and support the others.

To some extent, the divisions between these activities are artificial, for all must happen in a complimentary fashion if effective management is to take place. It may be useful to think of management as being like a rope, constructed from individual fibres that twist together to form strands. Strands, in their turn, are also twisted together. It is the combination of all the strands, and their individual fibres that gives the rope its strength and utility. So with management, Fayol's five functions form the strands of the rope and each of those functions is composed of various activities which we might liken to the individual fibres. The reader should bear in mind that it needs the combination of these functions and activities to produce the strong and useful rope that is management. Later chapters in this book will pick out some of the individual activities (fibres) but, for now, we will be unravelling the bigger rope to examine the major strands of planning, organizing, commanding, co-ordinating and controlling.

Planning

This is the function on which all others depend, for without a clear plan it is impossible to know what resources the organization needs, what people should be doing or whether objectives are being achieved. Explicit plans are a necessary pre-requisite for effective leadership, or command, and for the co-ordination of the various activities within an organization, department or work group. Planning is an activity that occurs at all levels of management. For the highest levels, plans set the overall strategy for the organization and will typically lay the framework for activities in the long term. At intermediate levels planning will take on progressively shorter time-frames while even the most junior staff will need to plan what they are doing day by day.

The aim of the planning phase is to derive a set of objectives, or goals, that will focus the activities of everyone within the organization, and set the standards and timings for work efforts. These overarching objectives can then be split down to allocate more specific tasks to each subdivision of the organization, say, department, arm or corps. A well-constructed objective will state who will do what, by when, to what standard and under what conditions. An imaginary example could be that: 'the desk officer for reserve forces (who) will review the database of reservists (what) every three months (when), to include the last known contact details and medical fitness (standard), during peacetime (conditions)'. Many texts now use the acronym SMART to teach that objectives for people, departments or entire organizations should be:

Stretching
Measurable
Agreed
Realistic
Time-related

The planning process consists of a chain of decisions, each limiting the options for the next, but they must allow sufficient flexibility that they can be adjusted if circumstances alter. The alternatives to flexibility are either panic and indecision or a knee-jerk reaction to unexpected developments.

A good example of planning comes from Ghana, where the rehabilitation of barracks was recently assessed to be a priority by the Ministry of Defence. This was an enormous project, which included improvements to roads, water supplies and sewerage, that would cost millions of dollars.

The planning decision was to phase the work so that it could be completed in batches. Hence there was a clear plan about what was to happen and a timescale for its completion. The first phase of that work has been completed and, with a clear plan to guide progress, another 19 separate projects are underway (Ghana 2005).

Organizing

With proper planning the task of organizing becomes much easier. This involves setting up appropriate structures within the organization, and pulling together the necessary resources for everyone to achieve the objectives that they have been set.

Traditionally public sector organizations have been structured as bureaucracies. For at least 4 000 years, such typically hierarchical structures have provided stability and clear lines of authority as a basis from which to reap the efficiencies of job specialization with every post-holder performing according to specific rules and regulations (Weber 1947). Those same rules apply across all functions and departments so that work continues regardless of personal preferences or opinions. Some (Du Gay 2000) would argue that this in-built impartiality makes bureaucracy the single best form of structure for a public sector organization. However, as the operating environment becomes increasingly complex and liable to change it seems that the bureaucracy is simply too stable to cope with new demands. Other problems can occur as, for instance, people can too easily pass responsibility for their own work to others, or hide in the anonymity of the structure or behind the rules (Merton 1969). To avoid such difficulties managers need to carefully develop a structure that will enable people to do their work, rather than frustrate their efforts. Perhaps several structures are needed. For instance the production division of a defence equipment manufacturer would be likely to work best with a hierarchical structure and tight controls, while the research and development division of the same company would probably need a loose structure that would allow greater communication and encourage innovation.

The proper allocation of resources is key to our definition of management which gives an indication of how important that function is. Those resources will include finances, people and equipment.

Regardless of where they work, all managers are spending someone else's money and need to be held to account by that someone for spending decisions. In the private sector, which increasingly includes defence industries, managers report to shareholders, although customer service agreements now provide an additional mechanism for accountability to government. Defence is financed through public funds or, we might say, through the taxation of individual citizens. So, there is a great onus on public sector managers to spend that money wisely so that every dollar spent on defence might deliver a dollar's worth of defence capability. Here, the principles of good governance, as well as good management, apply for financial resourcing in defence is about the proper use of public funding. Len Nockles and Teri McConville give a richer insight of financial management in Chapter 12.

Any organization is only as good, effective, or efficient as the people within it. People are the most flexible, talented, intelligent and, often, expensive resource that an organization can have. For proper functioning, and to put plans into operation, the right people need to be recruited, in the right numbers. They need to be trained in how to do their work and allowed to keep their skills and knowledge up to date. Importantly, considering the investment that they represent, the right people also need the incentives or rewards that will encourage them to stay. These are what human resource management is about, but, as Alex Alexandrou and Roger Darby will explain in Chapter 11, management of the human resource is far too important to be shrugged off and abdicated to a team of specialists. The only way to realize the true potential of people is to consider their management as a strategic issue and include them in top-level plans.

Of course, people need equipment to do their work effectively and that is the third aspect of resourcing that needs to be organized. This will involve hard decisions, as defence equipment becomes increasingly expensive and requirements have to be balanced against other demands for public monies. When the cost of a new Eurofighter Typhoon exceeds the entire defence budget for states such as Fiji, Albania or Moldova (CIA 2005) then it is not sufficient to simply maintain that the armed forces need a new piece of kit. Priorities must be set, and based upon required capabilities. The entire acquisition process, from initial concepts through to final disposal, must be considered if the full benefit of equipment is to be realized. For more on through-life acquisition the reader is directed to Trevor Taylor's contribution in Chapter 13.

Commanding

By commanding, management educators are referring to that part of the task which concerns guiding others towards their objectives. It is often difficult to distinguish the differences between command, leadership and management. Indeed, a deal of thought and effort is dedicated to identifying their distinguishing features: a task made all the more difficult within the defence sector by the military emphasis on leadership. This is not the place to enter into that debate; readers who want to explore the issue further may find some of the suggested readings helpful. For now, let us return to the analogy of the rope. Within this particular strand there are fibres that we have called commanding, leading and directing, along with others including authority and motivation. At any point in a manager's work one strand may be more visible than others but it is their combination that gives the rope its strength.

In another part of his writings Fayol talks of the principle of unity of command which will be familiar to military officers. This is one management term that has retained its original meaning: that 'for any action whatsoever an employee should receive orders from one superior only' (Wren 1994: 186). While dual command may be a threat to stability, in a changeable environment it is recognized that stability may not always be desirable and many organizations are redesigning their structures in a way that undermines this principle in order to encourage a free flow of communication. Arguably such structures only work well where the workforce is made up of knowledgeable workers who know the limits of their own responsibilities and authority and who have been given the freedom to exercise their own judgement in response to conflicting requests or orders. Nevertheless, even in the most flexible of structures, there needs to be an ultimate arbiter to decide who should be doing what and to intervene in the event of conflict. In short there needs to be a named individual to take ultimate responsibility, be it for a specific project or for a particular sector.

With responsibility there must also be authority and it is authority that allows an organization to be guided towards its objectives. In this context authority means a legitimate basis for the exercise of power. Weber (1947) tells us that there are three ways to allocate authority to individuals. Tradition gives authority to someone because that is how it is always done so that, for instance, the son of a King will inherit his father's throne, but there is no guarantee that the new king will have either desire or aptitude for his new role. Charismatic authority derives from personality characteristics – perhaps past heroism – that makes people want to give loyalty and allegiance to the individual. History has taught us, through examples such as Adolf Hitler and Napoleon Bonaparte, that charismatic individuals might not always exercise their authority to the benefit of those that trust them. It is the third type of authority that forms the basis for proper management and governance. This is the rational-legal form of authority that elevates an individual to a position of power through the exercise of rational rules and processes. Rational-legal authority allows for the continuity of power in the organization, as does traditional authority, but does so by rational means. Rational principles ensure that individuals are given authority on the basis of their likely ability to perform rather than simply on whether other people like them, which would be the basis of charismatic authority. Further, the legal principle means that the scope of authority is clearly defined and that its bounds are also established. The use of authority, though, has its limits, for compulsion will only extract the minimum of effort from subordinates. A good manager, rather than relying on their authority, will try to persuade or motivate others to do their job better, faster or more efficiently.

The task of building up motivation in others has always taxed managers, for motivation is an internal force and the factors that may motivate one person might not apply to another. Within a market-based economy, money will always be an issue for people and is the single greatest reason that people go to work (as cleaners, soldiers or even senior executives). It would be a mistake, though, to see pay as some panacea or as the only means to motivate people to perform. While we can accept that people can be spurred into greater effort by the promise of better pay or some form of bonus, especially where those people have difficulty meeting their material needs, motivation theories show us that non-financial rewards can have just as great an impact. This is important in the public sector as managers will normally have very little influence over how much pay or bonus a worker receives.

The key to spurring people to greater efforts is to know them well. From a managerial perspective it is worthwhile to realize that objectives can serve to energize people (Hollyforde and Whiddett 2002). Where workers are sure of what is expected of them, when they see an objective as difficult but possible, and provided they have the necessary skills, then they are liable to work harder or more thoroughly than if they are unsure of what is required, or if they see the task as too simple or too hard.

Co-ordination

The co-ordination task deals with uniting and combining the efforts of all parts of an organization (or all members of a work group) in the achievement of the mutual goals that were defined in the planning stage. It involves integrating the various sections involved in the task(s), ordering and linking the various activities that need to be carried out, and maintaining effective communications.

The most obvious aspect of co-ordination, and which links with planning, is to order, or schedule, the different aspects of a job, and get them in the right order so that the work is carried out as efficiently as possible. For complex jobs many managers find it useful to use graphical techniques such as Gantt charts which are easily constructed using either graph paper or, for those with the technology, specialist software. One such tool, the Programme Evaluation and Review Technique (PERT) offers another example of a defence concept being taken up by managers elsewhere. (PERT was developed to manage the development of the Polaris submarine.) The concept has been taken up widely within management (and systems analysis) as Critical Path Analysis.

While the plan can link the different aspects of a particular job, if the entire organization is to work towards a common goal, then different groups and departments also need to be linked and co-ordinated. Sometimes that is a role (the linking role) that sits squarely on a manager's shoulders. There are, however, other mechanisms that can help. These are the organizational structure, or design, and communications.

As a general rule, the more specialized (differentiated) an organization is, the more managers need to act to hold the various parts together, to promote the common goals. The structure of an organization can be the means by which this is achieved but it depends very much upon the structure matching the purpose. In a formal bureaucracy, the rules and regulations will serve as integrating devices but with looser structures there needs to be much greater emphasis on teamwork and on establishing channels of communications across, as well as up and down, the organization.

It has been said that up to 80 per cent of a manager's job is about communicating (Armstrong and Stephens 2005). While this may not be absolutely accurate, it demonstrates how important communication is if an organization is to do its job effectively and efficiently. It is only when they know what is to be done and how one job links to another, what sort of progress is being made and whether circumstances are forcing any changes, that people can make a worthwhile contribution. The need for communication increases as the environment becomes less certain, so the need for good information management is as important to co-ordination as it is to planning. Annie Maddison has much more to say about this subject in Chapter 10.

An especially important aspect of communication, within the defence sector is the need-to-know principle. This will limit the extent to which an individual can know the purpose of their work, task or role, and people who are told that they do not need to know something may feel that they are not trusted and find it hard to become motivated. For multi-national operations it can also lead to trying, and sometimes ludicrous, situations where one country's policies may keep secret information that another state releases under Freedom of Information laws or, more seriously, a failure to share intelligence could put operational troops at risk.

Controlling

The final task in Fayol's list is a process that begins with the standards, which were determined in the objectives of the planning role, and only ends with a satisfactory completion of a task or project. Managerial control concerns making sure that the final product or service, that a group or organization delivers, matches that which was planned (although it may be that the plan was adjusted over time). Like any process, it can be shown visually (see Figure 8.1) as a series of steps, which in this case has an internal, iterative loop, to deal with any shortfall in performance.

Proper controls begin with good planning. If clear objectives have been devised, not only will people know what is required of them, clear standards will also have been set. The control part of objective-setting deals with deciding how best to measure outputs, or performance, against those standards (see also Chapter 14). In those parts of a defence sector that deal with finance and materials clear, quantifiable standards will have been set. This may be in the form of, for instance, a statement of costing or the delivery of products. Measurement becomes a problem, though, when organizations are dealing with values. Notions such as security, justice or liberty are difficult, if not impossible, to measure for they are subjective concepts. When politicians and defence leaders talk of security, for instance, they are likely to be thinking about border controls or counter-terrorism measures. Individual citizens, thinking about security, may well be considering how safe the family home is from burglary or whether they feel confident to walk out in their locality at night.

In such cases managers need to devise proxy measures, or indicators, that will represent the value that is being set. There are two problems here. First,

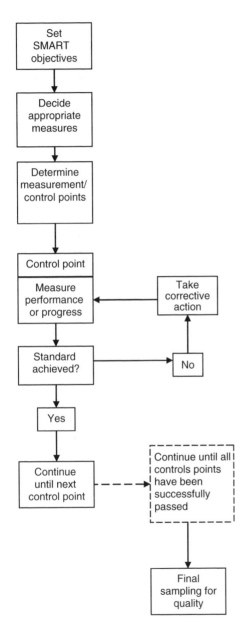

Figure 8.1 The control process.

is the need to be sure that the proxy is a true indicator. For instance, does the absence of suicide bombers in a given city really indicate good security, or simply good luck? Second, if people are being assessed by proxies, or indicators, they are likely to perform in a way that will meet the requirements of the indicator. For control purposes, managers do well to give serious thought to what, when and how to measure; for measuring the wrong thing, at the wrong time, or in an inappropriate way, is a waste of time, effort and resources.

Measurement needs to occur at appropriate points. It is insufficient and wasteful to wait until the end of a task to check whether it was done correctly. Rather, measurement needs to occur at a time when any shortfall in performance can be corrected, before further work is compromised by an earlier problem. A training unit would not wait until the end of training to assess a recruit's competence. Instead, directing staff and others involved in the training process will test recruits at regular points during training to make sure that that are achieving the desired standard, or to take corrective action with anyone who is likely to fail. Any complex task can be broken down into various elements, and the start or end of each of these elements is an appropriate point for measurement. There may be certain points in a job that present a risk to end-users or to other workers. At these points other controls, such as a written record of procedures completed, can be added to the measurements. These are control points.

Example: food safety for space travel

HACCP (Hazard And Critical Control Point) is an internationally recognized food safety control which was developed originally, by NASA, to ensure the safety of food being supplied to astronauts during the early days of the United States manned space programme. It has become a standard control tool in food production.

HACCP systems allow a methodical assessment of hazards to be conducted through the audit of processes and the listing of any characteristics which will affect the integrity of the final product (Whittle 1998). Where a hazard or risk is identified, then preventive measures are devized and controls put in place. Test points are established to monitor likely hazards. At each of these points HACCP forms record the delivery details of each ingredient as well as preparation times. Operators sign for each element of the procedure and are held accountable for specific hazard controls.

The particular strengths of the system are: that it can monitor and control a range of hazards, particularly contamination by germs, chemicals or foreign bodies; and that there is an audit trail to confirm that procedures were carried out properly, and by whom.

The sole purpose of measurement and control points is to ensure that work is continuing as planned. If there is any indication of things going wrong then the control function of management requires that corrective action is taken before the work progresses further. This is not a one-off process but something that should be repeated at various points throughout a job. This ensures that organizational efforts are being focused on high quality output, in accordance with intended goals.

The general body of classical management theory has been the focus for a deal of criticism and it is important to recognize that it has limits, especially in complex organizations and uncertain environments. What has been presented above is only one aspect of the theory and it can be argued that Fayol's 'functions of management', remain useful, for they are universal functions and show that management skills and knowledge are portable – that they can be used in any form of organization – and that the basic job of managing is the same no matter where it takes place. However, no organization, or sector, remains the same and there are always new challenges to be faced. For public sector organizations, such a challenge has come in the form of New Public Management (NPM). This is a slightly ridiculous label and something of a misnomer as the concept has now been around for some twenty-five years, at least in the economically strong states. NPM represents a shift in the way that policy-makers think about public services and makes demands for greater efficiency, transparency and accountability in the administration of those services. It is, therefore, appropriate to devote some time and attention to this aspect of managing public affairs.

The new public management

Over the last twenty-five years there has been a transformation in the way that public sector organizations, all around the world, are managed. It is a trend that began in richer states but that quickly spread throughout the Organization for Economic Co-operation and Development. This new pattern of public management has become the norm for the administration and reform of public sector services.

Change came about alongside, or maybe as a result of, four major trends (Hood 1991):

- During the 1970s massive inflation in the great economies, combined with major oil crises, put enormous pressure on public funds. The costs of maintaining huge bureaucratic organizations and expensive social welfare programmes became intolerable without increasing taxation and government borrowing.
- The election of conservative governments around the world, including Britain, the USA, Australasia and South America heralded a more international agenda in political strategy and decision-making.

- It also brought in a new approach to political economy, called monetarism, which advocated that governments should concentrate on core services. This lead to the sale of formerly nationalized industries, and increasing use of private sector organization and finance for the provision of new projects and for ancillary services such as catering and cleaning.
- The development of information technology allowed the collation and distribution of information on a scale that would have been nearly impossible using manual systems. It became much easier to develop databases on costs and service delivery, to compare the performance of organizations, and to inform the public of the results. While the defence sector has recognized a Revolution in Military Affairs, the corresponding Revolution in Business Affairs (Matthews and Treddenick 2003), enabled by information technologies, has been underestimated by those who manage or administer defence services.

The resulting approach to managing public services, NPM, brings together two main streams of thought. On the one hand is institutional economics which advocates that public sector policy and doctrine should uphold the principle of choice for service users. On the other hand there is school of thought called managerialism which maintains that management expertise should take precedence over other professional or technical knowledge. While these two approaches do not necessarily lead to the same conclusions, the fusion of the two leads to a clear set of doctrinal principles (Hood 1991) which stand in stark contrast to the traditional idea that public sector organizations should be administered by well-ordered and impartial bureaucracies.

Doctrinal components of NPM

Traditionally, public sector organizations have been regarded as being like machines where, provided rules and procedures were in place, and people worked according to those rules and procedures, then the organization was bound to work efficiently. All that was needed was someone at the top to administer – ensuring that resources were in place and enforcing the rules. NPM takes a very different view, emphasising responsibility and accountability (Lane 2000). If the public sector is to be engineered for performance, managers cannot be anonymous bureaucrats but must take active and visible control. This means that public organizations need professional managers who know the range of best practices available within the private sector; and they must be given the right and power to manage their own organizations (this is called the managerial prerogative). There could be no place for blanket regulations that might restrict managerial initiatives and neither could professional judgement, be it from generals or politicians, over-ride well-reasoned managerial strategy.

NPM shifts the emphasis in public sector work. Doing things right is no longer the key concern, rather organizations are required to do the right things so that outputs rather than process become the foci of activity. Rules and procedures need to be replaced by explicit standards of performance and clear indicators of success. These then determine how resources, and even personal rewards, should be allocated. The principles of transparency and accountability require that the basis for such allocation is clear and, hence, the reporting of outputs (preferably in quantitative format) is one of the enduring features of NPM.

Some of the (many) disadvantages of bureaucratic structures, especially in the large-scale organizations that make up the public sector, are that it is often difficult to distinguish who is doing what, where activities are duplicated, which functions are consuming resources, and where performance can be improved. For managers to exercise their prerogative, and for the effective assessment of performance, smaller, manageable units are needed. So, NPM advocates the separation of units within the public sector. This allows for resources to be targeted on those areas where they are most needed, and for managers to identify those functions that most require their attention. It also means that core functions can be separated from support activities, rather like the armed forces will distinguish combat, combat service and combat service support. Where an activity is not central to producing the final output, NPM allows that the public sector can franchise the activity to other departments, or even to the private sector, to take advantage of economies of scale.

The establishment of smaller units, with clear output targets and performance measures makes it much easier to compare costs and outputs. This allows the next doctrinal principle, which is to encourage greater competition within the public sector. The reasoning is that exposing a service to the rigors of the market will reveal its true value and that rivalry will lead to better standards and lower costs. By shifting the way resources are allocated, from government departments to representatives of the end-users, users have a degree of choice in areas such as healthcare and education. Thus, quasi-markets have been developed so that the best organizations get more resources, as well as more clients, and poorly-performing units are exposed as inadequate or inefficient. There are, however, some public services where it is difficult to identify competitors and defence is one of them. (Admittedly some smaller states do engage private military companies to supplement their defence and security provision.) Even so, there are segments of these functions, such as training, medical support, engineering or procurement, where the principle of competition can operate.

These principles have fundamentally altered the way that public sector organizations operate. Above all they stress the need for greater discipline and thrift in the way that public resources are used. The public purse is not a bottomless well and those who manage public services have a duty to ensure that resources are used to greatest effect. While there are some who see NPM as gratuitous and philistine destruction of the public service ethic there is an equally valid argument that former practices had failed irretrievably and that drastic measures, including a re-assessment of why governments and the public sector exist, were the only way to bring about improvements.

Conclusion

Defence is a unique function within any given society, for it is the basis of national security and can ultimately safeguard, or otherwise, the very existence of a state. It is a function that can consume massive resources, including human life. It follows that the management of defence is a key task whether it occurs within the corridors of power or in a barracks. However, the management task is not so very different in the defence sector than elsewhere.

In the past there has been a tendency to assume that, because military commanders are practised in the arts of leadership, then they must also be good managers. History has shown us repeatedly that that is not so. If we fail to accept the lessons of the past we are guilty of leaving a crucial public function to run itself. That could only lead to the sector becoming stagnant and complacent when what it needs is to be continually improving both what it does and how it does it.

Effective managers require skill and specialist (management) knowledge if they are to do their job well, if true value for money is to be achieved, and if all components of the defence sector are to be fit for their purpose. They also need courage and integrity for, if the interests of the nation (or state) are to be properly served, public management practices must be open to scrutiny, and individuals must be held accountable for their own actions as well as organizational outcomes. Public sector reforms do little more than underline these needs.

All public organizations, including those dealing with defence, need a strong rope to pull them in the right direction; and that rope is skilled, professional, and knowledgeable management. In this chapter we have unravelled the rope slightly to show how it has been constructed. Later chapters will do a little more unravelling. The readers' task is to splice that rope back together, and to use all its strength and function, to deliver an efficient and effective defence service to a public that expects, and deserves, nothing less.

Questions to consider

1   Does your current job include specific objectives for each task that you would normally undertake? Can you identify the who, what, when, and the required standards and conditions?

    a   If not, as part of your own management development, try to construct a set of objectives for your most regular work and pass them to your boss to see if you both agree.

2   Try to remember a time when you felt that you wanted to put all your energies into doing a particular task. Was it really because the job was going to bring some extra payment, or were there other factors? Perhaps the work presented a challenge to your skills and knowledge or, maybe, you believed the task to be really important. It may be that you were going to get some other benefit such as the chance to travel or to leave work early.

   a   Now do the same for a job that you couldn't find the motivation to complete. Was it really a matter of not getting paid enough?

3   Remember a time when a colleague would not or could not share information that, later, proved to affect your job. How did you feel? You possibly experienced a mixture or anger, frustration and bewilderment that someone should consider you to be unimportant or untrustworthy. You probably had to put in extra effort to put right what you had done because you did not know to do it differently. Remember, too, a time when the reverse applied – when you held back information. If you could re-live that time, what might you have done differently?

4   What is the main output of your current job? How might you measure that output? Can you see any potential difficulties with that measure? (Sylvie Jackson gives a vivid example in Chapter 14.)

5   Not all activities in the defence sector need to be, or even should be, carried out by service personnel.

   a   Think for a moment and make a list of the range of activities that are currently performed by the armed forces in your country.

   b   Now consider which of those simply must be done by a trained, full-time soldier, sailor or airman?

   c   Which could reasonably be assigned to a reservist? This probably still leaves quite a long list. Look at those functions that remain. Which jobs should be tasked to civil servants?

   d   Anything that is left over could possibly be contracted out to some other organization, and it is entirely possible that a specialist company could do the job more efficiently or most cost-effectively than it is done at the moment.

Suggested reading

Armstrong, M. and Stephens, T. (2005), *A Handbook of Management and Leadership: A Guide to Managing for Results*, London: Kogan–Page.

Defence Leadership and Management Centre, www.da.mod.uk/dlmc, accessed on 12 November 2005.

McConville, T. and Holmes, R. (eds) (2003), *Defence Management in Uncertain Times*, London: Frank Cass.

Maylor, H. (2002), *Project Management* (3rd Edition), London: FT Prentice Hall.

Moskos, C. C., Williams, J. A. and Segal, D. R. (eds) (2000), *The Postmodern Military: Armed Forces After the Cold War*, Oxford: Oxford University Press.
Shaffritz, J. M. and Ott, J. J. (2001), *Classics of Organization Theory*, Fort Worth: Harcourt College Publishers.

Bibliography

Armstrong, M. and Stephens, T. (2005), *A Handbook of Management and Leadership: A Guide to Managing for Results*, London: Kogan–Page.
CIA. (2005), *World Factbook*, www.cia.gov/cia/publications/factbook, accessed on 29 October 2005.
Crainer, S. (1996), *Key Management Ideas*, London: Pitman.
Du Gay, P. (2000), *In Praise of Bureaucracy*, London: Sage.
Fayol, H. (1916), *Administration Industrielle et Generalle*, trans. C. Storrs (1949) as *General and Industrial Management*, London: Pitman.
Ghana. (2005), www.ghana.gov.gh/governing/ministries/governance/defence.php, accessed on 10 September 2005.
Hollyforde, S. and Whiddett, S. (2002), *The Motivation Handbook*, London: Chartered Institute of Personnel and Development.
Hood, C. (1991), 'A public management for all seasons?' *Public Administration* 69: (Spring): 3–19.
Lane, J.-E. (2000), *New Public Management*, London and New York: Routledge.
Matthews, R. and Treddenick, J. (eds) (2003), *Managing the Revolution in Military Affairs*, London: Palgrave.
Merton, R. K. (1968), *Social Theory and Social Structure*, New York: Free Press.
Parker, L. D. and Ritson, P. A. (2005), 'Revisiting Fayol: Anticipating Contemporary Management', *British Journal of Management*, 16 (3): 175–94
Weber, M. (1947), *The Theory of Social and Economic Organization*, trans. A. M. Henderson and T. Parsons, New York: Free Press.
Whittle, V. (1988), 'Putting HACCP in the QMS Bundle', *Quality World* (March), 10–11.
Wren, D. A. (1994), *The Evolution of Management Thought*, New York: John Wiley & Sons.

9 Strategic management
Avoiding analysis paralysis

Derrick J. Neal

Introduction

Strategic management is the process and practice of establishing and delivering an organization's strategy. In this regard it is necessary to manage a number of aspects of the organization that are of strategic significance. In particular aspects such as,

- Recognition of core competencies
- Understanding environmental changes
- Identification of threats and opportunities
- Balancing stakeholder expectations
- Evolving an appropriate culture
- Embracing the impact of technology and innovation
- Understanding the motivations of staff and customers
- Being able to understand the significance of elements within the value chain
- Recognizing the impact of critical success factors

This list is by no means exhaustive and, within the topic of strategic management, issues need to be addressed in the areas of Finance, Production, Human Resource Management and Sales/Marketing.

Many textbooks exist on the subject of strategic management (including those under the headings of Corporate Strategy, Business Policy or Strategy) but they all have one thing in common, namely, the assertion that strategic thinking is about testing boundaries and challenging assumptions. In order to achieve this, the strategy process needs to be rigorous and be prepared to challenge the current paradigm (culture) within the organization in a positive and constructive manner.

Strategic management is a relatively new subject and over the past 30 years academics have been busy in producing a wide literature that approaches the subject from different perspectives. The study of strategy by Mintzberg, Ahlstrand & Lampel (1998) is instructive in this matter as they chart some 10 schools of strategic management that cover very different perspectives as shown below.

- Design School
- Planning School
- Positioning School
- Power School
- Cognitive School
- Entrepreneurial School
- Cultural School
- Configuration School
- Environmental School
- Learning School

Each of the above has produced a large number of books from academics making the case for their perspective. In the real world most organizations either knowingly or by chance use a combination of these approaches. The Planning School is of particular interest in this book because it will be shown that it fits most closely with the processes and practices used by the military to develop overall strategy both in terms of operations and non-operational activity.

At this point it is useful to have a working definition of the process of strategy formulation as it will ground some of the topics that are to follow. The particular definition used in this text comes from Johnson and Scholes and has been used on strategic management courses for many years.

> Strategy is the *direction* and *scope* of an organization over the *long term*: which achieves *advantage* for the organization through its configuration of *resources* within a changing *environment*, to meet the needs of markets and to fulfil *stakeholder expectations*.
>
> (Johnson and Scholes 2005: 8)

The key element in this definition is the identification and need to understand the organization's stakeholders. This aspect is something that the UK Ministry of Defence (MoD) has only recently given an appropriate level of attention and rigour. The emphasis in the strategic analysis section of this chapter will reflect the significance of stakeholders and will show how it is important to take the widest possible perspective of stakeholders in strategy formulation.

In the past, it can be argued that public sector organizations took a very simplistic view of strategy where the objective was to spend the full monetary allocation each year to ensure that the budget for the following year would be maintained or increased. However, most public sector organizations today operate in a very different environment where accountability, transparency and social responsibility are high on the agenda. In addition to this many public sector organizations find themselves working in partnerships of various forms with the private sector. The growth in the use of commercial good practice in public service delivery has had a major impact on organizations as diverse as railway transportation, health, education and even the provision of military capability in defence of the nation.

Increasingly, public sector organizations find themselves having to compete for scarce resources, needing to demonstrate efficient and effective use of their assets and having to adopt a more commercial model of organizational structure and operation in striving for greater efficiency.

Changes within the defence sector in the last decade or more are such that an understanding of strategic management is now an essential requirement and not simply an option. Meaningful application of strategic management principles and concepts involves far more than simply changing structures, employing consultants or producing glossy documents that speak of vision statements and awards of civilian standards of excellence.

The Planning School

The Planning School came to maturity in the 1970s and was really a development from the design school that had been the adopted approach during the 1960s. It was consistent with the general move during the 1970s towards more formalized organizational systems, structures and processes. The corresponding response from the academic community was the development of a wide range of strategic analytical tools and techniques to support more formalized strategy processes.

Of all of the strategy schools of thought the Planning School most closely resembles the approach associated with military operational planning. Indeed, many of the terms used in management generally and marketing in particular have been borrowed from the military in the first instance. Many militaries around the world, when planning a military campaign, use an operational planning process known as 'the estimate'. The estimate process involves working through a series of questions (typically varies from seven to nine depending upon which of the services you are dealing with) and these questions form a checklist to ensure that the commander has worked through all of the key aspects of conducting an operation. The process involves a number of steps including,

- understanding your superior's strategic intent (an element within the concept of mission command);
- having knowledge of the battle ground where the operation will take place;
- assessment of your strengths and weaknesses and those of your enemy;
- identifying the enemy's centre of gravity and then developing possible courses of action.

Each course of action is then tested against the strategic intent and, upon selection of a specific course of action, the detail of the implementation is addressed. Although this might sound rather mechanistic it does allow the commander to introduce his/her experience and apply novel solutions to problems. Increasingly, the issue of the time available for decision making is becoming a critical factor, which is being compounded by the explosion in the amount of information available to the commander at any given time. In such a situation it can be very helpful to the commander to have a structured analytical approach as this lends itself to being able to delegate specific tasks within a formal process.

Given that the military are very comfortable with this approach to strategy formulation for operations it makes sense to adopt the Planning School approach in strategy formulation for non-operational activities within an MoD. This area of an MoD is often referred to as the business space and is concerned with issues of the provision of training, personnel management, equipment acquisition, logistics functions, project and programme management, financial management and the establishment of management performance metrics.

The Planning School approach has a number of advantages and disadvantages (see Table 9.1) but organizations that adopt this approach generally feel that the structure that this gives to the organization outweighs the disadvantages. The significance of structure becomes more significant when the organization is large and has diverse activities that need to be coordinated.

Table 9.1 Advantages and disadvantages of the Planning School of strategy formulation

	Issues
Advantages	
Check lists	Means that you know that you have covered set issues
Confidence generation	Having worked through the process you have confidence that you have completed your elements of a much larger process
Easy to put into systems	Very helpful in very large diverse organizations to help ensure coherence
Disadvantages	
Check lists	May stifle innovation and true strategic thinking if the commander fails to consider beyond the first cut analysis
End unto itself	The approach becomes a mechanistic process that needs to be in compliance with target dates and forms
Focus is on the preparation of the plan	Key risk is that the plan is not considered from an implementation perspective

The latter point is depicted graphically in Figure 9.1 which shows, in element (a), how the creation of the strategic plan is the focal point and that the focus is lost in the implementation stage. Evidence that this is often the case is given, in the academic literature, in the widely held belief that more than 80 per cent of strategies fail and that the failure is due primarily in the implementation. (Many reasons for this state of affairs can be identified and these will be discussed Chapter 15.) The ideal scenario is given in element (b) and highlights the need for creative thinking in the strategy formulation process followed by a high degree of focus in the delivery of the strategy.

The main generic activities within most Planning School models include the activities as shown in Figure 9.2.

It is particularly important to recognize that the strategy process is not linear. When developing strategy it is necessary to continually go backwards and forwards between the three elements. This dynamic should continue through the formulation process into the implementation process and should result in the constant process of feedback and evaluation.

Although all of the models developed within the academic literature contain a range of words to describe the process, in essence they can all be reduced to the three stages given above. In plain English this is often stated in three very simple questions, namely,

- Where are we now?
- Where do we want to go?
- How do we get there?

Organizations, both large and small would be well advised to ensure that they continually ask these three questions and that they approach the

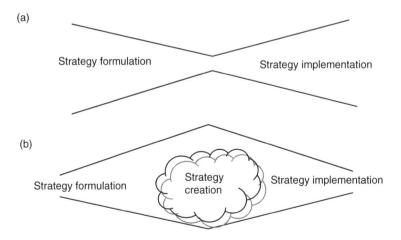

Figure 9.1 The problem of (a) and solution to (b) a mechanistic application of the Planning School approach.

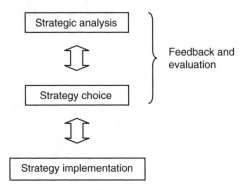

Figure 9.2 The activities of strategy planning.

production of the answers with a degree of rigour and professionalism. All too often it can be seen that senior management have already decided the answer to these questions and simply go through a process to deliver the answers that they want.

The question needs to be asked as to why an organization should feel that it needs to review or change its strategy. The most common reason is that there has been change in the external environment. Failure to acknowledge this and reflect it in the organization's strategy will at best lead to under-performance and at worst see a commercial company fail totally. Public sector organizations or departments do not fail and vanish, as commercial firms might, but when things go badly wrong there is usually some form of public enquiry. Typically the outcome may result in the offending department being restructured, perhaps given new terms of reference and would probably see the removal of a number of senior staff. The latter may be valid or as is often the case they are seen as scapegoats.

Failures in health, education, transportation and a range of social services become public news very quickly because they help to sell newspapers. Equally, military operational failures are painfully obvious; however, failures within the military business space tend to be highlighted when very large sums of taxpayer's money are involved.

Major problems within the UK MoD have centred on issues such as over-spending on major pieces of equipment and/or the late delivery of equipment. Even when the equipment has been delivered the MoD has had to face difficult questions about its reliability or suitability when it is being used in specific conditions, such as the poor reliability of the Apache helicopters and the Challenger tanks when deployed in desert conditions. The US DoD has been heavily criticized for its poor performance in managing the cost of new platforms such as the F22 Raptor and their missile defence systems.

It is not only the developed Western nations that have these problems and it is not always equipment that gives cause for concern. As Indonesia moves forward on the path to being a democracy the future roles for the Police and the Military are thrown into question. It is clear that the strategy pursued by the TNI (Tentera Nasional Indonesia (Indonesia Military)) prior to the election of Sulsio Yudhoyono will not be viable in the future and that they will need to develop new strategies to pursue their future roles within Indonesian society.

Similarly the Ghanaian armed forces have recognized that given the financial constraints within which they need to be able to operate they have to seek additional sources of funding if they are to be able to maintain a credible military. Part of their strategy has been to identify a niche market as UN Peacekeepers, which they are performing with great credit.

Equally, consideration of a number of South American nations highlights that they are having to come to terms with significant changes in their internal and external environments and are being driven by a number of political, financial and socio-cultural factors that require them to review and change their strategies to ensure that they are able to meet changing stakeholder expectations.

Given that the external environment is constantly changing it is often the case that organizations are able to follow the changes through incremental adjustments to their strategies. However, when they fail to do this, or when the rate of change in the environment accelerates, and goes unnoticed, the organization runs the risk of strategic drift. This concept is depicted in Figure 9.3 and clearly shows how the gap between the organization's incremental change efforts and the changes in the environment grows. The specifics of the individual elements will be discussed more fully in Chapter 15, but suffice to say at this stage that if an organization fails to fully appreciate the need for change and the drivers behind that change they face the prospect of trying to implement a new strategy and change in a highly reactive manner. This situation commonly leads to initiative fatigue and to ill-considered changes of structures, systems and processes – a state of affairs that clearly helps explain the 80 per cent failure rate.

One of the causes for failure to see the problem is the onset of complacency. The danger of complacency is that it can be a very slow-onset problem and the inertia associated with this situation means that making the necessary changes can take a long time. For example, the Indonesian military operated almost as a private army to the President under the rule of Suharto for several decades. During this time they established questionable practices that became part of their culture. It has been very difficult for them to accept that such practices are no longer deemed acceptable, to the point where the current administration has needed to pass new laws to make senior military leaders realize that they cannot continue the practices that have made them very wealthy for many years. It also follows that the government now also has to realize that it will cost the public purse far more to maintain the military in the future, given that personnel will no longer be able to subsidize their income by other means.

In the past many defence companies have been seen as national champions and have been afforded preferential treatment by their governments. However, with the move to globalization and the consolidation of the defence sector, defence companies today find themselves in a difficult position. In some ways they have a more difficult situation because in many cases they are locked into long term business arrangements developing equipment for the MoD and it can be very difficult to explore other opportunities whilst ensuring that such contracts are honoured. For this reason many defence companies have elected to pursue growth through acquisitions, mergers and strategic alliances. This approach permits the existing businesses to continue intact whilst growth opportunities are pursued through the new ventures.

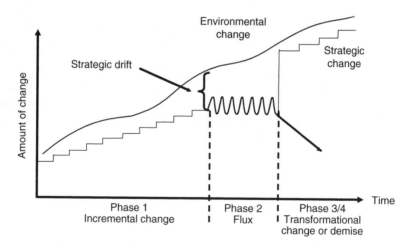

Figure 9.3 The concept of strategic drift (Johnson and Scholes 2002: 81).

Strategic analysis tools within the Planning School

In conducting the strategic planning process, irrespective of which Planning School model is being used, a number of tools have application and typically they are intended to answer the question, 'where are we now?' In achieving this a number of perspectives need to be included such as,

- The nature of the macro environment.
- The internal strengths and weaknesses of the organization.
- An understanding of the impact of organizational culture.

PESTLE analysis

The PESTLE analysis is a very useful tool for establishing the nature of the environment within which an organization operates now, and can give some indications of the possible changes that may be appropriate for the future. The elements within this analysis are as follows:

P – Political What is the political environment like at present? Is it stable, are the politicians talking about making changes that will affect the company/organization?

E – Economic What is the state of the economy at the local and national level? If the organization has significant overseas interests then consideration of economic conditions in other countries might also be appropriate.

S – Socio/cultural Consideration of changing social norms and values appropriate to the sphere within which the organization operates. The impact of specific cultural values or practices needs to be taken into account especially if they affect the potential strategic options under consideration.

T – Technology Most organizations will find that technology has and will continue to have an impact on the way they operate. It may be the case that government initiatives or even legislation will require the organization to adopt particular capabilities in order to comply with regulations. The application of technologies within industries can also form a dynamic with working practices that may be influenced by social and cultural considerations.

L – Legal With the increase in litigation, both between organizations and between organizations and private citizens, it is increasingly important for the strategic analysis process to consider the implications of legal obligations during the development of strategy.

E – Ecological This factor has been included in the analysis process quite recently as organizations and governments realize that the planet has finite resources, and that their utilization and disposal requires a responsible approach. To this end issues such as the disposal of computer equipment and refrigerators have caused organizations to rethink their approach to these issues.

Putting the PESTLE analysis into a defence sector context reveals a wide range of issues and highlights that several of the areas are interrelated thus making the analysis potentially very complicated.

Defence officials conducting such an analysis would be acutely aware that their political masters are likely to have a track record of changing direction on matters of international relations and in requiring their military capability to be infinitely flexible and responsive. This makes it particularly important for the military strategic planners to have a very clear understanding of the scope and scale of political input and interest in the military strategy formulation process. Politicians are often strongly guided by the general state of the economy and the vote winning value of their decisions. Running a professional military and equipping it with modern capabilities is a particularly expensive exercise and affordability issues need to be considered. The military have to be aware of the views of society about the way they conduct their business and recognition that cultural diversity exists in society generally and should expect this to be reflected in the military personnel. Failure to confront this issue will leave the military open to criticism when performing civil roles of discrimination. In many developing nations, as found in Africa, it is often the case that international funding is linked to major reform within the military in that country.

The SWOT analysis

A second very useful tool in conducting a strategic analysis is the Strengths (S), Weaknesses (W), Opportunities (O) and Threats (T) analysis. American texts often refer to this as a TOWS analysis and often set the strengths and weaknesses against the opportunities and threats in the external environment. The culmination of this process is that strengths and weaknesses are scored as positives (+) and negatives (−) and some form of summation is applied, leading to guidance on strategic options. Such a process, to the inexperienced, can cause problems if the calculated figures are used as an answer rather than a prompt for further questioning.

The key factor to the successful use of SWOT is the realization that the S and W are factors that are *internal* to the organization and that the O and T are *external* factors. Failure to apply this correctly usually leads to the strengths being converted to opportunities and the weaknesses to threats. A classic scenario of this problem is given below in the example:

Gregor had just finished reading a piece about the SWOT analysis and decided to use it in his strategic analysis work for his aerospace company. He greatly enjoyed doing the S and W part as he felt he could find details to fill the boxes with ease, although he was disappointed at the number of weaknesses he was able to produce. When it came to the O and T elements he felt that he was making very good progress as he was generating a large number of opportunities. For example, he had noted that his company had financial strength and he was also confident that the technical/engineering skills in his company were a particular strength. Combining these factors led Gregor to identify that new product development was a major opportunity. Was he right to make this assessment?

The answer is a clear 'no' because new product development is an internal factor. However, if Gregor had made the following statement as his opportunity then he would have used the SWOT correctly: 'There is a market demand for products that are well suited to my company's technical/engineering capabilities'. This change is not merely a case of being a wordsmith; it makes clear that the opportunity is beyond the control of Gregor and his company. Ultimately, Gregor has to make a decision about going ahead with product development and this decision is indeed an internal decision but the opportunity remains external.

The final problem that occurs with SWOT analysis is that the analyst often spends a great deal of time trying to have a balance between the number of factors in each box. Generally, the number of S and W will outweigh those in the O and T boxes. This is to be expected given that one would expect to know more about the workings of ones organization and have little difficulty in identifying them as strengths or weaknesses.

Stakeholder analysis

The importance of stakeholder analysis cannot be overemphasized. It is central to the definition of strategy given at the beginning of this chapter, which highlights that an organization's strategy needs to deliver stakeholder expectations. Consequently, it is critical that, in formulating strategy, stakeholders are identified and their expectations are understood.

A number of tools and approaches can be used to capture the essential stakeholder information; however, one of the most useful is the Power/Interest matrix (see Figure 9.4). This is particularly helpful because when large organizations, such as an MoD, look at the list of stakeholders it quickly becomes apparent that a very large number exist and turning this into something useful can be challenging. The P/I matrix is a framework that helps prioritize stakeholders so that an appropriate focus can be maintained.

It should be noted that all stakeholders are considered and that none are ignored in this matrix, even the low-power and low-interest groups deserve effort to keep them informed of performance. The logic of the axes

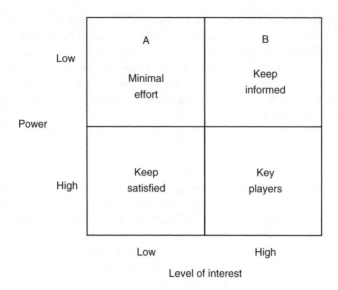

are simple, if stakeholders have power it can be exercised either in your favour or against you. Similarly, stakeholders may be interested in what you are doing or may simply leave you alone. In both cases groups can move from high to low or indeed from low to high. To this end it must be recognized that a P/I matrix is dynamic and it is important to recognize when stakeholders have moved on the matrix, in particular when a change of power is involved. Naturally, it is essential that the strategy being formulated meets the expectations of the key players. Failure to achieve this can lead to only one thing, overall failure. Whilst it is not intended that the stakeholders are plotted on this matrix with a map-maker's precision it is helpful to locate them in a relative manner within each box, thus the bottom right-hand corner is more significant than the top left-hand corner in the key players box and this gives a further degree of prioritization within the process. Having identified the stakeholders the second phase is to ensure that the expectations of the stakeholders, especially the key players, are well understood.

In situations where a mismatch exists between the strategic intent of the organization and the expectations of key stakeholders it is the responsibility of senior management to establish a communications strategy, to try to change or shape the expectations of stakeholders, to facilitate the delivery of the strategy. If it is not possible to gain 'buy-in' from essential stakeholders then it may be necessary to re-visit the strategy. An alternative approach can be to develop a phased strategy approach and use success in the delivery of phase one to convince stakeholders to change their views and accept the general strategic intent.

Critical success factors

The final tool considered in this chapter is that of critical success factors (CSFs), for failure to establish what they are is likely to leave a strategy that is doomed to failure. As the name suggests there are relatively few of these factors and even for a very large organization such as a multi-national corporation or a public sector department, such as the UK MoD, there are probably in the region of five to seven CSFs. It can be most informative to ask people in your own organization to list the CSFs as they see them. If they try to impress by putting forward ten or more you will have at least established that they do not know what CSFs are and, more importantly, they do not fully understand the critical things in their day to day operations that will deliver success for the organization.

Having considered the CSFs from an internal point of view it is particularly helpful to take these findings to the marketplace and cross-check with the views of the customers and suppliers because if a mismatch exists managers can find themselves trying to improve things that either, do not need improving, or are not important. Equally, it may be that some things which need to be addressed are not being considered because people within the organization do not see them as being important.

In addition to specific analytical tools it is important to remember that organizations are collections of human beings and that the issue of organizational, regional and national cultures need to be considered when conducting an analysis of the now and the possibilities for the future. Similarly it would be a naïve manager who ignored the issue of power balance, within the organization and between stakeholders, when considering the subject of strategy.

Having established the current status of the organization, the next stage of the process is to generate strategic options for further analysis. Many tools and techniques exist for this purpose including decision tree analysis, cultural mapping and ranking techniques. Whilst some of the strategy analysis tools are of a generic nature as is the case for PESTLE, SWOT, stakeholder analysis and CSF analysis this is not the case with tools for strategic option evaluation. It is beyond the scope of this chapter to go into this area in any great detail as the tools selected need to be chosen for the specific circumstance and applied in an appropriately weighted manner. However, it is also the case that strategic options can utilize several of the strategic analysis tools to good effect. For example, having generated a strategic option, such as using elements of outsourcing, it is a relatively simple matter to assess this option in terms of how it meets customer critical success factors, and to judge it against the organization's strengths and weaknesses. Equally, the use of outsourcing can also be considered from the perspective of key stakeholders in forming a view as to how acceptable or unacceptable this strategic option will be.

The three key tests that need to be applied to the strategic options are:

Is the strategy suitable?   That is, does it fit with our view of the organization. For example, if the organizational culture is one of a family that cares for its staff, a strategy that requires 'hire and fire' would be inappropriate. However, if the organization is in crisis and such drastic measures are needed then senior management need to ensure that they have the necessary transformational change skills (see Chapter 15) to tackle the problem.

Is the strategy feasible?   This is a reality check as it is often found that senior management are so detached from the organization that the strategy is no better than a wish list from the top. This situation can be difficult to manage because staff below senior management level see the strategy for what it is and consequently the organization lacks buy-in from those tasked with the implementation.

Is the strategy acceptable?   In this case the acceptability has to be linked to knowledge of the key player stakeholders, as any strategy that does not have their support will struggle to gain the right levels of commitment needed to put the ideas into action.

Conclusion

Within a defence sector organization the breadth of stakeholders is significant and their particular interests can be highly varied. They will include political sensitivities at local, national and international levels, economic considerations, matters of staff morale, of ongoing commitments and the impact of technology on modes of operation. The pressure on defence budgets around the world is relentless and the days of senior management simply saying that we need to tighten our belts and continue to deliver more with less resource are rapidly diminishing. Consequently, senior management in defence organizations around the world need to take a long hard look at their strategy formulation processes to ensure that they conduct the process with rigour and a high degree of professionalism.

The selection of the means for implementing strategy must not be overlooked at this stage. Indeed, at each stage of the development of strategy alternatives it is necessary to think through exactly how the strategy will be delivered. It should not be the case that strategy and implementation are considered as independent events. The implementation of strategy is covered in Chapter 15 as change management.

Questions to consider

1   Think about the 10 schools of strategy and consider how your organization approaches the development of its strategy. Is it a matter of who has power, is it guided through informal power paths or formal paths, is it highly structured or does it evolve over time.

2 How clear is your understanding of where your organization is heading and how it proposes to achieve its objectives? Do you have a clear picture of what you have to do in support of this strategy?

3 Think about your own organization from the perspective of strategic drift. Can you identify issues of flux (often seen as failed change initiatives), and are the current strategies closing the gap with changes in your environment? What factors are changing or influencing the strategic environment in which you operate?

4 Conduct a PESTLE analysis for your organization and reflect on the key aspects that are responsible for shaping the strategic direction of the organization

5 Conduct a SWOT analysis of your organization. What are you able to do to minimize the effects of the weaknesses and to take advantage of the strengths? How do the opportunities and threats relate to your findings from the PESTLE analysis?

6 Prepare a Stakeholder map of your organization. Consider how well your current strategy is delivering against those stakeholders defined as key players. How could your strategy be improved in this regard?

Suggested reading

Hamel, G. and Prahalad, C. K. (1994), *Competing for the Future*, Cambridge, MA: Harvard Business School Press.

Johnson, G. and Scholes, K. (2005), *Exploring Corporate Strategy Text and Cases*, (7th edition) [there is also a version without the cases] London: Financial Times, Prentice Hall.

Mintzberg, H., Ahlstrand, B. and Lampel, J. (1998), *Strategy Safari: A Guided Tour Through the Wilds of Strategic Management*, London and New York: Prentice Hall.

Bibliography

Johnson, G. and Scholes, K. (2005), *Exploring Corporate Strategy: Text and Cases*, (7th edition), London: Financial Times, Prentice Hall.

Mendelow, A. (1991), *Proceedings of 2nd International Conference on Information Systems*, Cambridge, MA, Cited by Johnson, G. and Scholes, K. (2005), *Exploring Corporate Strategy: Text and Cases*, (7th edition), London: Financial Times, Prentice Hall, p. 81.

Mintzberg, H., Ahlstrand, B. and Lampel, J. (1998), *Strategy Safari: A Guided Tour through the Wilds of Strategic Management*, London and New York: Prentice Hall.

10 Information and its management

Annie Maddison

Introduction

In 1988, Peter Drucker tried to imagine what the typical organization of the twenty-first century would look like. The picture he drew was of a flatter, less hierarchical structure. Work would be carried out by interdisciplinary teams of knowledge specialists, forming as required, tackling a project and then dispersing to create new teams with new challenges. Most critically, the driving force behind this organization, the vital component, would be information. Almost 30 years after Drucker made these predictions, how close has the contemporary organization come to meeting his vision? Have workers evolved into knowledge specialists and has information become their driving force?

The answer to these questions must surely be 'yes'. We live, so we are told, in the Information Age. It is widely reported that both private and public sector organizations around the world see information as one of their most critical, strategic assets (Leonard-Barton 1995). The United States, Japan, Germany and other major industrial powers are being transformed from industrial economies to information-based service economies, while manufacturing has been moved to the low-wage countries (Laudon and Laudon 2002: 5). However, although this scenario may suggest otherwise, the Information Age is not solely the province of the so-called first world. Even in developing countries, information has become a key ingredient in creating wealth.

India, for example, has undertaken a programme of public sector reform focused on increased efficiency, decentralization, increased accountability and improved resource management (Heeks 1998) – a programme not dissimilar to the UK's 'Modernising Government' agenda (Great Britain, Cabinet Office 1999). As in the UK, these reforms are being achieved through greater use of information technology with a more overt role given to information.

The African Development Forum, convened in 1999, is a representative group of leaders from private sector organizations in Africa as well as from global corporations (ADF Private Sector Focus Group 1999). This Forum sees tremendous potential in the information economy for Africa, with a knowledgeable workforce as a fundamental component.

These examples demonstrate how easing access to high quality information and ensuring its use is seen as a means of improving business performance, a means of delivering an increased return to shareholders in the private sector and of delivering value for money to governments and their citizens in the public sector.

This transformation into an 'information age' economy began at the turn of the twentieth century and has gradually accelerated over time. Technological advances have made the production, distribution and retrieval of information much easier and speedier, resulting in an explosion in the amount available. Whereas it used to be a scarce commodity and having more was considered to be a good thing, we are now reaching saturation point and seeking ways to optimize and limit our use of it. It is evident that the need to manage information has never been greater.

However, information has become intrinsically linked to the technology that delivers it and management concerns tend to focus on the management of that technology. This narrow approach ignores the other issues, such as managing the people who use the technology, the processes supported by the technology, the organizational context in which the technology operates and, not least (although often left until last or simply overlooked), the information that is central to the whole system, the vital component. To misquote T. S. Eliot, where is the information we have lost in technology? In the days of typewriters, paper documents, files and filing cabinets, we were much more planned, systematic and structured in our information management but now, in managing the technology, we seem to have forgotten how to manage the information.

> Where is the Life we have lost in living?
> Where is the Wisdom we have lost in Knowledge?
> Where is the Knowledge we have lost in Information?
> (T. S. Eliot, *The Rock* 1914)

As already seen in the case of India, there has been a move in recent years for governments around the world to make their services electronic. So-called 'E-Government' provides a way to deliver better, more efficient public services by improving the administration or 'back office' of government.

Alongside this is the intent to make the 'front of house' more effective, to give the public the information it wants when it wants it, thereby improving relationships with citizens. Governments are applying these principles to all their departments, including those administrations responsible for national defence.

Leading defence manufacturer, Lockheed-Martin, highlights how information is as important in the defence environment as it is to any private sector organization, from McDonald's to Microsoft:

> Our warfighters must see first, strike first, and come home safely. To do that, they need the best possible information, from myriad sources, fused into a common picture of the battlefield.
>
> (Lockheed-Martin 2005)

The 'best possible' information is required on the battlefield and also in the defence 'business-space', which provides the capability and manpower for the battlefield. Of course, at the core of this provision is more effective information management, rather than simply a reliance on technology.

This chapter sets out to find the information that we have lost in technology and to remember exactly what information management is. In doing so, it will consider why managing information is still an organizational issue, explore how it can be managed for optimum return and, finally, assess the benefits to defence of ensuring the best possible information in both the business-space and the battlespace.

Why manage information?

During most of history, information has been a scarce resource, of greatest value to the small elite that were able to access it. In former times, there were natural selection processes in place to ensure that only the most important information was transmitted, such as the length of time that it took to send a letter by courier on horseback. However, supply has increased spectacularly over recent years due to efficiency gains in the transmission and processing of information (see Table 10.1). This is governed by the increasingly low marginal cost of using technology. Moore's Law states that the speed of microprocessors doubles every 18 months while the price is halved (Webopedia 2005). This gives the same computing power for half the price (or twice the power for the same amount of money) every 18 months. Alongside this, networks have grown. Metcalfe's Law states that the cost of networks expands linearly with increases in size, while the value increases exponentially (Wikipedia 2005). Factors such as these mean that information is generated and communicated more quickly than ever before.

This means that people have to cope with increasing amounts of information. Nowadays, a weekday edition of the New York Times contains more information than the average person was likely to come across in a

Table 10.1 Advances in the speed of communication (derived from Heylighen 1998)

In earlier times, people communicated by letters delivered by couriers on horseback. If the average letter is taken to be 10 000 bytes and the journey time one month, then the average speed of information transmission was 0.03 bits per second
With the invention of the telegraph, this was reduced to 3 bits per second
In the 1960s, the first data connections using computers gave an average information transmission speed of 300 bits per second
Nowadays, new technologies, such as fibre optic cables, give transmission speeds of billions of bits per second

lifetime in seventeenth century England (Wurman 1989: 32). In 1900, the average person received 1 000 new bits of information every six months but, by 1960, that was reduced to a week and, by 2001, to an hour (Gammon 2001: 12–13). We are no longer reliant on hand written letters and horses. We can type a message in minutes and then send it by e-mail to thousands of people. This has led to an explosion of irrelevant, unclear and low quality information.

A prime reason for trying to manage this situation is that humans have natural limits on the amount of information that they can process at any one time. In 1959, the psychologist, Miller, showed that people can only keep seven items at once in their working memory and they are also hampered by limits on the speed that the brain can process them (126 bits per second) (Heylighen 2002). Long term memory is more powerful and can store millions of concepts, but it is short term memory that we use to think. Whether Miller's estimations were correct or not, it is an irrefutable fact that we all have limits on the amount of information that we can process at any one time.

So, on the one hand, there is too much information and, on the other, humans have a limited ability to process that information. This means that the potential for having the wrong information, or for not having the right information, is growing. It also means that the situation for the organization is becoming increasingly complex: too much information and limited ability to process that information, while operating in a faster and more competitive world that demands faster and better decisions. It is evident that organizations have to manage their information asset.

What is information management?

In order to manage information, we first need to decide what it is that we are trying to manage. In everyday life, we use the word 'information' in a fairly random way, whether talking about data, information or knowledge.

This is an understandable inaccuracy, as it can be difficult to discern where one ends and the other begins. Data merges into information and information merges into knowledge: it is a continuum. In addition, it has to be acknowledged that it is not normally necessary to be particularly precise or careful in choosing which of these words applies. However, such precision and care is far more imperative if you are trying to work out where an organization is and what it needs to do in terms of managing its data, information and knowledge requirements.

Data can be defined as raw facts and figures, observations and measurement. Data stands in isolation. In other words, it has no intrinsic meaning until it is organized in some way. It only makes sense to the person who receives it when it is put into some sort of context, and it is only then that it becomes of real organizational value. From this, it is evident that data needs to be processed and transformed before it becomes meaningful. It needs to be organized, interpreted, formatted, analysed and summarized for a distinct purpose. The first step in this process is identified by Checkland and Holwell who draw a distinction between the mass of raw facts and figures, the data, and the sub-set that is actually of interest and relevance to the organization, which they term 'capta' (Hinton 2006). Capta are the result of some form of selection, the process of forming a category of relevant data.

DATA – from the Latin *dare* meaning 'to give'
CAPTA – from the Latin *capere* meaning 'to take'

Having selected or created some data, turning it into capta, it can then be processed to become information. To quote Peter Drucker, information is 'data endowed with relevance and purpose' (Davenport 1997: 9). It can be interpreted and understood by the recipient. Not surprisingly, the purpose of information is to inform. This means that, while data can often be expressed simply as numbers, information is more often expressed in language, adding the complexity of the communication process to any system that is designed to retrieve and use information (Myburgh 2000: 4–13).

The information that we have about people, objects or events increases our understanding and results in knowledge. Knowledge is bits of information pulled together into a coherent whole and it is humans who have to do the work to achieve this, applying logic to the item of information before internalizing it and modifying their actions as a result. The logic that humans apply includes comparing one bit of information with other bits that are accessible to them, considering the consequences of that information, making connections between various bits of information and having conversations with other people about the received piece of information (see Table 10.2).

Table 10.2 The human side of information processing

Comparison	How does information about this situation compare to what else we know?
Consequences	What does this information suggest we should do?
Connections	How does this bit of information relate to others?
Conversation	What do other people think about this information?

Source: Adapted from Davenport and Prusak (2000).

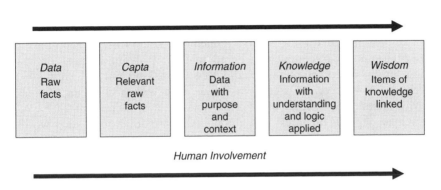

Figure 10.1 The data – information – knowledge continuum.

There is a final step in this continuum: wisdom, which can be defined as the ability to use knowledge for a purpose, making links between separate items of knowledge in response to an unexpected situation (see Figure 10.1). Ultimately, organizations are seeking to capture and exploit this intelligence, held by their employees. It is this, above information and knowledge, which will enable them to leverage their information resource and so gain competitive advantage. However, at present, most organizations are having enough trouble trying to sort out their data processing, information management and knowledge sharing requirements. The problem of capturing the wisdom in an organization can, thankfully, be set to one side for the time being.

An important point to note from this discussion of the data-information-knowledge continuum is that, not only does the organizational value increase as we move along it, but so does the amount of human involvement. Ultimately, information and knowledge are created by humans: we use data for a purpose and bestow meaning on information. While computers are well suited to processing data into an understandable form, they are less good at information management and even less competent at knowledge sharing (Davenport 1997: 10).

Armed with a much more precise definition of information, we also need to consider the word 'management'. We need to understand what we mean by 'information management' before we can go on to consider how we might approach the actual task. The Classical Management theorist, Henri Fayol, a French engineer who died in 1925, identified five functions of management that still form the basis of much modern management thinking: 'to manage is to forecast and plan, to organize, to command, to co-ordinate and control' (Fayol 1949). For detailed explanations of these functions, see Chapter 8.

All of these management activities involve making decisions and those decisions are made with the ultimate goal of achieving the organization's objectives. Making such decisions involves understanding the nature of the problem, finding the information that is most relevant to it and then interpreting that information to reach a judgement. To do this, decision makers need relevant, clear, complete, accurate and available information because these factors affect the quality of the decision making and so have a direct bearing on whether an organization can cope with a changing business environment. The success of decision making and, indeed, of all Fayol's activities, depends on access to high quality information or, in other words, information that is relevant, timely and accurate.

However, as already seen, managers at all levels have to make decisions in an uncontrollable environment with less than perfect information. In today's global and pressurised marketplace, they have to work hard and fast to keep up, trying to process large amounts of information without time to reflect in a leisurely way. However, although information is fundamental to the decision making process, it should be noted that it does not determine totally the decisions that are made. Other human qualities play a part, such as professional expertise, intuition and discretion (Hinton 2006: 2). Accessing these qualities, trying to manipulate them, share them and use them to underpin decision making throughout the organization moves us into the realm of knowledge management, 'connecting people who need to know with those who do know' (Denning 2000: 97). Arguably, the control of information, 'the knowledge stocks', needs to be confronted before these 'knowledge flows' are tackled.

So, if management concerns forecasting and planning, organizing, commanding, co-ordinating and controlling, then the same definition can be applied to information management: to manage *information* is to forecast and plan, to organize, to command, to co-ordinate and control. Information management is the provision of relevant information to the right person at the right time in a usable form to facilitate situational awareness and, ultimately, decision making. Therefore, it should take the form of a conscious process by which information is gathered and used to assist decision making throughout the organization (Hinton 2006: 2). The use of the word 'conscious' demonstrates that this process requires thought. Information is not simply gathered for its own sake – although, in some organizations, it might seem that way. It is gathered to be used. The ability to assess the organizational information needs and to collect, process and analyse relevant information is vital. It enables the efficient exchange of information and so results in improved decision making. In order to improve decision making, the process of information management should start with the decisions that have to be made.

How to manage information

As already noted, information has become bound with the technology that delivers it. It follows from this that the solution to information management is often thought to be the creation of an information system and, when most people talk about an information system, they refer only to the technology. However, an information system actually consists of more than that. It is the people in the organization who use information as part of their work systems or processes. The role that technology plays is to make it easier to gather and store the large amounts of data to feed the information requirement. Therefore, an information system actually consists of the people and the processes they perform, as well as the technologies that collect, manipulate and disseminate data to be transformed into information through human involvement.

The Israeli Defence Force has been making great efforts to improve the levels of learning in the organization (Lipshitz, Popper and Oz 1996). In the case of the Ordnance Corps, a breakthrough in the process came when it was discovered that each unit had developed its own unique maintenance information system. These were based on experience and, hence, contained wisdom as well as information that needed to be shared. The distinctly non-technological solution was to hold a series of seminars where each unit in turn would present the details of their system to the others. Participants enjoyed these seminars as they made for a change to routine, while remaining relevant. They allowed a degree of social integration between the units. Most importantly, the outcome was that knowledge was shared so that each unit could use the best practice of others.

The key to success for the organization lies in transforming this data into information and so into intelligence and knowledge, and then using that more effectively than the competition. This demonstrates that implementing an information system is markedly more complex than simply installing technology. It is also evident that organizations will not be good at managing information or knowledge until people and their work processes take the primary role in terms of an information system, rather than the technology (Davenport 1997: 3).

So, if information management is not simply a matter of applying technology, how can we approach the problem of too much information and too little time to process it? According to Davenport (1997: 135), information management consists of four elements that fit well with our adaptation of Fayol's definition of management: determining the requirement (forecasting and planning), then capturing (organizing and commanding), distributing (co-ordinating) and using that information to best effect (controlling) (see Figure 10.2).

Determining information requirements

The first stage in managing information is to understand the processes that people carry out, to identify the decisions that underpin these processes and then to isolate the information that feeds these decisions. In carrying out this examination, it is insufficient to simply focus on 'hard' information, which is taken to be the documentary-based or formal sources that are available within an organization. The 'soft' information, in the form of news, ideas, gossip or rumour accessed from other people, also needs to be taken into account as this gives context and richness to the hard information.

> Hard information is often limited in scope, lacking in richness and often failing to encompass important non-economic and non-quantitative factors...
>
> Much hard information is too aggregated for effective use in strategy making...
>
> Much hard information arrives too late to be of use in strategy making...
>
> ...A surprising amount of hard information is unreliable.
>
> (Mintzberg 1994: 259–64)

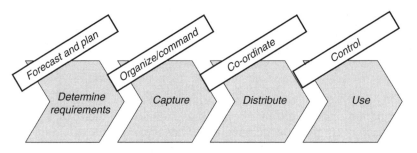

Figure 10.2 Management in information management (adapted from Davenport 1997).

Common problems encountered at this stage are that the required information is simply not available or, simply, that it is available but not used. There may be gaps in the available information resources or, conversely, too much information so that the necessary items are hidden by all the irrelevant information. In addition, when looking at people's work cycles, it may become apparent that a lot of time is spent gathering information for the use of others and achieving little organizational value in the process (Hinton 2006: 57).

Capturing information

Capturing or gathering the information requirement should be an ongoing activity. It involves scanning the information environment for the relevant sources. Davenport (1997: 143) identifies three broad sources of information for the organization: 'outside expertise', 'cognitive authorities' and 'inside scuttlebutt', which is slang for gossip or rumour and refers to the soft information sources discussed below (see Table 10.3). This latter is difficult to scan and is often considered to be inaccurate. However, as already noted, hard information can be equally inaccurate. Increasingly, these informal types of information are being acknowledged by organizations to be a valuable source of organizational learning and knowledge sharing.

Technology can be used to scan for relevant information. However, the risk in machine-based scanning is that it simply becomes a filtering process, adding little value to the information. The captured information needs to be analysed to make it more useful to the decision making process – the transformation of raw data into meaningful information. Evidently this involves human intervention to add context, interpretation, comparisons and local implications to the information that is captured – value, in short. Therefore, a combination of automated and human approaches has been found to work best (Davenport 1997: 141).

The best scanning environment is where everyone scans and shares captured information. This requires a range of issues to be addressed, such as accountability, data definition, standardization, quality monitoring and,

Table 10.3 Sources of information (adapted from Davenport 1997)

Outside expertise	Published materials or other formal sources like conference presentations
Cognitive authorities	Individuals or institutions that have gained credibility in a given field – for example, the information and data analysis empires that have arisen over the past decade
Inside scuttlebutt	Your own organization's grapevine

not least, ensuring that staff have the relevant skills (see Table 10.4). It is also likely to require a significant change in the organizational culture, to make people more aware of their information needs and more involved with its management and, from there, to ensuring the sharing of information around the organization. As Drucker has noted:

> We will have to learn, before understanding any task, to first ask the question, 'what information do I need, and in what form, and when?'...The next question people have to learn to ask is, 'To whom do I owe which information and when and where?'
>
> (cited by Davenport 1997: 28)

Once the information has been located, it needs to be categorized into meaningful groupings using some form of structured, classification system. This helps people to retrieve the information rapidly and reliably. Again, this is a human activity: people define the initial classification scheme, mediate between others with differing views, ensure that there is continuous monitoring in case new categories need to be added and make updates as necessary. It is a labour-intensive process to do well.

In addition, a lot of the information gathered has to be stored. For some types of information in some countries, there are statutory regulations determining what must be kept and for how long. Decisions need to be taken about issues such as who needs access, how long it should be kept and what kind of protection it requires.

Distributing information

The purpose of the third stage in the information management process is to connect managers and employers with the information that they need. However, sharing information around an organization is no simple task to

Table 10.4 Management issues in data capture

Accountability	Responsibility for who collects what should be made clear
Data definition	Agreement on what items a particular type of information should include
Standardization	Ensuring everyone is collecting the same information in the same way
Quality monitoring	Ensuring that the information of the right quality is being collected
Skills	Helping staff improve their information-gathering skills

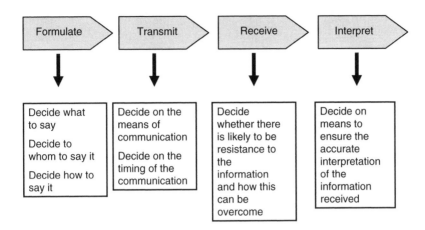

Figure 10.3 The information distribution process.

achieve. Most people working in large organizations would identify problems with the distribution or communication of information. However, if the definition of the information requirement and the capture of the information are working, then this should present less of a problem. The process of defining an organization's information requirement helps to increase awareness of what information is available, while scanning and categorizing it helps to increase understanding.

In defining a distribution process, issues such as the formulating of the information need to be addressed, alongside the transmission, receipt and ultimate interpretation. This is demonstrated graphically in Figure 10.3.

Information distribution is based on either a 'push' or 'pull' strategy. To date, we have tended to focus on 'push' where the information is sent out to the users based on the premise that they do not know what they do not know. This makes people the passive receivers of information that someone else sees as important. A 'pull' strategy assumes users are the best judges of what they need and also that information is best distributed at the time of that need. In order to pull the right information, users have to be motivated to do so. The initial step of determining information requirements will encourage a move towards a 'pull' strategy by identifying the relevant information for the decision making taking place within the work processes. However, many organizations, like the Turkish Air Force (below), adopt a combination of the two strategies, pushing some information out to the users and allowing other types to be pulled in by the users.

The Turkish Air Force has designed an integrated Command and Control System (TICCS) that is to be a central resource for all its core functions through a series of sub-systems: battle management, operations, intelligence, training, resource management etcetera. By linking the different sub-systems with each other and with, for instance, the NATO Air Control and Command System, TICCS is able to push information to where it is obviously needed and to act as a resource for people to pull out other information as and when they need it (Jane's 2004).

Using information

Information is no good unless it is used. Encouraging its use is the final stage in this process of information management. How information is used depends on a range of factors, including the nature of the problem around which the decision revolves, which will have an impact on the way the information is interpreted. Inevitably, an important decision may require more careful analysis of the available information. In addition, decision makers will interpret a problem differently depending on their position. Given the same information, the human resource director will see people problems, while the accountant will see financial problems.

Information management can be viewed as a generic and structured set of activities that start with the people and the processes and then look for the relevant information. In discussing these steps, the technology has largely been ignored but it is evident that it can add benefit and value at each stage. However, it should be viewed as an enabler, providing the right information at the right time in the right form, rather than continuous provision of a mass of unformatted and unfocused information. The major gain from working through these information management activities is in understanding of how people tackle their work processes and how this can be made more effective with the right kinds of technology. This can bring fundamental changes to the way an organization operates.

Why is information management critical for defence?

Defence is no different to other public and private sector organizations in that decision making is the means of achieving its objectives and in that it requires high quality information to feed that process. Making decisions involves understanding the problem, finding relevant information and then reaching a judgement. Military commanders seek to achieve and maintain decision superiority in the battlefield:

> In order to deliver a wide range of effects, we need...an improved ability to exploit information that can then be translated into

synchronized responses to achieve decisive military effect. ... It relies on the ability to collect, fuse and analyse relevant information in near real-time so as to allow rapid decision making.

(Ministry of Defence 2003: 11)

The information management processes currently in use in defence administrations have been developed and established over hundreds of years and have worked well to date. Large volumes of data are captured and analysed, then distributed as information to pre-determined users, based on a 'push' strategy. This distribution is guided by the command process and by security constraints, which means that information tends to flow vertically from the top of the organization downwards.

Managing information in this way was developed when the security risk centred on large-scale armed conflict. This risk has now reduced. The current perceived threats are reckoned to be low intensity, increasingly involving terrorists or other non-state actors and requiring rapid reaction with joint and combined forces. The rigid, structured information management processes of old do not allow the flexibility required in a battlespace that is operationally agile and needs better cross-functional, cross-force and cross-ally communication processes. More suitable information management techniques need to be developed with the emphasis moving towards a 'pull strategy', allowing users to rapidly exploit information that is relevant to the context in which they are operating and available when they need it.

Commanders have always worked in the so-called 'fog of war', recognizing the impossibility of ever having all of the necessary information provided to the right people at the right time (Ministry of Defence 2005: 2.2). However, modern technology provides the possibility for much improved representations of the battlefield. It also creates the potential to fundamentally reconfigure the command role. For example, it could significantly alter the application of control, allowing options to be chosen: ranging from more decentralized control, more centralized control; to over-control. It could also allow commanders to be physically remote from their subordinates, operating from secure positions, yet with as clear a view of the scenario being confronted as if in the same location (Ministry of Defence 2005: 2–12).

Technology also provides the capability for much greater collaboration across all the relevant decision makers: the command components, the military functions, the supply chain, the coalitions, allies and governments. Such collaboration is not simply about passive acceptance of information but rather an exchange of information that adds value. Well-integrated joint forces can achieve better shared awareness, a common understanding and so more potential for speed, precision and agreement in their decision making processes. Logistics can be networked to the operations to provide greater tactical responsiveness, enabling the logistics commanders to be involved in operational planning from the outset (Ministry of Defence

2005: 2–12). This provides them with information about the Commander's intent, increases their understanding and so enables them to deliver focused logistic support, rather than merely responding to orders and co-ordinating instructions.

It is apparent that new technology has the potential to deliver innovation to the way in which information is managed and used in the defence arena. However, there are other issues that need to be examined if this information is to be fully exploited. For example, successful command is not simply about providing information to the commanders; it is about how that information is used to command. It is humans who gain the competitive edge in the battlespace, thinking in innovative and flexible ways, to understand and counteract the decision cycles of an opponent. In addition, commanders who are physically remote from their forces could cause a loss of trust and confidence in subordinates who remain in harm's way. Moreover, a greater information flow will not, by itself, remove the inherent cultural barriers, power struggles or political manoeuvrings that will inevitably exist in any collaborative environment.

In the United States, information is already viewed as being critical to the battlespace and the United Kingdom is coming to a similar conclusion with its focus on Network Enabled Capability (NEC). This emphasis on the importance of information means revisiting information management. As with the generic information management process discussed above, defence information management needs to stem from the decisions, the people and the processes around those decisions, and then to use technology as an enabler. Taking this approach will ensure that the technology assists commanders, and managers, at all levels by creating relevant structures and meaning from the large volumes of information with which they are faced. Working through the four elements of information management, determining the requirement, capturing, distributing and encouraging the use of the information, is likely to result in a new understanding of how people engage with work processes and how the right kinds of technology can be used to enhance their decision making capability. Potentially, this could also lead to fundamental reconfigurations in the way defence is structured, resulting in a model which is potentially flatter, more responsive and offering shared situational awareness through collaboration.

Conclusion

To fully engage with the Information Age, both public and private sector organizations need to move beyond simply being able to transmit and access information in volume and at speed. In terms of defence, countries like the United States and the United Kingdom are recognizing that information is their vital component. However, in order to fully exploit it as such, the basic skills of information management need to be dusted off and given much greater priority. Working from the information that people and processes require to feed decision making means that the most relevant information can be differentiated from the exponentially multiplying mass of non-relevant information. Drucker's image of the organization of the twenty-first century can then become reality: flatter structures, knowledge specialists and information as the driving force.

Questions to consider

1 How do you turn data into information in your daily work?
2 Why is there a need for information management within your country's defence sector?
3 What are the key challenges facing information management in your organization?
4 How would you go about determining your organization's information needs?
5 What are the drivers for improved information management in defence?

Suggested reading

Davenport, T. H. (1997), *Information Ecology: Mastering the Information and Knowledge Environment*, New York: Oxford University Press.
Hinton, M. (ed.) (2006), *Introducing Information Management: The Business Approach*, Amsterdam: Open University/Elsevier.

Bibliography

ADF Private Sector Focus Group (1999), *Plenary Report*, Version 1.0, 66.102.9.104/search?q=cache:wuc9sj3KZyMJ:www.uneca.org/adf99/worddocs/ADF%2BPrivate%2BSector%2BFocus%2BGroup%2BReport.doc+private+sector+%22+information+age%22&hl=en (accessed: 3 September 2005).
Davenport, T. H. (1997), *Information Ecology: Mastering the Information and Knowledge Environment*, New York: Oxford University Press.
Davenport, T. H. and Prusak, L. (2000), *Working Knowledge: How Organizations Manage What They Know*, Boston, MA: Harvard Business School Press.
Denning, S. (2000), *The Springboard: How Storytelling Ignites Action In Knowledge-Era Organizations*, Oxford: Butterworth–Heinemann.
Drucker, P. (1988), 'The coming of the new organization', *Harvard Business Review*, 66 (1): Jan/Feb.
Fayol, H. (1949), *Adminstration Industrielle et Generale*, Paris: Dunod. (trans. C. Storrs as *General and Industrial Management*), Pitman: London.
Gammon, M. (2001), 'Look after your people and they will look after your business', *British Journal of Administrative Management*, 25, May/June.
Great Britain, Cabinet Office (1999), *Modernising Government*, Cm 4310, London: Stationery Office.

Heeks, R. (1998), 'Information age reform of the public sector: the potential and problems of information technology in India', *Information Systems for Public Sector Management, Working Paper Series*, Paper No. 6. Manchester: Institute for Development Policy and Management, University of Manchester, unpan1.un.org/intradoc/groups/public/documents/NISPAcee/UNPAN015479.pdf (accessed: 4 September 2005).

Heylighen, F. (1998), *Technological Acceleration: Principia Cybernetica Web*, pespmc1.vub.ac.be/TECACCEL.html (accessed: 26 September 2005).

—— (2002), *Complexity and Information Overload In Society: Why Increasing Efficiency Leads to Decreasing Control*, pcp.vub.ac.be/Papers?Info-Overload.pdf (accessed: 28 September 2005).

Hinton, M. (ed.) (2006), *Introducing Information Management: The Business Approach*, Amsterdam: Open University/Elsevier.

Jane's (2004), 'Turkish Air Force integrated command & control system', *Jane's C4I Systems*, www4.janes.com (posted 29 September 2004).

Laudon, K. C. and Laudon, J. P. (2002), *Essentials of Management Information Systems*, Upper Saddle River, NJ: Prentice Hall.

Leonard-Barton, D. (1995), *Wellsprings of Knowledge*, Boston, MA: Harvard Business School Press.

Lipshitz, R., Popper, M. and Oz, S. (1996), 'Building learning organizations: the design and implementation of organizational learning mechanisms', *Journal of Applied Behavioural Science*, 32: 292–305

Lockheed Martin (2005), *Information Superiority*, www.lockheedmartin.com/wms/findPage.do?dsp=fec&ci=12973&sc=400 (accessed: 17 September 2005).

Ministry of Defence (2005), *The UK Joint High Level Command Concept: An Analysis of the Components of the UK Defence Capability Framework*, London: Ministry of Defence, www.mod.uk/linked_files/jdcc/publications/hlocnew.pdf (accessed: 29 September 2005).

—— (2003), 'Armed forces capabilities' *Delivering Security in a Changing World* Defence White Paper, Supporting Essays, Cmnd 6041-1, London: The Stationery Office.

Mintzberg, H. (1994), *The Rise and Fall of Strategic Planning*, New York: Free Press.

Myburgh, S. (2000), 'The convergence of information management and information technology', *Information Management Journal*, 34: 2, April.

Webopedia (2005), *Moore's Law*, www.webopedia.com/TERM/M/Moores_Law.html, (accessed: 3rd September 2005).

Wikipedia (2005), *Metcalfe's Law*, en.wikipedia.org/wiki/Metcalfe's_law (accessed: 5th September 2005).

Wurman, R. S. (1989), *Information Anxiety*, New York: Doubleday.

11 Human resource management in the defence environment

Alex Alexandrou and Roger Darby

Introduction

Any discussion of HRM begins with the question, 'What is HRM?' The answer usually suggests a question, wrapped in a puzzle, shrouded in an enigma. To understand the concept, it helps to begin by viewing HRM's temporal and geographical beginnings. As Storey (2001: 2) succinctly points out 'it is scarcely more than a decade since the time when the term "human resource management" (HRM) was rarely used' at least outside the United States where it has its origins. It was during the 1980s that HRM emerged onto the global scene and now it is a familiar term around the world. However, it is still the subject of great debate amongst academics and practitioners alike. It is also a concept that defence organizations are coming to terms with around the world, be they established armed forces of industrialized nations such as the United Kingdom and the United States or developing democratic states in Africa, Asia, Central and Eastern Europe and South America. It is fair to state that many nations' armed services are experiencing rationalization and restructuring that has occurred as a result of the ending of the Cold War, changes in defence budgets, and new defence priorities since 2001.

One of the difficulties in defining HRM is the enormous diversity in HRM practice, dependent on several factors including: products or service provided, public or private sector orientation, sector of activity, culture – organizational and national, employment laws and the type of personnel required and used by organizations. Inevitably, HRM has been used in a variety of ways to focus on a wide range of issues which has created, in some cases, more problems than it has solved.

For example in the United Kingdom as Alexandrou, *et al.* state:

> Our understanding of the underlying ideology of HRM within the Armed Services is that it is dominated by the need to recruit and retain the best available talent, contraction of the core workforce (i.e. armed personnel) and constraining demands on the public purse. The aim has been to deliver and yet at the same time to improve efficiency,

effectiveness and flexibility. In practice, it seems to be characterized by a significant decrease in the number of service personnel, overstretch, low morale and difficulties in recruiting the next generation.

(2001: 1)

However, it is clear that there are similarities in a number of the key issues that the defence organizations of emergent democratic states face, particularly during the transition period. In order to overcome the difficulties and issues highlighted above, there is a need to understand what HRM means particularly from a public and defence sector perspective. The remainder of the chapter will identify this based on a theoretical and practical understanding of what HRM is and its implications for the defence environment. Further, it addresses the question of what challenges need to be faced in the future, based on the three central pillars of leadership, empowerment and ethics within the defence environment.

Defining HRM

HRM is a relatively new term even in western societies. Storey (1995) argues that its main initial contribution was to differentiate between personnel management and administration, and HRM. Human resource management focuses on regarding people as resources to be invested in, as opposed to viewing labour as a commodity and a cost to the organization. Such human resources are seen to have strategic importance and to support the creation of competitive advantages for organizations in both the public and private sectors. Further, HRM seeks to develop an internal fit among human resource functional areas and an external fit between HRM policies and practices with the organization's strategy (Beer *et al.* 1984; Schuler and Rogovsky 1998). In terms of power and the contribution to overall strategy, it is suggested that shifting perspectives, by involving senior management in HRM responsibilities, encourages a significant change. At the same time a shift of competences away from centralized personnel departments to line management encourages strategic integration. The goals of HRM have also dramatically changed perspectives on managing people in all types of organizations. Much more emphasis is placed on commitment, quality and flexibility than on previous outcomes such as employees' compliance with rules and regulations, efficient organizational administration or standard performance and cost minimization (Guest 1991).

Models and concepts

Given the diversity of businesses and services both in the public and private sectors, all have a surprising number of factors in common. For example, most have corporate missions that need to be achieved within the allocation of resources available. One key resource is people. Such resources need to be managed, which implies controlling their actions and behaviours. In essence, there is a fundamental division in most organizations, namely between the aspirations of individuals and the needs of organizations. Effective HRM maintains a delicate balance between these two key factors in the working environment. Central to maintaining this equilibrium is the importance of two key contracts. First, the formal, legal, employment contract which sets out the terms and conditions of employment, remuneration, and the rules that govern the employment relationship. Second and fundamental to the efficacy of HRM, is the psychological contract (see, for example, Guest and Conway 2000, 2001). This refers to the expectations that employees have about their role and to what the employer is prepared to give them in return. Furthermore, as external and internal environments inevitably change over time, so do the psychological contracts – placing more pressure on organizations to manage the change in employee relationships in order to overcome attitudinal and behavioural drift as its workforce reacts to the constantly changing direction of organizational objectives.

In order to manage human resource in organizations effectively, a number of models have been developed (e.g. Beer *et al.* 1984; Fombrun *et al.* 1984; Wright *et al.* 1994). Figure 11.1 identifies those key functions within the HRM cycle, which play a major role in managing human resources in all types of organizations.

The utility of this model is that it provides a framework which identifies the key HR functions of resourcing, development, rewarding and relations, all geared to the broader goal of employee performance. It highlights how functions within HRM can be integrated and designed to support an organization's strategic needs. Briefly, these key functions include:

Resourcing

The initial key activity of HRM is to supply the organization with the people required to make it successful. It is increasingly likely that these people might not necessarily be full-time employees, as flexible working practices may meet needs better by utilizing consultants or subcontractors – on a variety of working contracts, including full-time, part-time or casual. Recruitment and selection involves a two-way relationship and processes aimed at satisfying the needs of both employer and employee. It is firmly linked to other employment issues such as sustaining interest and motivation. In both the armed forces and the civil service there is an assumption that those joining will commit themselves for a number of years so, effectively recruitment is important, and even more so as, around the world, conscription is being ended with the move to professional forces. Careful recruitment is at the heart of any strategy to improve retention.

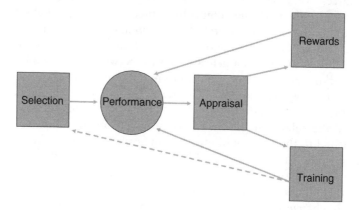

Figure 11.1 The human resource cycle. (Formbrun *et al.* 1984: 41) (Reproduced by permission of Pearson Educational.)

Development

Development occurs on two levels. First is the development of general skills which could apply in any organization, but which make a person inherently employable. This skill set has implications both as an incentive for people to want to work for a particular organization; for retention, where it may enhance later work prospects; and for life beyond the Forces, or Civil Service, where enhanced skills may serve to build up the public image of work in the defence sector. Second, carefully constructed development activities can build up skills and knowledge that are particularly needed within the organization. As a result, the individual who possesses such skills becomes more valuable to the employer. This may be why so much investment and prestige are attached to Command and Staff course, and why civil service placements on such courses are viewed as a confirmation of potential leadership.

The provisions of skills and knowledge is a continuous process that needs to occur in line with, and alongside, other business activities for they are all aimed at the same target, or goals. There is an inextricable link between performance and the acquisition of skills and knowledge, which combine to bring about the success of organizational objectives.

Relations

Employment is a relationship between the employer and the employee. An essential feature of HRM is the range of activities that are intended to uphold that relationship and prevent alienation of the workforce. There are two contracts that need to be maintained: the formal, legal contract of employment; and the unwritten, or psychological, contract.

Effective employee relations management occurs at both the individual and collective levels and includes the recognition of equity. Employee relations practice concerns the management of perception (and power) and necessitates effective communication between parties to maintain harmony and to achieve organizational objectives.

Reward

At the heart of the employment relationship is the effort-reward bargain. Reward is a transaction involving benefits given by an employer to an employee in exchange for skills, knowledge, loyalty and labour. HRM, then, involves aligning an organization's reward system with its performance objectives. It includes a bigger picture of financial and non-financial rewards (such as status, health care, or housing) to encourage employees to be motivated to give special effort, or to be more creative, so that their work adds value to the end product (or service). This is to the mutual benefit of the individual and the organization.

> ### *Example*
>
> A senior civil servant in the Ghana MoD told of how he uses reward-management as an incentive for people to stay in the organization. His ability to give pay raises or promotion is restricted by law and local regulations. Instead he takes time to find out which aspects of the work a particular person finds interesting or fulfilling. He will offer specialist training to people who will commit themselves to an agreed number of years, beyond the original contract, of extra service.

A final point to note here is that the discussion of HRM presents a major debate about the central issues of *best fit* and *best practice* which relates to the way HRM is utilized. An important question for developing and transitional states is whether or not there is a single, identifiable way of managing human resources which is universally appropriate.

Strategic human resource management

Any discussion of the functional nature of HRM needs to be viewed within the overall perspective of strategic management, including the external environment of an organization, which is illustrated in Figure 11.2, below.

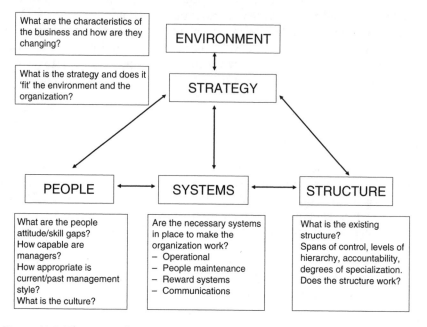

Figure 11.2 The external environment and HRM (Darby 2005).

There is a crucial interplay between the key variables when managing strategically. Tyson provides a useful starting point in defining strategic HRM (SHRM), were he states that it is:

> the intentions of the corporation both explicit and covert, toward the management of its employees, expressed through philosophies, policies and practices.

> (Tyson 1995: 3)

Budhwar (2000) points out that one of the central features of the recent debate on HRM has been the importance placed on integrating HRM with the business and corporate strategy, concentrating on how and when HR issues are considered in the formulation of corporate strategy. He further argues that the term 'strategic human resource management' was one of the outcomes of the debate, highlighting the growing proactive nature of HRM and its importance in the success or otherwise of the organization. This highlights the argument that such a shift in the nature of the HR function will see it change from 'being reactive, prescriptive, and administrative to being proactive, descriptive and executive'(Budhwar 2000: 141).

Gratton *et al.* argue that the cornerstone of SHRM

> is the creation of linkage or integration between the overall strategic aims of the business and the human resource strategy and implementation

[and]...managing the various human resource interventions, such as selection, training, reward and development, so that they complement each other.

(Gratton *et al.* 1999: 7)

Basically they are pointing out that SHRM is a set of interrelated practices with 'an ideological and philosophical underpinning'(Storey 1989: 3).

Wright and Snell (1998) and Gratton *et al.* (1999) also note that SHRM emphasizes what can be termed 'vertical fit' – integration between the business/corporate strategy and the human resource strategy and 'horizontal fit' – integration among the various HRM practices. Lengnick-Hall and Lengnick-Hall (1990) have emphasized that SHRM requires flexibility to adapt to adverse and changing environments and that it must deliver the corporate strategy, not only in terms of managing the performance of people, but also ensuring that this is turned into a competitive and economic advantage.

Developing and implementing SHRM

For the application of SHRM, Schuler *et al.* (2000) have developed their own Four Task Model. Each task has a set of questions:

Managing employee assignments and opportunities

- What number and type of employees are needed, with what qualifications?
- Where are they needed, and when?
- Where will they come from?
- What opportunities for growth, development, and rewards will attract them to the organization?

Managing employee competencies

- What competencies do employees have now?
- What new competencies will be needed in the future?
- What competencies will be less important in the future?
- Which specific employees need which specific competencies?
- Can/should needed competencies be purchased or developed?

Managing employee behaviour

- What behaviours does the organizational culture value?
- What behaviours are detrimental to the strategy and need to be eliminated or modified?
- How do employees' behaviours affect customers' buying patterns and satisfaction?

Managing employee motivation

- How much more effort are employees willing and able to give?
- What is the optimal length of time for employees to stay with the firm?
- Can production costs or customer service be improved by reducing absence and tardiness?

Strategic IHRM

Just as relevant today for the defence sector as any other organization, public or private, is the international context. The importance of an international perspective has enhanced the development of the field of strategic international human resource management (SIHRM). The main driver for SIHRM has undoubtedly been the multinational corporations (MNCs) and their influence on international concerns and objectives. For example, BAE Systems are a key player in the global defence industry and are influential in the partnership between business and defence. Their sphere of influence, by necessity, includes the rapidly changing area of managing people. Therefore, the focus of attention is on HRM in MNCs and the importance of linking HRM policies and practices with organizational strategies of the multinational organization. Of similar importance within the defence sector is the growing number of force coalitions and the use of multi-national forces. What is significant for this chapter is the increasing number of independent variables acting to influence international human resource management (IHRM). These include: political, social, technological and economic factors as Derrick Neal identifies in Chapter 9 of this book.

In terms of the conceptual framework of SIHRM, the key principles which have been developed and have been influential over time, can be linked with: issues related to organizational design and the development of strategy and structure (see, for example, Hedlund 1996); the development of integrative contingency frameworks based on the need to differentiate and integrate HRM policies (Schuler *et al.* 2000); and the focus on life-cycle models linked to the notion of fit between the stages of international operations and HRM (see Perlmutter 1969).

Figure 11.3 identifies the important link between strategic and functional HRM.

One final point to note in this section, which is of major importance to the relationship between strategic and functional HRM, is the question of culture and its influence on internationally-oriented organizations. The effect of this multicultural perspective for individual employees can be summed up by the cliché 'think locally, act globally'.

The salient issue of cultural diversity on a global scale cannot be overlooked either when managing employees or serving clients. Within HRM, the implications of cultural diversity on management include key

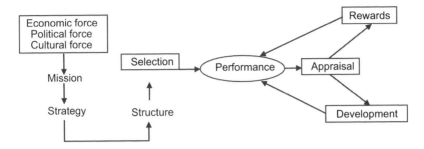

Figure 11.3 The human resource cycle and 'fit' with organization strategy (Darby 2005).

issues such as, organizational loyalty, the focus of control, rewards and performance, risk, time frames for planning commitment, communication and decision-making. Military personnel who have served in multinational peace keeping forces for example, will be well aware of the different demands cultural diversity places on their management of not only the battle space but also the increasingly important business space in the changing twenty-first century defence environment.

HRM in defence

As in the business world, success in managing people in the defence environment often rests on a manager's interpersonal skills. Successful results are achieved through the combined efforts of all parts of the larger organization. Motivation is not merely a matter of earning admiration but of inspiring people to work both individually and collectively. The manager's task can be seen as creating a working environment in which team efforts are organized towards the achievement of agreed objectives. To achieve that managers must understand human needs, aspirations, differences and the psychology of those being managed. In this respect, the importance of the psychological contract, which was discussed earlier, becomes apparent. It also places an onus on the organization to be more transparent about what it requires from its people, and what it offers in exchange, to attract, retain and support its employees through their careers in the organization.

In an attempt to apply the theory a recent example of the British armed forces and Ministry of Defence (MoD) will be used. Their *Armed Forces Overarching Personnel Strategy* (AFOPS) declares that:

> AFOPS is part of the Department's overall corporate planning and programming processes. It informs and is informed by Defence

Strategic Guidance and the Defence Corporate Plan, the Strategic Plan for defence Individual Training and Education, as well as the Department's Future Strategic Context and UK Joint Vision work.

(MoD 2003: 6)

AFOPS principles cascade down into key values and into policies and procedures for managing people in the armed services. Five stages highlight the 'cradle to grave and beyond philosophy' (ibid.):

Cultivate – prepare the ground for obtaining personnel.
Obtain – attract, acquire and train high quality, motivated personnel.
Retain – provide personnel with a rewarding career which stimulates and develops them and provides the foundation of a second career on leaving the Services.
Sustain – provide an environment in which Service men and women and their families will be willing to maintain their commitment.
Remember – provide ex-Service personnel and their dependents with help and support, particularly with resettlement back into civilian life.[1]

This cascades further down into the context of individual arms; balancing the rights of the individual with operational capabilities; meeting the challenges of recruitment and emphasizing leadership skills.

Table 11.1, below extends the AFOPS personnel policy and procedure guidelines to include the Navy Personnel Strategy. What is of particular interest is the proliferation of policies engendered by AFOPS. This raises interesting questions regarding the future capability or necessity for the Armed Services to provide full support for its employees from 'cradle to grave and beyond'.

SHRM in defence

If an organization in the defence environment is to pursue SHRM, it is imperative to ensure that it has an adequate number of employees and it has the right type of personnel, with the right skills set and competencies, to help it achieve its overall strategic goals and targets. As Gratton (1987) points out there are explicit links between individual performance, human resource processes and organizational strategies. She uses the following four questions to examine the links. They appear to be especially significant for the defence environment:

• How does the linkage between the organization's strategy and human resource strategy work?

- What are the key internal and external contextual variables that affect the design and implementation of human resource strategies?
- What are the key HR activities that link organizational strategy to performance?
- What role does line management play in influencing outcomes?

HRM has long term implications. It is not the fire-fighting function that used to be expected of personnel managers. Rather, its purpose is to gain the compliance and commitment of employees and, for HRM to survive and flourish, senior managers must be committed to it – so it can be transmitted all the way down the leadership and or management chain. There is a greater chance of HRM being successfully implemented if it is supported from the top.

Table 11.1 AFOPS/NAVY personnel policies and procedures (Darby 2005)

AFOPS	Naval Personnel Strategy	AFOPS guidelines as linked to NPS
Cultivate/Obtain	Recruit and Train	Youth Policy Recruitment Policy Reserves Policy Individual Training Policy
Retain	Career Management	Career Structures Policy Manpower Structures Policy Mobility Policy Career Management Policy
	Conditions of Service	Allowances Policy Pay and Charges Policy Education Policy Non-Financial Conditions of Service Policy Equal Opportunities Policy Discipline Policy Complaints Procedures Policy
Sustain	Health Welfare and Recreation	Living Accommodation Policy Pastoral and Spiritual Policy Sports and Recreation Policy Health and Safety Policy Families Policy Welfare Policy Health Policy
Remember	Recognition	Resettlement Policy Veterans Policy Bereaved Families Policy End of Service Benefits/Pensions Policy

Senior managers at the Ethiopian Ministry of National Defence identified the need for training and development of officers and officials to bring about transformational change. A suitable programme was devised and taught by a foreign university. Among those attending the first course was the Chief of Defence Staff, the Minister of State and several other 1* and 2* officers. Their attendance said much more than any edict from their offices. Not only did they lead by example but they demonstrated their commitment to both the training programme and to the change that it was to facilitate

It is justifiably argued that HRM will not be successfully implemented if it is used as a vehicle for a straightforward push in productivity with no shared aims and objectives and no sign of rewards. Advocates of HRM state that if it is seen as a fad with no real change, that does not solve or address organizational problems, it will fail. It will be unsuccessful if it does not bring together every aspect of the organization's overall strategic plan, so that all the functions and individuals are co-ordinated and interact.

Many organizations declaim that 'employees are our most important asset'. It may be an overused cliché but, as a number of commentators have pointed out, further down the management chain, leaders and managers must give greater consideration to the more effective management of human resources. As its name implies, HRM regards people as a resource to be managed and the aim of any HRM strategy is to maximize the potential of people. This is best achieved through a co-operative approach, which means that people must understand, and believe in, the organization's core vision, values and mission. This is especially pertinent for the armed forces, for values form the core of the moral component of fighting power and, as a famous commander once said, 'the moral is to the physical as three is to one' (attributed to Napoleon Bonaparte).

Values are basically guiding principles (which are not to be confused with specific cultural or operating practices) and they must not be compromised for financial gain or short term expediency. Values are not goals, specific targets or mission statements. They are beliefs that a particular end-state (such as honesty, liberty or justice) is a good thing in its own right. Blessing White Consultants (1999) argue that values are the beginning from which everything is built upon, and matters such as goals, targets and the mission follow. Values are timeless principles that drive the manner in which an organization operates.

Increasingly, armed forces have recognized the need for explicit values. For example, the Royal Air Force's published *Ethos, Core Values and Standards* emphasizes the place of respect, integrity, service (assistance) and excellence in service life:

> It is about the way in which tasks are undertaken; it is about excellence; and it is about taking responsibility and ensuring a job is well done no matter how difficult the circumstances. Key qualities include: Self-Disciple and Control...Personal Excellence...Excellence in the use of Resources [and] Pride.
>
> (Royal Air Force 2004: 4–8)

The creation and implementation of an HRM strategy, that will work in practice, for a defence organization is dependent on the same factors that are needed for good governance. Within them, are three aspects that are crucial to the effective management of people. They are leadership, ethics and empowerment.

Leadership and HRM

A plethora of articles and books have been written about leadership and, in turn, their authors have produced a multitude of definitions of what leadership is and what it means from various perspectives. It is not the aim of this chapter to definitively state what leadership is but, more importantly from an HRM perspective and taking into consideration the later discussion on ethics, the discussion will centre on how managers and leaders of organizations need to challenge their assumptions on leadership, if they are to meet the demands of a new era; particularly from a military perspective in developing democracies.

Defining leadership

As stated above, this chapter will not attempt to debate the definition of leadership but, in the context of addressing leadership from an HRM perspective, it needs to select a working definition from some of the thousands available.

The Leadership Trust (a UK based educational foundation), defines leadership as 'using our personal power to win the hearts and minds of people to achieve a common purpose' (Edwards *et al.* 2002). It argues that the only

The Iraq conflict of 2003 provides a pertinent illustration of a military commander articulating what is meant by leadership in a theatre of war, where Colonel Tim Collins states:

> Command of a battalion is as much about setting a standard as delegating and giving orders. You have to be seen as the man in charge. Soldiers must have the confidence in their leader's professional abilities and standing. Above all they must trust and respect them as a person
>
> (Collins 2005: 28)

way a leader's personal power can be expressed is through communication, be it verbal or non-verbal.

The aim of a leader should be to build relationships and create a positive atmosphere. This in turn will win the hearts and minds of the people who work for leaders, and inspire and motivate them to achieve the common purpose of the organization. The Trust goes on to argue that a leader's personal power should not only inspire and motivate, it must also give employees direction by communicating a path they should take within the working environment (ibid.). Another key point is that a good leader will lead in such a manner that allows success to be shared amongst all their team and that he/she is not regarded as a glory seeker, taking all the credit for a success for their own self-gratification. This is especially significant in the military context where ethos and *esprit de corps* must be nurtured.

There can be little argument that if this challenge is to be met then, as Winstanley and Stuart–Smith (1996) have pointed out, there must be an ethical dimension to leadership that provides a clear direction based on personal conduct; clear communication of what is expected of employees and the rules and codes to which they must adhere.

Gill (2001) offers a solution of sorts to the challenge based on the following three themes:

- *Realities*: leaders earn respect by demonstrating their willingness to serve the team, creating solid relationships, and continually learning and developing.
- *Effectiveness*: leaders win the hearts and minds of employees through a shared vision and values, using emotion and showing fortitude.
- *Language*: leaders communicate in a manner that everybody understands and that excites and inspires them.

Ethics and HRM

There has always been an ethical dimension to HRM but it has, until relatively recently, either remained hidden or safely tucked away in the background. As Woodall and Winstanley (2001: 37) point out, there has been little debate 'around the ethical basis of human resource policy and practice'. They argue that there has been some discussion around the development of ethical awareness among managers and 'the ethical dimensions of the change management process...[but]...the detail of HRM policy and practice has escaped ethical scrutiny' (Woodall and Winstanley 2001: 37).

There are many definitions of ethics but very few that are related to the working environment. Woodall and Winstanley (2001) have attempted to take the discussion forward. From an HRM perspective, they define ethics, as:

> the consideration and application of frameworks, values and principles for developing moral awareness and guiding behaviour and action.

At the individual level ethics guides individual judgement and conduct faced with moral dilemmas and choices, whereas morals may reflect a more personal intuitive and unexamined stance which may operate out of an individual's awareness.

At the collective level ethics represents common values enshrined in rules, and codes of practice for guiding behaviour, and which underpin professional and organizational life. Morality on the other hand is the customary values held about what is right and wrong which become embedded or fostered in a society or culture.

(2001: 43)

The helpful aspect of this definition is that it highlights the ethical dimension from organizational, individual, cultural and societal perspectives. All these factors have a bearing on how people are managed and behave in a work context.

As the MoD warns:

In defence, as in other areas, recent years have seen increasing scrutiny of the ethics and morality of Government policy, partly fuelled by the dramatic proliferation of specialist pressure groups and NGOs. Both at national and an international level, such organizations have proved increasingly influential in shaping policy, the most notable example being the accession of many countries to the Ottawa Convention banning anti-personnel land mines. Other areas of international defence activity are coming under scrutiny. More effort will be required to ensure that such public debate is properly informed, particularly where there is a possibility that these pressures will affect our ability to fulfil military objectives.

(MoD 2005)

The issues highlighted and the warnings given by the MoD are directly relevant to developing and transitional states, and their military organizations. All organizations should create their own ethical code (which may also be known as an ethical policy, code of conduct, statement of practice or a set of principles). No two codes will be the same, for they must reflect the concerns of the employees of the particular organization and the context of the relationships and environment in which it operates.

A code should be regarded as a management tool for establishing and articulating the corporate values, responsibilities, obligations, and ethical ambitions of an organization and the way it functions. Critically, however, having a code of conduct is not enough It can only be effective and practically useful with committed dissemination, implementation, monitoring and embedding at all levels so that behaviour is influenced.

Empowerment and HRM

Empowerment became an extremely popular concept in the 1990s (Holden 2004) and a trend that is set to continue for a number of years to come. Citing Arkin, Holden asserts that empowerment is:

> ...strongly associated with culture change initiatives, delayering and restructuring and usually involves devolving power and responsibilities to teams at workplace or customer level.
>
> (2004: 575)

Cook and Macauley (1997) take this further arguing that the working environment must be constructed in such a way as to encourage employees to use their initiative and not be constantly worried about the consequences of all their actions and decisions. They believe that empowerment is:

> ...a change management tool which helps organizations create an environment where every individual can use his or her abilities and energies to satisfy the customer.
>
> (1997: 54)

However, empowerment works in different ways for different situations and what managers need to decide is how best empowerment will work for their organization. Empowerment, if it is correctly implemented, should improve performance in three main ways (Wall 2002). These are: by motivating employees, reducing costs, and improving the employees' knowledge, competence and initiative. A good example of this is the UK Defence Aviation Repair Agency (DARA) which is the largest publicly owned aircraft maintenance facility in Europe (Rana 2002).

DARA has transformed itself. Formerly, it was a typical governmental bureaucracy, stuck in its military past. Now it is a forward-thinking, flatter organization where people take more responsibility for their actions and decisions; are more involved in decision making and are more aware of the needs and wants of their customers. It can be regarded as a model for empowerment.

DARA's *New Ways of Working* programme was an essential element of the organization's change programme. It created a new pay system based on broad banding and employees were given an up-front pay increase for accepting the changes and committing themselves to the new culture. Thus DARA moved from a rigid public sector pay structure to a more flexible private sector model that would recognize the competencies, efforts and skills of its employees. This operated in conjunction with a self-directed teamworking system and a restructuring scheme that reduced the workforce by 3 000 in order to eliminate duplication of work and to improve competitiveness, efficiency, effectiveness and performance.

At first there was suspicion and scepticism amongst the workforce when this programme was announced. It was totally different from the customary public sector/military style, when employment was guaranteed. They saw no need to change things, and were in denial about the need to change in order ensure future survival.

These obstacles were overcome by first, management and unions signing a partnership agreement that ensured both parties signed up to the change programme and supported and recognized the need for the changes. Second, DARA undertook a series of corporate briefings outlining the business and customer needs for change and thirdly, introducing the concept of empowerment. Rana tells how the organization sold a: '...new vision of high-performance working [that] involved talk of cross-fertilisation' and not working in isolation, multi-disciplined teams, hands-off leadership, flat structures and open-door policies' (Rana 2002: 33–4).

Individual employees and teams now have greater ownership of decision-making as they have been given the autonomy to solve their own problems. They can even control their own annual leave, provided that the targets set for their teams have been achieved by the specified dates. The concept of empowerment has filtered through to employee development and today employees will 'actively participate in identifying their own development needs and work closely with their Line Managers to define career path meets their personal ambitions as well as the changing realities of the Agency' (ibid.).

Holden (2004) provides an impressive list of the potential benefits of empowerment, for individuals as well as the organization. These include:

Benefits for organizations

- Greater awareness of business needs among employees
- Cost reduction from delayering and employee ideas
- Improved quality, profitability and productivity measures
- Enhanced flexibility, loyalty and commitment
- Decrease in staff turnover
- More effective communication.

174 Alex Alexandrou and Roger Darby

Benefits for employees

- Greater job satisfaction
- Increase in day-to-day control over tasks
- Ownership of work
- Increase in self-confidence
- Creation of teamwork
- Acquisition of new knowledge and skills.

Futures

As in all sectors, defence faces an uncertain future. Various critical questions about manpower requirements, costs, and suitably trained staff have emerged in conjunction with future challenges to a country's economic, social, political and military environment.

Although the emphasis at present is on recruiting and retention, many would suggest that the AFOPS approach adopted by the United Kingdom still has validity when managing key human resources in the future. The focus for the armed forces will still be on a 'cradle to grave and beyond' philosophy incorporating the themes to cultivate, obtain, retain, sustain and remember their crucial human capital. However, unlike in the past when manpower planning was mainly about determining size; planning for the future is shifting away from a quantitative to a more qualitative approach. Strategies are aimed more at enabling existing workforces to carry out tasks that may emerge in the future. This in turn requires a more flexible workforce with transferable skills to match changing needs in a multiplicity of locations and diverse environments.

Hosek (2003) suggests that versatility and leadership are top of the requirements list for the soldier of the twenty-first century. In Figure 11.4, he offers an interesting vision of a future and the needed changes which directly impact on HRM in the military.

In line with the changing environment of the future, the issue of organizational architecture is a key component in overall HRM. The management functions of strategy, structure and control all influence HRM in all types of organizations and organizational design often determines how HRM functions, both negatively as well as positively. As future demands point to the defence sector being more flexible, versatile and responsive to immediate needs so too must organizations be designed to reflect and support those changes. Figure 11.5 identifies a number of crucial issues for organizational designers to address the challenges the future presents to organizations:

Conclusion

In conclusion, three key considerations for the future management of human resources have been identified within this chapter. These are based on the fundamental concepts of leadership, ethics and empowerment. However, in the future they will require more clarification in the defence

Comparing visions of the future and needed changes

Vision	Org. change	New technology	Manning requirements	Personnel quality
Cyber soldier	Yes	Yes	Decrease	High
Information warrior	Maybe	Yes	Increase	High
Peace operations	Maybe	Maybe	Same	Same
Rapid response	Yes	Maybe	Same	Same
Low-manning vessels	No	Yes	Decrease	High
Evolutionary change	Gradual	Gradual	Gradual	Gradual

Figure 11.4 Visions of the future and changes in personnel (Hosek 2003). (Reproduced by permission of RAND Corporation.)

QUESTIONS FOR ORGANIZATION DESIGNERS

■ **Specialization**
Should jobs be broken down into narrow areas of work or should specialization be kept to a minimum?

■ **Hierarchy**
Should the organization be 'tall'or 'flat' in terms of its levels of management and spans of control?

■ **Grouping**
Should jobs or departments be grouped together functionally, by product/service, by geographical areas served or by some other criterion?

■ **Integration**
What methods of integration should be used?

■ **Control**
Close or loose? Centralized or decentralized? Formal or informal?

Figure 11.5 Organizational architecture for the future (adapted from Child 1984).

sector if HRM is to be more effective. The concepts identified with resultant consequences, are as follows:

• Changing organization forms, processes and psychological contracts, which relate to *trust* in the employment relationship.

- Developing partnerships in the employment relationship to give everyone a *voice* in the workplace.
- The pursuit of multiple and parallel flexibilities which goes to the heart of how *work* is organized.

Questions to consider

1 Think about how the key task in the Four Task Model in relation to your organization. Ask the questions to highlight strengths and weaknesses.
2 Look back at Gratton's questions on strategic HRM. Try to answer them in relation to your organization. They will help to identify the strengths and weaknesses of your current system.
3 The Institute of Business Ethics has created a simple ethical test for leaders and managers when making decisions. Reflect on a recent managerial decision and answer the following questions:
   a *Transparency* Do I mind others knowing what I have decided?
   b *Effect* Who does my decision affect or hurt?
   c *Fairness* Would my decision be considered fair by those affected.
4 Give examples in your organization of the potential benefits of empowerment to both the organization and its personnel.
5 Thinking about the future, consider how specific changes in deployment, or personnel-related policies and procedures, affect your force readiness and the availability of individuals and units for deployment? You may want to think in terms of: recruitment and retention; training and development; performance, reward and cost of personnel; organization design; and ethical behaviour of leaders and others.

Note

1 During our international courses we have found that many people have difficulty in understanding this aspect of AFOPS. In the UK it has been decided that the care of veterans, widows and orphans should remain the responsibility of the defence sector. This does not imply some form of best practice, merely that this is the way Britain has decided to organise this aspect of its HRM practice, in keeping with the '... and beyond' in the AFOPS philosophy. TMcC.

Suggested reading

Alexandrou, A., Bartle, R. and Holmes, R. (eds) (2001), *Human Resource Management in the British Armed Forces: Investing in the Future*, London: Frank Cass.
Beattie, R. and Osborne, S. (eds) (2006), *Human Resource Management in the Public Sector*.

Budhwar, P. S. (ed.) (2004), *Managing Human Resources in Asia-Pacific*.
Budhwar, P. S. and Mellahi, K. (eds) (2006), *Managing Human Resources in the Middle East*.
Budhwar, P. S. and Yaw, D. (eds) (2004), *Human Resource Management in Developing Countries*.
Cooke, F. L. (ed.) (2005), *HRM, Work and Employment in China*.
Davila, A. and Elvira, M. M. (eds) (2005), *Managing Human Resources in Latin America: An Agenda for International Leaders*.
Johnson, S., Libicki, M. and Gregory, F. (eds) (2003), *New Challenges, New Tools for Defense Decisionmaking*, Santa Monica: RAND Corporation.
Kamoche, K. N. and Yaw, D. A. (eds) (2004), *Managing Human Resources in Africa*.
Routledge (London and New York) are publishing an excellent series on human resource management in international contexts. Titles to date include:
If your country or region is not already included, it is probably coming soon.

Bibliography

Alexandrou, A., Bartle, R. and Holmes, R. (2001), 'HRM in the armed forces: options for change to AFOPS', in Alexandrou, A., Bartle, R. and Holmes, R. (eds), *Human Resource Management in the British Armed Forces: Investing in the Future*, London: Frank Cass.
Beer, M., Spector, B., Lawrence, P., Quinn Mills, D. and Walton, R. (1984), *Managing Human Assets*, New York: Free Press.
Blessing White (1999), *Millennial Values*, Princeton, NJ: Blessing White.
Budwar, P. S. (2000), 'Evaluating levels of strategic integration and development of human resource management in the UK', *Personnel Review*, 29 (2): 138–53.
Child, J. (1984), 'Organization structure, environment and performance: the role of strategic choice', *Sociology*, 6 (1): 1–22.
Collins, T. (2005), *Rules of Engagement: A Life in Conflict*, Headline: London.
Cook, S. and MaCauley, S. (1997), 'Empowered customer service', *Empowerment in Organisations*, 5 (10): 54–60.
Darby, R. (2005), HRM Course materials, *Managing Defence in a Democracy Course*, Cranfield University.
Edwards, G., Winter, P. K. and Bailey, J. (2002), *Leadership in Management*, Ross-on-Wye: Leadership Trust.
Fombrun, C., Tichey and Devanna, M. (1984), *Strategic Human Resource Management*, New York: John Wiley and Sons.
Gill, R. (2001), *Essays on Leadership*, Ross-on-Wye: Leadership Trust.
Gratton, L. (1997), 'The art of managing people', in Bickerstaffe, G. and Dickson, T. (eds), *Mastering Management*, London: Financial Times Pitman Publishing, pp. 251–8.
Gratton, L., Hope Hailey, V., Stiles, P. and Truss, C. (1999), *Strategic Human Resource Management*, Oxford: Oxford University Press.
Guest, D. (1991), 'Personnel management: the end of orthodoxy?' *British Journal of Industrial Relations*, 29 (3): 149–75.
Guest, D. and Conway, N. (2000), *The Psychological Contract in the Public Sector*, London: CIPD.

Guest, D. and Conway, N. (2001), *Public and Private Sector Perceptions on the Psychological Contract*, London: CIPD.

Hedlund, G. (1996), 'The hypermodern MNC – A heterachy?' *Human Resource Management*, 25 (1): 28–43.

Holden, L. (2004), 'Employee involvement and empowerment', in Beardwell, I., Holden, L. and Claydon, T. (eds), *Human Resource Management: A Contemporary Approach* (4th edition), London: Financial Times Pitman Publishing, pp. 539–83.

Hosek, J. (2003), 'The soldier of the 21st Century', in Johnson, S., Libicki, M. and Gregory, F. (eds), *New Challenges, New Tools for Defense Decisionmaking*, Santa Monica: RAND Corporation.

Institute of Business Ethics (2005), *Codes of Conduct*, London: Institute of Business Ethics, www.ibe.org.uk (accessed 30 August 2005).

Legge, K. (2005), *Human Resource Management: Rhetorics and Realities*, (Anniversary edition), Basingstoke: Palgrave Macmillan.

Lengnick-Hall, C. A. and Lengnick-Hall, M. A. (1990), *Interactive Human Resource Management and Strategic Planning*, Westport, CT: Quorum Books.

Ministry of Defence (2003), *Armed Forces Overarching Personnel Strategy*, London: Ministry of Defence.

—— (2005), *The Future Strategic Context for Defence*, London: Ministry of Defence, www.mod.uk (accessed 31 August 2005).

Perlmutter, H. (1969), 'The tortuous evolution of the multinational corporation', *Columbia Journal of World Business*, 4: 9–18.

Rana, E. (2002), 'Flying information', *People Management*, 7 November 2002, pp. 30–4.

Royal Air Force (2004), *Ethos, Core Values and Standards of the Royal Air Force*, Innsworth, Gloucester: Royal Air Force.

Schuler, R. and Rogovsky, N. (1998), 'Understanding compensation practices variations across firms: The impact of national culture', *Journal of International Business Studies*, 29 (1): 159–77.

Schuler, R. S., Jackson, S. E. and Storey, J. (2005), 'HRM and its link with strategic management', in Storey, J. (ed.), *Human Resource Management: A Critical Text* (2nd edition), London: Thomson Learning.

Storey, J. (1995), 'Human resource management today: an assessment', in Storey, J. (ed.), *Human Resource Management: A Critical Text* (2nd edition), London: Thomson Learning.

Tyson, S. (1995), *Human Resource Strategy*, London: Pitman.

Wall, T. (2002), 'Empowerment', *People Management*, 25 October 2002, p. 43.

Winstanley, D. and Stuart-Smith, K. (1996), 'Policing performance: the ethics of performance management', *Personnel Review*, 25 (6): 66–84.

Woodall, J. and Winstanley, D. (2001), 'The place of ethics in HRM', in Storey, J. (ed.), *Human Resource Management: A Critical Text* (2nd edition), London: Thomson Learning.

Wright, P., McMahon, G. and McWilliams A. (1994), 'Human resources and sustained competitive advantage: A resource-based perspective', *International Journal of Human Resource Management*, 5 (2): 312–28.

Wright, P. M. and Snell, S. A. (1998), 'Toward a unifying framework for exploring fit and flexibility in strategic human resource management', *Academy of Management Review*, 23 (4): 744–59.

12 Basic concepts in financial management

Len Nockles and Teri McConville

The sinews of war are infinite money

(Cicero: *Philippics*)

Introduction

Whatever your role: officer, manager or clerk, you probably feel that you spend too much time filling in reports. But, if your organization is going to be properly managed, information is needed. Such is the case in financial management but the management accounting system will give information in return. The purpose of this chapter is to introduce defence managers to some of the basic terminology and concepts used in financial management, to help them to get the best out of the accounting information systems and enable them to make better decisions.

The main branches of accounting are: bookkeeping, cost accounting, financial accounting, management accounting and financial management. You do not have to be able to do bookkeeping (or cost accounting) to understand accounting – they are methods of recording information.

Bookkeeping is a mechanical task involving the collection of basic financial data using a method of recording information, consisting of three stages:

- Recording – introducing a transaction into the accounting system
- Analysing – grouping similar transactions together
- Summarizing – preparing statements showing the result of the recording and analysing for a given period.

Cost accounting involves the recording of cost data, which is the collection of information for internal management purposes.

The nature of costs

Almost every decision a manager makes has an effect on cost. It is essential that you have an understanding of the types of cost and how they should be used for cost management.

Cost classification

Total operating costs usually comprise staff costs (including salaries and wages, social security costs, pension costs and severance) and other operating costs. This second category includes stock consumption, equipment support, property management, research and ICT costs. In resource, or commercial, accounting this will also include depreciation and interest. These are the overheads, which are the usual focus of management control in service industries.

Costs are classified in a number of ways so that they can be grouped for analysis and reporting. The two major classifications are direct and indirect costs, or fixed and variable costs.

A *direct cost* is an expense, which can be easily identified with a specific product or service. In manufacturing, examples would be the cost of materials and the direct cost of labour For an RAF repair facility, direct costs could include property costs (depreciation, rent, heat and light etc.) for dedicated hangars and stock consumed. These costs can be charged to specific aircraft. Table 12.1 illustrates some of the differences.

Indirect costs – overheads – are all those costs that cannot be easily identified with a particular service (or job). In this example the costs of running the general airfield infrastructure, systems and staff would be regarded as indirect. This category might also include a share of general management operating costs (e.g. Strike Command HQ). We shall see later that staff costs etc. can be allocated to a 'product'.

A *fixed cost* remains the same, for a given period, whether activity is booming or slack. However, this is true only within a given range of activity. If there were an emergency; for example, extra premises might be needed for logistics operations, which would increase rent. Such major changes in scale are infrequent, so the fixed cost is a practical concept for short-term business planning such as annual budgeting. Of course, in the long-term, all costs are likely to change through price increases but fixed costs do not alter because of increases in volume. They can also be broken down into:

- *Committed costs* are mostly associated with maintaining the company's legal and physical existence, over which management has little or no discretion. Obvious examples are ministers' salaries and rent.

Table 12.1 Classifying costs

	Fixed costs	*Variable costs*
Direct costs	Depreciation of hangar Rent	Stock consumed Heat & Light
Indirect costs	Property costs Strike Command	ICT costs

- *Managed costs* include staff salaries that are related to current operations but must continue to be paid to ensure the continued operating existence of an organization.

A *variable cost* is a constant amount per unit of output; hence total variable costs change in proportion to the volume of output. For an equipment manufacturer, higher levels of production will increase the cost of materials used. The relationship between output and material costs would probably be directly proportional, unless the volume changed enough to provide economies of scale, for example bulk purchase discounts. The obvious parallel in defence is the cost of equipment and stores consumed, which will vary with the number of operational commitments.

In deciding how to categorize costs, you need to consider time. The example of a combat operation is based on the short-term. During this time, say a year, some of the cost inputs cannot be changed; and would usually involve barracks, staff costs and equipment running costs (including depreciation). Over time, however, the scale of the operation may change or there may be a change in capability. It follows that, in the long-run, all costs are variable and, in making decisions, the time boundary needs to be considered.

To classify costs as fixed or variable depends upon whose viewpoint is being taken. For instance, an IT department would probably regard depreciation and personnel costs as fixed. But, if it charges other departments in proportion to usage, those departments will view computer services as variable costs. In larger companies groups of costs may be regarded as variable – for instance a local HQ might be regarded as variable cost on the principle that individual bases, and the network, can be expanded.

- *Discretionary costs* Some costs are neither fixed nor variable nor in-between. Spending on advertising, training or research, for example, may change, not in line with changes in volume, but because of management's discretionary decisions. For instance, if recruitment fell, advertising might well increase.

Discretionary costs need not be committed for the long-term (in the way that rent is) because managers can decide to reduce advertizing costs by cancelling future advertising campaigns at short notice. Spending on advertising, training or research is usually determined by managers' subjective assessment of the (often long-term) benefits to the organization compared with the (immediate) measurable cost. (Because these benefits may be highly uncertain, financial accounts normally write off such discretionary costs as expenses when they are incurred.)

Costs in similar industries tend to be classified along the same lines. Recent studies suggest that, for manufacturing companies in Europe, fixed costs are some 35 per cent of the total; and, of these, about 20 per cent (of the total) are indirect. Table 12.2 shows how the cost structure would differ between manufacturing and service sector organizations.

- *Average cost* is often a good first rule of thumb to assess profitability. It is calculated as the total cost divided by the total number of units produced. All costs are included whether they are fixed, variable, direct, indirect etc. Therefore, in the case of a training unit, the average cost would be total cost per graduating recruit.
- *Marginal cost* is the extra cost incurred every time you produce one more unit of output. In the short run, with normal capacity constraints, marginal costs equal variable costs. For instance, each graduating recruit will require uniform and other kit. For most short-term business decisions, it is marginal, rather than average, costs which are relevant.

Costs and revenues

In commercial enterprises the management of cost is often dealt with in isolation from revenue, and vice versa. At some levels, however, managers (usually senior management) need to look at the interaction between them. If defence managers are to be accountable for how they spend public money, they need to monitor the relationship of revenue (or non-financial targets, such as states of readiness) and costs. To achieve value and to keep spending within the available budget, costs must not exceed income (revenues) in the long-run, given that revenue may be fixed. Market forces often drive achievable prices, which then set a ceiling to long-term costs for a given volume of output. It is rare that defence managers can pass on whatever costs they incur, as higher prices to customers, so a more typical problem may be matching costs to capabilities.

Costs and revenues usually vary with output; and managers need to know which level of output and which type of business are likely to realize the maximum value from the defence budget. We turn now to look at short-term tactics, where existing facilities limit the scale of business.

Table 12.2 Comparing cost structures in manufacturing and service sector organizations

Manufacturing				Service sector		
Total (%)	Direct (%)	Indirect (%)		Total (%)	Direct (%)	Indirect (%)
35	15	20	Fixed	10	0	10
65	55	10	Variable	90	75	15
100	70	30	Total	100	75	25

Full costing (Apportioning indirect cost)

Full costing, or absorption costing, is the term used to describe the approach whereby products (or services) each absorb a share of the total overhead costs in addition to their direct cost, so that:

Total (or full cost) = Direct costs + Share of overheads (indirect costs)

Manufacturing industry often uses time, machine hours or labour hours to allocate indirect costs but this is not usually practical in the case of service industries or in the public sector. Apportioning indirect costs in non-manufacturing concerns relies on a measure of output which can be determined as a benchmark. For example, in the case of the training school, you could allocate the indirect costs to various courses on the basis of taught hours or trainers' salaries.

In recent years, full costing has fallen out of favour but it remains a quick and reliable, if flawed, process for apportioning costs to calculate profits by product. In relating costs to revenues (or outputs), it is important to attribute variable costs to products or services. This process allocates fixed cost, which is arbitrary and has a large margin of error.

Marginal costing

We need a method of calculating profits which can be used to make decisions but which does not contain arbitrary figures. The most common method uses a technique called marginal costing which relies on the principle that variable costs are those that change in line with output.

- *Cost centres.* A cost centre is simply the smallest grouping in the organization for which costs are collected separately and usually have a manager (or supervisor) responsible for the budget and performance. In most organizations there is a breakdown between functions – for example, supplies, recruitment, finance. As companies become bigger, large departments are sub-divided so, for instance, supplies might become purchase, stores and distribution. An Army, for instance might treat regiments as cost centres and these may have departmental cost centres of their own.

Marginal costing analyses each cost centre, deciding first, which costs are fixed and then which are variable. It then attributes the variable costs to each product in a manner which seems reasonable. The fixed costs for all cost centres are totalled and deducted from the sum of the contributions.

Budgets and forecasts

It helps to understand budgets, if they are considered in the context of strategic planning. This highlights some of the issues surrounding the generation and use of budgets. Budgeting is an essential tool, for managers to plan and control their firms' operations. Organizational strategy will influence senior managers' approach to budgets.

We have seen that organizations are often sub-divided into cost centres in order to allocate responsibility for operations. A MoD cost centre would have targets for a given period, say, every three months. In this way, the Director of Naval Recruiting, for instance, would have targets for every quarter. This would not only include numbers of new recruits, but also the total advertising spend, staff salaries and their training costs, rent on recruiting offices and selection centres, and related overheads.

At the two extremes, plans could be dictated from above (top-down), or simply emerge from below (bottom-up). In practice, different levels of management often agree plans through a process of negotiation. The final budget will often lie between what top management would really like, and what junior managers reckon is feasible (but ambitious junior managers might even budget for better results than top management demands). Typically, the process will include a combination of these processes with the first detailed plans being developed bottom-up.

Budgets are business plans, expressed in money, covering a shorter period of time than the strategic plan (usually a year). Most companies prepare budgets for balance sheet items (e.g. fixed assets, debtors, stocks), as well as for profit and loss account items (e.g. sales, expenses). As well as internal planning and objective setting, budgets will often be needed to satisfy external financing bodies – governments are more inclined to allocate extra money to departments that demonstrate sound financial planning. A budgets should not be a neutral forecast or idealized target. It must be achievable, and managers need commitment to make it happen. Although they are often regarded with mistrust and dislike, budgets simply involve forward planning. Problems, arising out of the budget system normally result from how the information is managed. Hence, budgets have implications for human behaviour. Budgets are like any performance measurement system, if they are to be fully effective, managers should:

- Agree targets and believe they can be achieved.
- Receive information in a form relevant to their work – such as number of units produced or delivered.
- Be trained to understand the need for budgets and how they are used.

It is not sensible to judge a department's performance entirely based on financial indicators since many decisions have longer-term effects. Using more than one yardstick to measure success is wiser than judging managers or business units by any single accounting figure, however cleverly it has been devised. This is no less true in the public sector. Income is difficult to manage and costs can fluctuate for reasons beyond managerial control. It is better to judge managers on their record of accomplishment over a period of years.

Finally, a budget is not intended either to be either an academic exercise or a decorative object. Budgets help in all management functions (see Chapter 8), and starts with the planning process, of which it is an integral part.

Budgets help managers to

Plan and organize

Budgets force managers to look ahead, setting targets, anticipating problems and giving the organization purpose and direction. The budget demonstrates that managers have thought ahead about how they will utilize resources in their area to achieve organizational objectives. The total defence spend will be cascaded downwards, as departmental limits, and these will set limits on how much administrative, and other operational departments, are allowed to spend in the period. A word of caution, though is that budgets can be overly bureaucratic and it is too easy to focus only on matching predictions and results. Diligent thought in the budgeting process can highlight certain future events which could cause problems, especially in relation to resources. For instance, the broadcast of television programmes about service life usually bring a surge of inquiries to recruiting offices. Good planning should anticipate this and ensure that resources are in place at the right time, but not before they are needed.

Example

Suppose the operations budget has been prepared for an air movements squadron. From that data, and knowing the amount of traffic moving on a particular route, capacity requirements can be derived, by day and by route. This might involve, for example, talking to civilian carriers about availability and pricing.

There are further multiplier effects. For example, there will be questions about the availability of warehousing and road transport. There could be concerns about the correct mix of skills, which should inform decisions about recruitment and training, or even changes in working practices such as shift patterns.

Command

The value of a budget is further enhanced if it motivates managers to strive towards objectives. A realistic budget has the benefit of encouraging people to achieve planned targets. Two levels of attainment can be set: a minimum expectations budget, and a desired budget, which can present some sort of challenge. Like other targets, a budget that is either too easy or too difficult to achieve will usually prove to be less motivating than one which is difficult but achievable. Likewise, business managers tend to work more effectively if they know that their performance (and that of their business unit) is to be compared with an agreed budget. Managers may feel greater commitment where they have been involved in preparing the budget. Top management may expect junior managers to not-quite achieve their (stretching) budget targets. Budgets can be coercive, but good managers should be able to control and motivate a workforce without resorting to coercion with all its negative and 'Theory X' connotations.

Co-ordinate

Budgeting helps to ensure that there is a unity of purpose and that people within the organization will work towards a common goal. For example, the transport department should have its budget based on expected movement requirements. In turn, the movements budget should be based on operational expectations. A budget provides a formal system for communicating plans and is a useful way of ensuring that each person is aware of what they are supposed to be doing. The construction of the budget can be a powerful aid to clarifying the lines of communication within the organization.

Control

By setting agreed targets for performance, budgets form an integral part of control and review procedures. As a yardstick, the budget provides indicators of where action may be necessary. *Variances* – differences between actual spending and the budget – can act as an early warning for management action.

Once a budget is formulated, a regular reporting system needs to be set up, just like control points for activity. This helps to ensure that managers focus on problems which need corrective action – a principle known as management by exception. While budgets can be useful for evaluating how a manager or department is performing, it is important that the budgetary control system keeps the organization fit, monitors progress, and informs the decision making process. This is a two-edged sword and, if budgetary targets are over-emphasized, managers might overlook other important aspects of their jobs such as maintaining quality or staff morale (Sylvie Jackson shows this well in Chapter 14). The wise manager will be vigilant to ensure that budgets are not being achieved through manipulation of either the budget or results, or both.

Budget processes

Most managers accept the need for budgeting in theory but too often tend to rely on accountants to do a lot of the work for them. The result will be very well presented – but not always based on business reality. Nevertheless, you still have to provide the basic information – they do not know, for instance, how much extra training you expect to undertake for a particular platform next year. Accountants need to know how many extra staff you need next year and whether they will need extra equipment etc.

The stages in the budget process

In a large organization, the budget will contain, literally, thousands of targets and objectives for each measured item: people, prices, manufacturing cost, etc. Together, these make for an extensive and extremely detailed exercise. For a comprehensive picture, the figures overall must be reconciled, to ensure consistency, and then consolidated to form the top-level budget. Managers working in large organizations will usually receive budget guidelines which will indicate performance targets, as well the factors that will be used to calculate the budget. (These might cover exchange rates, employment costs, external costs such as rent, local taxes and energy costs.) Parameters and assumptions about the range of capabilities, major equipment changes, expected force growth, exchange rates, etc., need to be set early, and disseminated, to form the base of the plan.

When all the budget information is collated, the master budget for the operating costs can be prepared. Then follows a review of the departmental limits for each unit and sub-unit. From the various data, work can begin on constructing the budgeted cash flow, which will include consideration of a capital equipment budget. Some organizations concentrate on profit and loss account budgets and overlook the need for cash budgets at the operating unit level. Such an approach risks ignoring the high cost of over-investment in assets such as debtors, or fixed assets. Therefore, a cash flow budget should be worked out in parallel with other budgets, to assess affordability. This helps to ensure that the final budget is consistent with the broad financial targets and does not, for example, assume unrealistic borrowing requirements.

Once individual budgets have been prepared and collated, they must be approved; certain aspects of the budget may need revising, or contentious aspects of the budget defended. The budget is issued to the operating areas, possibly after being phased for use on a month to month basis. The annual budget is normally divided into months, but not necessarily equal. Where business is seasonal or is changing rapidly, setting realistic monthly budgets will need great care.

Choice of budgeting systems

An organization preparing its budgets has a choice between a number of systems usually, Incremental Budgeting, Zero Based Budgeting, Flexible Budgets and Rolling Budgets.

- *The incremental budgeting system* is the most straightforward approach. It looks at the current year's results and adjusts these results for changes in activity levels, and the effects of price inflation. One of the weaknesses of this system is that it encourages past inefficiencies to be perpetuated. Being simple, it is the preferred system of budgeting but it can prevent a critical, or vigorous, consideration of all the costs of running an organization.

- *A flexible budget* is designed to change in response to shifts in output levels or other relevant factors, but allows that some costs are fixed. Flexing does not have to be restricted to output levels. It can incorporate changes for any factor which differs from that which was anticipated, for example, different states of the economy. In this way, flexing is saying 'If I knew then what I know now what budget would I set?' It is a useful concept but can cause some concern. If taken to extremes, it undermines many of the budget principles – targeting, motivation etc. and managers can become confused and frustrated if, throughout the year, they face the proverbial moving goalposts.

- *A rolling budget* is one that is constantly being updated: adding a further period (e.g. month or quarter) and deducting an earlier period. It is basically used for control purposes, and to reduce the influence of uncertainty from factors such as inflation or world events. Rolling budgets are time- and labour-intensive.

- *The Zero Based Budgeting system* (ZBB) was developed to eliminate some of the weaknesses of incremental budgeting. It is based on the idea that, if budgets are automatically prepared according to existing levels of expenditure then past inefficiencies can be replicated. With ZBB, each item of expenditure included in the budget must be justified. A case must be made for each item of expenditure included in the budget of a coming period, hence unnecessary expenditure is more likely to be excluded. The ZBB system is complex and not often used. In most cases expenditure can be argued as necessary although this approach will highlight discretionary costs and ought to point to marginal items of revenue and expenditure.

The budgetary control process

The starting point for any budgetary control system is the actual preparation of the budget, and when this has been agreed and issued, activity can be monitored against it. Later, when measured information is reviewed and investigated, the reasons for variances with the plan/budget can be considered. This is part of the feedback process. Inefficiency can be corrected and any potential for savings exploited.

If conditions change, the budget figures may no longer represent a good estimate of the current year's results, nor continue to act as a meaningful plan. Monthly reports may, then, include a latest estimate for the current year which can help to show whether a variance in one month is merely a function of timing which will reverse itself next month, or the start of a trend towards large cumulative variances by the year-end. Clearly, these would require different management actions. Flexible budgeting can allow for changes in operating conditions. Managers may become demoralized if actual results are compared with budgets that have become unattainable, or complacent if budgets are now too easily achieved. Therefore, despite the time involved it may be desirable to revise budgets.

Budgetary control with monthly reporting may help managers to answer the following kinds of questions:

- What has recent performance been like? How and why does it differ from budget?
- How, if at all, will these events cause latest estimates of current year results to differ from budget if we take no action?
- What, if anything, can be done to counter unfavourable variances from budgets, or to increase favourable one ? (Successful managers cash in on good luck!)
- How soon will such action be effective? How much difference will it make?
- After all proposed actions, what is now the latest estimate of current year's results?

Decision-making and problem solving

We have already defined a number of cost categories but in decision making it is important to recognize costs and benefits which are relevant to the decision and to filter out irrelevant items. Even someone who cannot distinguish cash and operating costs can discuss a proposed decision provided that they simply consider whether benefits will outweigh the expense.

The costs which should be used for decision making are often referred to as *relevant costs*. In particular these are cash outflows or cash inflows, which would follow a particular course of action. Decisions are always about the future – they cannot alter the past – hence, relevant costs are also *future costs*. The concept that bygones are bygones relates to all historical costs, including labour, materials, machinery and other items. A cost that has been incurred in the past is totally irrelevant to any current decision. Costs and revenues that increase (or decrease) are relevant whereas those that remain unchanged are not.

Eighteen months ago FitCo won a significant sub-contract to refurbish electronic components on minesweepers but it needed specialized handling equipment and a clean room at a cost of £50 000. The main contractor has just given three months notice that it intends to take the work in-house. The four operators working on the existing contract (total cost of £88 000 per annum) can be redeployed within the existing facility but FitCo are unlikely to find a use for the equipment and room in the *short-term*. Management are considering four alternative courses of action:

1   Leave the area and equipment intact until new business can be found.
2   Scrap it all and realize £1 500.
3   Dismantle the equipment and room and use the materials for spares at a cost of £500 but saving £8 000 on spares and fittings.
4   Spend £15 000 to dismantle, modify and reassemble the equipment, and move it for work on a similar contract saving £35 000 on new equipment.

Table 12.3 Options for FitCo

Option	Extra cost	Benefit	Net benefits
1	Nil	Nil unless a customer is found	Nil
2	Nil	£1 500	£1 500
3	£500	£8 000	£7 500
4	£15 000	£35 000	£20 000

The results of each option are set out in Table 12.3.

In each case the past costs of £50 000 and operator cost of £88 000 are ignored. That money has been spent regardless of what the company will do in the future. Only the future costs and benefits are relevant to the decision. The last option seems to be the best – with a net benefit of £20 000.

Make or buy decisions

In the era of New Public Management, outsourcing is a common practice as organizations try to concentrate on their core functions and/or to realize the economies of scale of specialist contractors. Additionally, outsourcing can improve quality, flexibility or control. It offers an alternative to expensive investment and may be useful for occasional, specialist work.

Example

The OC Motor Transport of Carpathian Barracks noted that his section was making a daily trip to transport personnel to hospital appointments. The round trip took two hours at a cost of £65 (= £16 500 per annum). He invited two private ambulance companies to bid for the business and received quotes of £46 and £43 – a potential saving of £19 (£5 500 per annum).

Before accepting the bids he decided to get an analysis of the costs (Table 12.4).

Table 12.4 Cost analysis for the hospital trip

Hospital trip cost sheet	(£)	
Labour cost	19.00	
Diesel fuel	6.00	
Vehicle operating cost	40.00	20% variable; 80% fixed
Total cost of trip	65.00	

Only 20 per cent of the vehicle operating costs are variable (i.e., £8.00), So the extra savings from outsourcing would amount to £33.00 (£8 + £6 + £19). Since the best quote is £43 a trip then it should continue to be done by the section. If the cost difference had been closer then other operating factors should be considered, for example, what could the vehicle do with the two hours released, are there cheaper outsourcing methods? Of course, OC should also ensure that the cost of pickup is built into a cross-charge to the medical section.

Capital expenditure decisions

Capital investment decisions are those that involve current outlays in return for income (or other benefits) in future years. As with discretionary costs, capital expenditures are made in the expectation of realizing future benefits. Time is the distinguishing feature between short-term decisions and capital investment decisions, and relates to the period between cash outlay and the realization of benefits. This time horizon is probably similar to the view that differentiates fixed and variable cost. The commitment of funds for a significant period involves an interest cost, which must be brought into the analysis. With short-term decisions the interest cost is normally so small that it can be ignored. Capital investment decisions often represent the most important decisions that a manager can make. They commit a substantial proportions of an organization's resources to actions that are likely to be irreversible and subsequent managers usually inherit the impact.

Investment decisions are taken at all levels of society. In the public sector they include new roads, schools and airports. Individuals' investment decisions include house buying and the purchase of white goods and cars. There are some basic principles that can be used to assess investment proposals.

Capital investment decisions are complex and would need input from other managers, accounts staff and other specialists. To simplify matters, what follows assumes cash inflows and outflows (or profits and expenses) are known with certainty, and that sufficient funds are available to undertake all profitable investments. The impact of tax and inflation are also ignored.

Evaluating capital projects

Typical decisions for defence managers could be:

- Whether to move to (or add) Barracks A
- Whether to move to Barracks A or Barracks B
- Whether to move to Barracks A or buy IT system X
- Whether to move Barracks now or later.

The MoD guidelines on appraisal and evaluation often form stages of a broad policy cycle that some departments and agencies formalize in the acronym ROAMEF (Rationale, Objectives, Appraisal, Monitoring, Evaluation and Feedback). This is shown in Figure 12.1.

The key steps are:

- *Rationale*: Need for the policy or programme.
- *Objectives*: Flow from the need identified as being unmet.

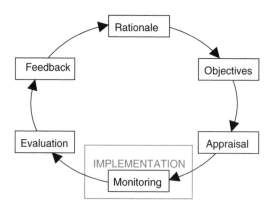

Figure 12.1 The ROAMEF framework.

- *Appraisal*: Assessment of the possible options to meet those needs. Appraisal methods are discussed in detail later. These are usually centred on the financial implications.
- *Monitoring*: Is the continuous review of the project operation/ implementation.
- *Evaluation*: Is the assessment of the full effects of the project against a previously determined baseline.
- *Feedback*: Communicating the results of evaluation to those concerned with the original project or with related projects.

Simple appraisal methods

The return on investment (or accounting rate of return method) is quick and simple and, unlike other methods, is not based on cash flows. It calculates the average rate of return (as a percentage) on the original investment. This method assumes that all the costs are written off and the project has no value at the end of a given period. If you deduct the initial cost from the expected benefits over the forecast period (in the example, seven years) and divide this by that number of years you will get the average annual return.

Example (Capital investment)

Table 12.5 illustrates three rival proposals for capital investment with benefits forecast over the next seven years.

Table 12.5 Three rival proposals for capital investment with benefits forecast over the next seven years

		Project A (£)		Project B (£)		Project C (£)	
Initial cost	Year 0		50 000		70 000		50 000
Benefits	Year 1	10 000		10 000		10 000	
	Year 2	20 000		10 000		20 000	
	Year 3	20 000		10 000		10 000	
	Year 4	20 000		20 000		13 500	
	Year 5	10 000		30 000		3 500	
	Year 6	5 000		30 000		3 500	
	Year 7	2 800	87 800	30 000	140 000	3 500	64 000
Net benefits			37 800		70 000		14 000
Average annual return			5 400		10 000		2 000
Average annual return / Initial investment		5 400 / 50 000 = 10.8%		10 000 / 70 000 = 14.3%		2 000 / 50 000 = 4.0%	

On this basis you might decide that project B looks best, but you might be concerned about the large returns expected in the later years. The average rate of return is a good indicator and easily understood but it ignores the timing of the profit or cash flow.

The pay-back method is popular and one of the simplest and most frequently used techniques of capital investment appraisal. The pay-back is defined as the length of time that is required for cash proceeds from an investment to recover the original cash outlay. If the cash income is constant each year, then the pay-back period can be found by dividing the initial outlay by the total income each year, to work out the number of years to pay-back the investment. For example, if the initial outlay was £50 000 and the income was £20 000 per annum then the pay-back would be:

£50 000 / £20 000 = 2½ years.

In pay-back calculations the profit is assumed to be even throughout the year.

Consider the three projects in Table 12.5 to assess the payback period.
  Project A can easily be calculated. The repayments (benefits) from Years 1, 2 and 3 equal the initial outlay, so the pay-back is exactly three years.
  In Project B, after four years, £50 000 has been earned (the income for Year 1 to Year 4) leaving £20 000 outstanding from the £70 000 initial investment. In Year 5 it will take eight months to earn this, so the pay-back period is 4 years, 8 months (or 4⅔ years).
  Project C is calculated in the same way as project B. After three years £40 000 has been earned (the income for Years 1, 2 and 3) leaving £10 000 outstanding from the £50 000 initial investment. It will take nine months in year 4 to recoup the remainder (£10 000 / £13 500 x 12, rounding up) so the pay-back is 3¾ years.

With this method Project A looks the best performer, paying-back the investment in three years. (When forecasting net profits or cash flows some years hence – approximations and roundings are acceptable as long as they are done consistently.)
Discounted cash flow (DCF). So far, the methods used do not consider the impact of time. To decide whether returns are acceptable you need a

technique which compares returns in the future with investment now, because a given amount of money now will be worth less in future. DCF techniques rely upon the principle that involves discounting, or scaling-down, future cash flows. The more familiar technique of compounding will help to explain this.

Example (Compounding)

Suppose you invest £1 000 in a savings fund paying interest at 20% per annum, at the end of one year you will have £1 200 (your original sum plus the interest). In year two, interest will be paid on £1 200, not just your original investment. Table 12.6 shows the figures for four years, and indicates that today's £1 000 will be £2 074 in four years' time.

Table 12.6 £1 000 Compounded over four years

		£
End of Year 0 (Now)		1 000
End of Year 1	£1 000 × (1.20)	1 200
End of Year 2	£1 000 × (1.20)^2	1 440
End of Year 3	£1 000 × (1.20)^3	1 728
End of Year 4	£1 000 × (1.20)^4	2 074

When compounding is applied to a sum of money, its value in future may be calculated, given a known rate of interest. Discounting is the reverse. Future cash inflows are discounted at a given rate of interest so that they may be directly compared to the present outlay of cash. Because discounting is the reverse of compounding, to calculate the real value of the project:

- Estimate the future cash flows for each year.
- Estimate an appropriate rate of interest (how much you think money will cost to borrow. A rate between 5 per cent and 15 per cent is more normal than the 20 percent used here.)
- Determine the discount factor. This is the inverse of the compound factor.
- *Reduce* the net cash flows to their present value by multiplying them by the discount factor.

For the above example, the compound and discount factors are shown in Table 12.7.

From the two examples mentioned earlier we can deduce that the *present value* of £1 000 earned in four years from now is £482 if the discount rate is 20 per cent.

Historically discount rates were obtained from tables (nowadays calculators or spreadsheets can be used). A rate table for a range of percentages is listed in Table 12.8 and we will use these to calculate the discounted cash flow (or net present value) of the projects in our example.

The Net Present Value method

If you convert the cash flows in Table 12.5 to the discount rates – using 10 per cent – and then sum them, you will get the *Net Present Value* (NPV), as shown in Table 12.9.

From this table – valuing future cash flows at today's value – the project assessment might be different. Project B seems the strongest contender

Table 12.7 Compounding and discounting factors compared

Year	Compound factor	Discount factor
Year 0	1	1
Year 1	$1.20 = 1.20$	$\frac{1}{(1.20)} = 0.8333$
Year 2	$(1.20)^2 = 1.440$	$\frac{1}{(1.20)^2} = 0.6944$
Year 3	$(1.20)^3 = 1.720$	$\frac{1}{(1.20)^3} = 0.5787$
Year 4	$(1.20)^4 = 2.074$	$\frac{1}{(1.20)^4} = 0.4823$

Table 12.8 Discounted cash flow factors

Period	Rate				
	5.00%	7.50%	10.00%	15.00%	20.00%
Year 0	1.0000	1.0000	1.0000	1.0000	1.0000
Year 1	0.9524	0.9302	0.9091	0.8696	0.8333
Year 2	0.9070	0.8653	0.8264	0.7561	0.6944
Year 3	0.8638	0.8050	0.7513	0.6575	0.5787
Year 4	0.8227	0.7488	0.6830	0.5718	0.4823
Year 5	0.7835	0.6966	0.6209	0.4972	0.4019
Year 6	0.7462	0.6480	0.5645	0.4323	0.3349
Year 7	0.7107	0.6028	0.5132	0.3759	0.2791
Year 8	0.6768	0.5607	0.4665	0.3269	0.2326
Year 9	0.6446	0.5216	0.4241	0.2843	0.1938
Year 10	0.6139	0.4852	0.3855	0.2472	0.1615

Table 12.9 Calculating net present value for three projects

Discount rate. 10%	Period	Discount factor	Project A		Project B		Project C	
			Cash flow	Present value	Cash flow	Present value	Cash flow	Present value
Initial cost	Year 0	1.000	−50 000	−50 000	−70 000	−70 000	−50 000	−50 000
Cash inflows/profits	Year 1	0.9091	10 000	9 091	10 000	9 091	10 000	9 091
	Year 2	0.8264	20 000	16 528	10 000	8 264	20 000	16 528
	Year 3	0.7513	20 000	15 026	10 000	7 513	10 000	7 513
	Year 4	0.6830	20 000	13 660	20 000	13 660	13 500	9 221
	Year 5	0.6209	10 000	6 209	30 000	18 627	3 500	2 173
	Year 6	0.5645	5 000	2 823	30 000	16 935	3 500	1 976
	Year 7	0.5132	2 800	1 436	30 000	15 396	3 500	1 796
Net profit			37 800		70 000		14 000	
Net present value				14 773		19 486		−1 702

Table 12.10 Three projects re-evaluated with a discount rate of 15%

Discount rate: 15%	Period	Discount factor	Project A		Project B		Project C	
			Cash flow	Present value	Cash flow	Present value	Cash flow	Present value
Initial cost	Year 0	1.000	−50 000	−50 000	−70 000	−70 000	−50 000	−50 000
Cash inflows/ profits	Year 1	0.8696	10 000	8 696	10 000	8 696	10 000	8 696
	Year 2	0.7561	20 000	15 122	10 000	7 561	20 000	15 122
	Year 3	0.6575	20 000	13 150	10 000	6 575	10 000	6 575
	Year 4	0.5718	20 000	11 436	20 000	11 436	13 500	7 719
	Year 5	0.4972	10 000	4 972	30 000	14 916	3 500	1 740
	Year 6	0.4323	5 000	2 162	30 000	12 969	3 500	1 513
	Year 7	0.3759	2 800	1 053	30 000	11 277	3 500	1 316
Net profit			37 800		70 000			
Net present value				6 591		3 430		−7 319

with the highest NPV at the end of the period, but it earns most of that in Year 7. Up until then, the NPV is negative (Years 1–6 add up to less than the initial investment). There is a greater element of risk in Project B.

If the project is re-assessed at a higher discount rate (15 per cent) then the weakness of Project B is further exposed and the NPV is lower than that of Project A and, of course, Project C is even less attractive (see Table 12.10).

The interest rate selected should be realistic – perhaps the cost of a bank overdraft or the income that can be earned from alternative investments. The current UK Treasury guideline to the MoD is 3.5 per cent.

Conclusion

People who are not trained in accounting or financial management often find the whole subject daunting. It is entirely possible that the list of numbers even in this short chapter have discouraged you from reading it. However, the purpose here was not to produce instant financial managers, but simply to introduce some of the terminology and concepts so that financial statements need not be quite so intimidating. Even a basic understanding of costs, budgets and methods for making financial decisions will help to yield information from reports, and will improve communication with finance professionals.

Questions to consider

1 Get hold of a copy of the MoD accounts (www.mod.uk/publications/ performance2003), look up the Consolidated Resource Account – Section 2 and familiarize yourself with some of the content. Turn to Page 130 which is a list of the operating costs. Try to categorize the costs between fixed/variable and direct/indirect. Most costs will cover a range of these. (There is no right answer.)

2 Consider your own car.

   a Try to breakdown the running costs over say a year.
   b Calculate the average cost per mile (average cost) and compare this with the cost of fuel per mile (marginal cost).
   c Which cost should you use when deciding to use public transport?

3 Try to calculate the total repayments on a house purchase and compare these with the NPV.

4 Use ROAMEF to justify buying an iPod.

5 Get hold of a copy of your unit's operating cost statement – try to analyse the costs by type.

Suggested reading

Atrill, P. (2004), *Management Accounting for Non-Specialists* (4th edition), London: FT Prentice Hall.

Robertson, J. and Mills, Roger W. (2000), *Accounting Principles for Non-Accounting Students*, London: Mars Business Associates Ltd.

13 Defence acquisition

Trevor Taylor

Introduction

Governments everywhere find the effective acquisition of defence equipment to be a challenging business. The capacity to buy the right things for a satisfactory price is elusive and even the United Kingdom, having put years of effort into improving its defence acquisition system, still suffers from continuing delays and cost overruns (Committee of Public Accounts 2005). However, richer larger countries, and in particular the United States, are better able to cope with acquisition problems, not least because they have a legacy of extant capability which they can maintain in service.

A fundamental source of difficulty in this area is that it involves so much looking into the future. Defence equipment, even when bought 'off the shelf', often involves a wait of a couple of years before delivery, and then remains in service for at least a decade and often more. Thus the defence acquisition community must constantly address such issues as what sort of adversaries will a country have, how will they behave and to what technology will they have access? There may also be domestic and international uncertainty about the roles that an armed force will be called on to perform. The Iraq experience has forced the United States to think much harder about protracted 'peace support' operations in a dangerous environment, rather than the brief high intensity conflicts on which it focussed before 2003.

Especially as far as the developing world is concerned, most academic attention has been devoted to size of the arms trade (IISS 2005; SIPRI 2005; and Grimmett 2005) and to why and how (developed) states decide to export arms. Attention on this topic grew from the late 1960s and during the cold war era (Frank 1969; Stanley and Pearton 1972; Thayer 1969). Although there are some studies (Murray and Viotti 1994; Singh 1998), the mechanisms by which governments decide to acquire defence equipment have attracted less analysis; not least because of the challenges of collecting information. Corruption, when it can be demonstrated, attracts the attention of analysts but, even then, most attention tends to be paid to the vendor companies and governments (Boulton 1978; Sampson 1977).

This chapter cannot provide detailed guidance on how to acquire defence capability, but it does dissect the primary tasks that are involved and explores the capabilities needed for the execution of these tasks.

Capability-based acquisition

A fundamental point is to stress that defence organizations should rest acquisition activities on what they want their armed forces to be able to do; that is, which capabilities they want them to have.

During the cold war, defence acquisition thought was dominated both by a desire to match and offset emerging Warsaw Pact systems and by a wish to replace ageing pieces in NATO with newer versions of similar pieces of kit. The first element can be summarized as a threat-based approach to acquisition and the second as replacement-based thinking. Both these lines of thought are recognized as inappropriate in the twenty-first century. The experience of the major western states is that it has become extremely difficult to identify future adversaries. At the beginning of 1990 neither rival or British governments expected to be undertaking a major campaign in Iraq and they would have been bemused to be told that they would soon also be off to the Balkans. Replacement thinking is also being discredited because it means that opportunities to solve problems presented by new technology could be missed, and because the costs of improving many established types of equipment, most obviously combat aircraft, have become so high.

An alternative is a capability-based approach which involves articulating the effects that armed forces need to achieve and the capabilities necessary for their attainment. While 'capability' is a very broad term, it can be given a greater precision by breaking it down into constituent elements. British Defence Doctrine (JDCC 2001)refers to seven areas of capabilities; Inform, Command, Operate, Systems, Project, Protect and Prepare. Figure 13.1 provides definitions of these elements. For a decade the leading Western states have been trying to direct more resources into the areas of Inform and Command (which are at the heart of information-based warfare) as well as to Project (to enable Western forces to reach threats away from their homeland).

Alternative approaches to breaking down capability can be found in NATO, with its Defence Capabilities Initiative of 1999 and the Prague Capabilities Commitment of 2002. The latter pointed to four areas that were recognized as needing particular attention: chemical, biological and nuclear defence; command, communications and information superiority, 'interoperability and key areas of combat effectiveness; and readiness, deployability, rapid deployment and sustainability of forces (Buckley 2002). In the United States the capabilities taxonomy is based on essential operational effects that the US warfighter must be able to deliver to be successful. The Joint Staff has now reorganized around new functional concepts.

'There are seven fundamental defence capabilities required to deliver fighting power. These are:

- A robust and responsive means of **Command** (the authority for the direction, co-ordination and control of military forces).

- A process to **Inform** the command (the acquisition, collation, processing, management and distribution of information).

- A means to **Prepare** forces for employment (all the activities needed to define, resource and deliver fighting power for operational employment, within readiness criteria laid down in policy).

- Measures and resources to **Project** and recover in a timely manner, a force that is appropriately packaged for the objective it is pursuing.

- The means to **Protect** and preserve fighting power, principally on operations (involves countering wider threats, natural, human and technological).

- The ability to **Sustain** the force (the maintenance of the necessary level of fighting power required to achieve objectives).

- All of which are necessary in order to discharge the prime function, namely to **Operate** by conducting military actions, primarily in combat (including movement, supply, attack, defence and manoeuvre).

These fundamental defence capabilities are inter related and supporting; none can be considered in isolation, and all are required in varying measure to meet the requirements of Government policy.'

Figure 13.1 Defence capabilities.
Source: JDCC 2001: 4-2–4-3.

The top of the landscape shows the joint functional concepts where materiel solutions play a major role: battlespace awareness, command and control, force application, protection and focused logistics (*Defense Industrial Capabilities Study: Protection*, December 2004: ii).

While these taxonomies vary somewhat in the way that how they break down the overall concept of capability, there is some considerable overlap, not least with regard to the importance of information, command and control, and protection. Emphasizing that, for successful acquisition, governments could well focus on desired capabilities, reflects a wider argument that purchasing is most likely to be successful when a buyer government that is clear about what it wants to be able to obtain from a purchase. The specification of requirements should be located within a framework of an agreed defence policy that analyses the environment of a state and the role of defence capability in promoting security.

> For many years Thailand had a largely autonomous military that both generated its own politico-strategic analysis and the equipment requirements needed. The results were at first ineffective – the excessive emphasis on a military solution to the insurgency issue, which involved the purchase of many light arms, arguably made things worse on the internal front. Then a miscalculation about the threat of conventional attack resulted in the import of many heavy weapons that proved to be of little relevance (Wattanayagorn in Singh: 219–20).

Traditionally governments looking at military equipment in these terms have sought to generate a clear military requirement statement against which offerings would be assessed. Until a decade or so ago such requirements were often written in continuous text but today purchasers appreciate the value of spelling out individual requirements in separate sentences and maintaining them, each with their own number, in an electronic document. An area of expertise known as Requirements Engineering has been borrowed from information systems specialists and adapted for defence. This involves the explicit articulation of user requirements (what the user needs to be able to do) and their link to system requirements (what the system needs to be able to do to meet the user requirement). Table 13.1 offers some illustrative user and system requirements relevant to a protected mobility need.

While this approach is intellectually demanding and requires an investment in training and education, its advantages include the possibility of operating clear criteria for the acceptance of equipment on delivery.

In specifying requirements, governments must of course be sensitive to what is already available on the market, technological possibilities and likely costs. There is little point in specifying requirements that are either unfeasible or unaffordable. Most governments buy defence equipment that is already in production, so they need to relate the definition of their wants to what the market has on offer. It is, nonetheless, an invaluable discipline to have the user specify what an armed force needs to be able to do, so that offerings can be assessed for their relevance.

Table 13.1 Illustrative user and system requirements

User ability	System requirement
The User shall be able to carry a 10 tonne load on road and a 7 tonne load off road	The system shall be fitted with a suspension system with a mean maximum pressure (MMP) of z kN/m^2
The User shall be able to recover the vehicle with in service and planned specialist recovery equipment without preparation of the casualty vehicle	The system shall be fitted with interface devices allowing connection to towing cables, towing bars, lifting devices and tractors
The User shall be able to tow the vehicle without preparation with another vehicle of the same type	The system shall be fitted with towing cable and towing arm locating points and shall be equipped with towing cables stowed externally
The User shall be protected within the vehicle from attack by enemy small arms fire	The system shall be fitted with armour protection of x mm throughout a full 360 degree arc around the crew compartment
The User shall be protected within the vehicle against attack from an anti-personnel mine	The system shall be fitted with blast and shock-absorbing seating to withstand the effects of an anti-personnel mine with y kg of explosive
The User shall be able to increase the level of protection against attack from anti-personnel mines for specific operations	The system shall be equipped with locating devices to permit additional armour to be fitted across the underside of the full hull width

All this suggests that governments striving to be effective defence purchasers need to devote human resources to both the formal consideration of user needs and the monitoring of relevant areas of the market and technology (comparatively few governments will be interested in advances in satellite technology). The governmental defence sector needs access to at least a small number of relevant scientists and technologists.

The generation of military requirements requires a focussed workforce which concentrates on that task. That workforce needs to be in regular contact with a wide range of stakeholders who will be affected by requirement choices and who will have an impact on the eventual utility of anything that is bought. These stakeholders include the eventual users of equipment in front line units, those who will be responsible for maintaining the equipment, those who generate operational doctrine, and those will need to recruit and train the individuals who will operate and look after any equipment. The generation of requirements that will result in useful and value-for-money equipment involves a wide range of consultation. It might then be perhaps unrealistic to think that the broad outline of requirements can be kept deeply concealed. Equipment bought in secret comes as a surprise to most of the purchasing armed forces as well as the potential adversary.

There was a dramatic demonstration of the dangers of this in 1956, when Russia delivered a mass of equipment to Egypt out of the blue after an arms co-operation deal in the autumn of 1955. Israel was alarmed by the unprecedented deliveries of jet combat aircraft and tanks, among other items, and launched an invasion of Egypt (in collusion with the United Kingdom and France) long before Egypt had developed any capacity to use its new equipment.

There is a further point linking the specification of requirements to the wider governmental defence sector. As noted, those generating requirements are often a specialized group, or up to four specialized groups (army, air force, navy and marines) in countries such as the United States and India where requirements generation occurs mainly within individual branches of the armed forces. It thus makes sense for a further group to be involved, most obviously representing the defence ministry as a whole, in the approval of proposed individual projects. In the United Kingdom this function is undertaken by the Investment Approvals Board where there are representatives of the armed forces as a whole, the logistics function, the purchasing function, the science and technology perspective, and the policy and finance communities. In the United States the major choices of the individual services must be endorsed by the Joint Requirements Oversight Council. For states such as France, Germany, the United Kingdom and the United States, where many acquisition choices involve an extended period of development, and so risk, there are at least two points at which projects are approved by representatives of the MoD or at least the armed forces as a whole. Needless to say, a process in which projects are initiated by one group and approved by another makes corrupt decision making more difficult. Those approving projects cannot initiate them: in some governments in the developing world, it is not unusual for the highest possible approving body, that is, ministers and even heads of government, seek to introduce projects without service staff work having been undertaken.

Planning and programming

A governmental system for identifying requirements needs to be integrated with the organizational arrangements for prioritizing those requirements into those that can be pursued immediately, those that can satisfied through future spending plans, and those that should be rejected as insufficiently valuable for the foreseeable future. In short, planned procurement needs to be accommodated within an equipment plan that estimates the annual expenditure on each item and indicates that all items in a specific year can be afforded within the expected financial arrangements.

In Britain financial planning for defence acquisition covers a ten-year period whereas France looks out to only five years. Around the world, five years is probably the most common planning period. Plans can be based on the expectation of lower, constant or increased funding, depending on the orientation of the government of the day and its security environment. Table 13.2 offers a simplified equipment plan for a hypothetical state which wishes to work on the basis that equipment funding will be constant. It has selected first to enhance its direct fire capabilities and then to improve its communications. Better transport will start to become available in the third year. The expensive single item to support Exclusive Economic Zone surveillance illustrates how plans have to be drawn up so that fewer of the less expensive items of kit are needed in years where a major mass of spending is need for a single item.

Of course a government may moderate the immediate expenditure demands of any single major item by taking out a loan (or indeed a lease) in order to spread payments. In Britain the Royal Air Force could not afford to buy C.17 transport aircraft and so arranged to lease four of them. Loans, leases and indeed Private Finance Initiatives are ways of avoiding the need to make single large capital commitments, and many states use loans to finance arms purchases. One disadvantage of this route is that it ties up significant elements of the defence budget sometimes for many years and so reduces the flexibility open to future governments.

Plans, of course, are often not implemented as laid out, and this is particularly true in the equipment area where things are often not ready when they are formally due and require more resources than was initially expected. A Government thus needs the capability to modify its equipment plan in the light of changing circumstances, with the role of the original plan being to provide a baseline from which a new course of action can be derived.

Risk management provides important tools for the effective management of resources. Especially in developing states such as Uganda, the defence ministry might not, during the financial year, receive all the money that was

Table 13.2 A simplified equipment plan

Item	Expenditure in £ million				
	Year 1	Year 2	Year 3	Year 4	Year 5
Individual direct fire capability	20	20	10		
Secure voice communications		10	10	10	
People and goods road transport			10	20	
Indirect fire	10				
EEZ surveillance					30
Total	30	30	30	30	30

specified in the budget at the beginning of the year. Circumstances, such as lower than expected tax revenues or unforeseen needs affecting other ministries, can result in an in-year reduction in defence spending. A risk-based approach considers this possibility and leads to contingency plans for adjustment in the equipment spend in the light of such an in-year cut.

Looking at a different aspect of risk, if a country's experience is that industry tends to deliver equipment a little later than originally contracted, it could conclude that it can safely order more equipment, in a period, than it could pay for if all that equipment was delivered on time. If £100 is available to pay out, and there is evidence that only 90 per cent of goods will be delivered on time, a country may feel it can order £110 worth of goods. Of course, the goods delivered late will probably be a commitment in the budget for the following year.

Thus designing and operating an equipment plan is not a straightforward activity, and it requires the careful study and indeed exploitation of risk. It is an area of defence where financial experts, who are often civilians, and those well-versed in defence capability needs (the latter usually include many military personnel) must all work in a co-operative and integrated manner.

Procurement

Moving through the overall concept of acquisition, this chapter has established that defence ministries should specify their requirements, establish priorities, and work out what can be paid for in the agreed period. The next step is to move towards selecting the particular equipment that will best enable the needed capability. In short equipment has to be procured.

If a country is seeking to buy something that is already in production, it will probably conclude that competitive tendering is the best way to proceed. The process of competitive tendering requires the effective purchaser to articulate precisely what is needed, that is, the capabilities and features that are required of the defence system. Those using a requirements engineering approach will base an Invitation to Tender (ITT)on a system requirement document whereas others will generate a statement, as precisely as they can, about what is needed.

However, prior to the issue of an ITT it is normally sensible to issue a broader statement about a project and to invite Expressions of Interest (EoI) from qualified organizations. This will provide a chance for interested parties to explain their particular capabilities and track record while not requiring them to make specific commitments. The information generated through EoIs allows the purchaser to select only the more promising prospective bidders for the ITT stage. This is significant because it costs money and time to prepare and to assess bids, and the procurer should not wish to waste resource by analysing bids that had very poor prospects from the beginning. Even prior to the EoI stage the procurer of defence equipment should think through whom should be regarded as an acceptable bidder from a political point of view. Certainly this must happen before the ITT stage. Simply releasing a defence requirement to an organization gives the recipient sensitive information about a government's aspirations and intentions, and it should not be done lightly.

With the ITT issued to selected parties, the procuring organization may usefully and equitably hold an Industry Day where prospective suppliers are invited as a group, to be briefed on the programme and have their questions answered. Such activities allow the competing contractors to better understand the purchaser's needs, and enhance the chance that they can develop suitable bids. In a similar vein, the ITT should include a reasonable outline of the purchaser's assessment scheme that will be used to evaluate the bids. This should make it easier for the bidders to understand the priorities and values of the purchaser, and so help them to make good bids. It is a further check on corrupt practices since the criteria for success are set before any bids are prepared.

Bidders need a reasonable period of time to prepare their bids, and may often have specific questions which they will need purchaser to answer. To ensure fair treatment, the questions asked by each bidder, as well as the replies, should be circulated to all the bidders. A specific deadline and procedure for bid submission should be set. Completed bids, properly received must then be assessed, and a winner selected.

For defence systems of any complexity, bid documentation is likely to be extensive. It needs to:

- explain the nature of the contractor's proposed solution to the requirements,
- explain the technology offered in the solution so that the buyer can assess its effectiveness and reliability,
- make proposals for the sustainability of the system,
- and to spell out costs, delivery and payments arrangements and so on.

The purchaser should ensure that an adequate number of competent people are available for bid assessment. Ideally the purchaser will break bids down into their constituent elements so that they can be assessed for their technology, performance in different military aspects, cost structures, in-service support arrangements and so on. The assessment scheme devized as part of the ITT should detail the relative weightings of each of the elements. The identifiable risks that can be associated with each bid also need to be taken into account. An assessment must be made of whether the bid as a whole is satisfactorily compliant with the demands of the ITT. If not, it should be rejected unless the ITT itself had specified that bids offering partial solutions could also be assessed for the value for money that they offered. Bid assessment is arguably an even more complex task than bid generation: it needs people and time, and thus money. It is clearly a waste of multiple resources if bids are prepared and examined when they could never have the political qualifications needed for success.

For simpler procurements involving straightforward goods (such as fuel or basic foodstuffs) where there are few variables to be taken into account, the procurement process may be more straightforward. Only two basic questions need to be addressed – which bids are compliant with the demands of the ITT and then which is the cheapest of them. This form of procurement gives the purchasing authority comparatively little discretion and, therefore, is useful as an anti-corruption tool. It is often favoured by inter-governmental organizations as well as national governments for this reason. However, it can mean that important chances to secure special quality, and so value for money, may be missed, and the risk present in some bids may be overlooked.

Once a preferred bidder has been selected, the procurement process can move to the finalization of a contract that will spell out the responsibilities of both parties and the consequences of either failing to meet their side of the bargain. Because contracts involve much more than a commitment to meet a requirement, an extended period of discussion may be needed before a contract can be signed. Particularly when long-life systems involving extended maintenance, spares supply and technical advice are being bought, the contract should cover the contractor's in-service support commitments as well as the initial delivery of the good. To help speed progress in some areas, a country may develop a series of standard terms and conditions for contracts with which companies can familiarize themselves before and while they submit their bids. In addition, an ITT can include a draft contract that the successful company will be expected to sign.

Contracts are legal documents and, if they are to have real impact, they need to be backed by effective legal systems. One significant choice, when a company from one state signing a contract with the government of another state, involves deciding which country's national legal system will under-pin the contract. Companies are well-practised in protecting their interests in this field and it is strongly desirable that purchasing governments engage very capable legal advice before committing themselves.

Because governments buying defence equipment from foreign firms may feel unsure of themselves in this area, they sometimes prefer to purchase equipment not from a company but from the government of the country where the company is based. Government-to-government sales are common in the defence world and the United States in particular runs a very extensive Foreign Military Sales (FMS) programme. The United Kingdom, too, will enter into government-to-government defence supply arrangements. However, governments also charge for purchasing services that they provide and any risks that they undertake, and many developing countries have found FMS deals, in particular, to be an expensive option.

If a country wishes to gain economic benefits from a procurement by securing offset commitments from a vendor, and particularly if it seeks to produce under licence a piece of military equipment for itself, sound decisions are likely to be even more complex, as governments must take account of the perceived military benefits of the equipment itself, as well as economic aspects (such as the provision of employment, the learning of new skills), plus security aspects associated with greater self-sufficiency in the defence equipment sphere. A decision to develop equipment nationally rather than to buy it from overseas has even more risks and uncertainties. India, China and South Korea are among the countries that for many years have shaped arms procurement choices to build up national industrial capability (Brzoska 1999; Jeshuran 1989; Siddia-Agha1999; Singh 1998). It is a cause of concern in the West that developing states may find it easier to develop ballistic missiles (such as the Indian Agni and Prithvi projects) than advanced combat aircraft, where India and China have both struggled to narrow the gap with the West.

A final consideration is that, because of the high costs of funding development and the increasing concentration of the defence industry, outside the United States, it is rare for a competitive procurement to be possible using only national firms. Thus a national development project normally means the early selection of the national contractor to do the job.

Acceptance

Purchasing countries should consider (and contracts should make provision for) formal acceptance arrangements for goods or services. The need to assure the quality of whatever is supplied means a range of possible activities need to be considered, going from oversight of manufacturing processes, inspection on delivery, the securing of warranties and random sampling (countries buying ammunition often test fire a random sample of rounds as a means of checking quality). Certainly countries should try to avoid paying for goods entirely in advance so that they have some leverage over a contractor in the event of a non-satisfactory delivery.

Sound acceptance arrangements are a further barrier against corruption, especially if those that conduct the acceptance arrangements are not those who placed the order. However, this is another field where a wish or a need to preserve secrecy can make things more difficult. Going back to the first Arab-Israeli War in 1948–49, Egyptian undercover arms buyers operating in Europe bought low quality equipment for personal financial gain. This practice was one factor that led Nasser and his colleagues to become so dissatisfied with the government that they mounted a military coup.

Support and the operation of equipment in-service

So far, this chapter has traced the main processes involved in the specification of requirements to the delivery of a product or service. In the case of equipment, this simply forms one albeit an important element in wider military capability. Before capability will be achieved, equipment needs to be linked to a range of other factors that in the UK have been designated as 'Lines of

Development'. The seven other Lines of Development accepted in the United Kingdom are:

People

Individuals with the right attitudes and intellectual and physical capabilities must be available to operate and maintain any equipment that is acquired. Normally such people will be employed within the armed forces of the purchasing state, but increasingly developed states are relying on contractor-employed staff for many storage, maintenance and repair tasks. In parts of the Arabian Gulf, expatriate labour is used for the support of much advanced defence equipment. Countries need not, therefore, rely on their own people, but they must make provision for suitable people to be available.

Organization

Equipment must be located within organizational structures and new types of equipment usually need new organizational structures which include career progression arrangements for those within them. The advent of aircraft led the UK to establish the Royal Air Force as a separate arm of the services in 1918, whereas the United States waited until after the end of the Second World War to take a parallel step. Governments buying equipment must consider closely the implications for organization and personnel structures.

Infrastructure

Some equipment requires a significant amount of infrastructure that may in itself involve a substantial investment. Aircraft need runways and hangars, ships need dockyards, vehicles need garages and so on. Because infrastructure can take time to prepare and can require significant expenditure, it clearly needs to be considered at an early stage in a project's life.

Support

Military equipment needs to be supported once in service, and repair and maintenance is often a major source of expense. There are many cases in post-1945 history of countries buying equipment that they could not support effectively, either because they lacked the money or the skills, or both. Singh has pointed to the poor level of serviceability of Indian equipment, during the 1990s, in part because of the limited technical education provided (Singh 1998: 80). However, it would be unfair to highlight India as exceptional. In 2002 the Nigerian Government (Kwankwanso and Oritsejafor 2002) posted an account of the terrible state of repair of the equipment that the new government had taken over in 1999 (and listed the improvements it had sought to make).

For platforms such as tanks, combat aircraft, helicopters, or ships, expenditure on fuel, lubricants, repair and maintenance for many systems will amount to five times or more the original purchase cost. Thus the support dimension needs to be addressed from the earliest stage in a project's life as a government should always work out whether it will have the funds available to operate a system once the money has been made available to buy it in the first place. Government's also need to consider the whole life cost aspect in addition to the initial acquisition cost when they are evaluating bids from competing companies (see earlier). Because many countries have separate budget headings, in the charge of different people, for the purchase of new equipment and its support, special managerial care needs to be taken to ensure that the in-service phase is given appropriate weight in tender evaluation activities. Australia, however, is among those that have established a single body, the Defence Materiel Organisation, which is responsible for both buying and looking after new equipment. It has an obvious interest in looking for equipment that will be comparatively cheap and easy to operate.

Wholelife costs or throughlife costs, which essentially have the same meaning, are clearly of financial and wider significance (Ministry of Defence 2004a; National Audit Office 2003). Their calculation is invariably a matter of judgement and calculation as to just what is included. There is an obvious need to include the employment costs for operators, trainers, and maintainers, and the costs of consumables (fuel and oil), spare parts and so on. There are also the cost of any services provided by external contractors and whole life costs must also include infrastructure costs. Some of these costs will be fixed over a year while others will vary according to the amount of use.

More problematic are decisions about whether to spread costs over defence-wide activities across operational units. Should an air defence unit be expected to bear the costs associated with the recruitment and basic training of its personnel or the operation of the services pay and allowances organization or the provision of a defence-wide information system? The response to questions such as these is very much a matter of judgement and may depend on why the question is being asked. Consideration of the affordability of a new equipment type should try to capture as many as possible of the extra costs that will be incurred. On the other hand, setting the budget for an operational unit can concentrate on calculating the money it will need to generate the right amount of capability.

The costs that will be incurred each year to operate a piece of equipment are often more relevant than though-life costs. In the United Kingdom this figure is often referred to as the cost-of ownership. Similar considerations apply as to the calculation of whole-life costs but an important consideration is how the initial capital cost of equipment is treated. In purely cash-based accounts the cost of ownership will include all the initial purchase costs in the year(s) that money was handed over, while an accounting system more similar to that found in the commercial world will spread the capital cost of a project over all the years of a its expected life. The cost of ownership is not necessarily uniform over a project's period in service, since a major overhaul or mid-life update may have to be factored in after five years or so.

Training

For equipment to be usable, people have to be trained as individuals, and often as teams, so that they can operate it both in a peace time and an operational context. Individual and collective training are normally involved, which is a further source of expense and sometimes difficulty. Singapore, for instance, has very little land or airspace available in which it can conduct training and frequently has to send its forces overseas to friendly countries for this purpose. Combat training can be particularly demanding: the authorities of one important state in Africa have recognized privately that they have aircraft in their inventory that they can fly and maintain, but cannot fight with effectively.

Because live training with vehicles, ships, aircraft, missiles or ammunition is usually very expensive, governments increasingly look to (cheap to use) simulators to carry more of the burden. Simulators themselves are sophisticated pieces of equipment in their own right and so require the same range of careful consideration as a frontline piece of equipment.

Doctrine

Items of military equipment are rarely used in isolation but, even when they are, they need doctrine to guide operators as to when and how they should be used. A basic form of doctrine needs to be available before equipment is delivered, not least so that it can be linked to training programmes. Of course doctrine can and is refined while equipment is in service. The United Kingdom has been working for some years on its doctrine for air manoeuvre warfare centred on the Apache helicopter fleet and this must of course address how the Apaches link to other elements in UK forces.

Information

British thought now stresses information as a further line of development because equipment needs to be linked into the information and command systems of the armed forces. As comparative advantage in military operations is expected increasingly to rest on information attributes, this factor can be expected to rise in importance. However, it is not necessarily an easy factor to deal with, since the integration of sensors, data processors, communications and command systems is not straightforward. There is always a degree of risk, and thus cost, in such a simple thing as integrating a national radio system into a vehicle or an aircraft.

Disposal

Once the utility of a piece of equipment is coming to an end, its disposal becomes a pertinent issue. Obviously some equipment may have a re-sale value, either as scrap or as a system that still has use in a different environment. Any sale of military equipment should be to a responsible third party, normally but not always a government, and the revenues from any such sale should have been taken into account in the calculation of whole life costs.

Other equipment, especially when it contains harmful elements such as radio-active materials or toxic chemicals, will have extensive disposal costs. The UK financial accounts include a provision of almost £8 billion for nuclear de-commissioning (Ministry of Defence 2004b: 145), a sum which future governments will have to provide at some stage. In simple terms a government should not plan to take ownership of something unless it has a clear idea for its disposal in an acceptable and responsible manner.

The identification of lines of development is a fairly straightforward matter, but managing the processes by which they are all prepared and delivered in a timely manner can be very challenging. This can be because some particular items can be difficult in themselves. For instance, the United States has opted to solve some of the personnel and organization issues associated with the deployment on operations of the Stryker Brigade by employing and deploying 120 civilian personnel. There are also timing issues to get right, and some lines of development take longer to put in place than others. The United Kingdom did not succeed in training Apache pilots until a couple of years after the aircraft were produced and delivered (NAO 2003). Lastly there are budgetary and management considerations. The generation of lines of development takes money and attention, and budget holders in different parts of the defence machine may not have coherent priorities. The coherent assembly of lines of development is a significant and challenging task (Taylor 2003). It must be stressed that, although Lines of Development need to be provided only once equipment is at or near delivery, their consideration or preparation must take place earlier, and often from the beginning of consideration of the requirement.

Conclusion

This chapter has addressed the most important tasks associated with defence acquisition, and it is clear that, once Lines of Development are taken into account, the management of acquisition mushrooms into the management of almost all the defence budget.

There are four points to underline by way of conclusion.

The first is that defence acquisition should always be closely linked to defence capability, to what it will help armed forces to do. Unless thinking is clear about the particular capabilities that a piece of equipment will support, about the relevance of those capabilities to a country's security context, and about the ability of the defence machine to provide all the lines of development needed for true capability, acquisition efforts are unlikely to be seen as successful.

The second point is simply to reiterate that the whole process of acquisition should be taken into account from the beginning of the cycle. Many governments, even in developed states, find this easier to say than to execute in practice.

Third, defence acquisition involves many specialists with different agendas and time scales in mind. Successful acquisition requires them to bring their focussed expertise to bear but it also requires them to work always aware of how their efforts fit into the wider defence acquisition scene. When people work in segmented units, rather than seeing themselves as part of a larger team, acquisition is likely to be slow, unbalanced and subject to extensive criticism.

Finally, while defence acquisition is frequently and sadly associated with corrupt practices, it is apparent that the challenges of effective acquisition merit the allocation of some of the best minds in defence to the many tasks in this area. Defence acquisition calls for people with integrity, diligence, commitment and intelligence as well as knowledge of specialist areas such as technology, contracting, logistics and requirements management.

This chapter should end with a reminder with how it began – with an emphasis on the many difficulties of defence acquisition.

Questions to consider

1   What time scales into the future need to be considered by those involved with defence acquisition?
2   As part of a competitive procurement activity, why should the assessment scheme be prepared before the competition is launched and released to bidders?
3   Equipment is one element in defence capability. What are the other factors that need to be in place for defence capability to be derived from equipment?
4   Why is it important to try to calculate whole life costs at an early stage in the acquisition process?

Suggested reading

Ministry of Defence (2004a), *The Smart Acquisition Handbook* (4th edition), www.ams.mod.uk (where much other material is available, including on requirements engineering), accessed on 24 April 2006.
Singh, Ravinder Pal (ed.) (1998), *Arms Procurement Decision-Making Vol. I: China, India, Israel, Japan, South Korea & Thailand*, Oxford, SIPRI/Oxford University Press.

Stockholm International Peace Research Institute (2000), *Arms Procurement Decision-Making Vol. II: Chile, Greece, Malaysia, Poland, South Africa and Taiwan*, Oxford, SIPRI/Oxford University Press.

English language web-sites

RAND Corporation, www.rand.org/, accessed on 12 November 2005.
The Australian government, www.defence.gov.au/dmo/index.cfm (which includes the Kinnaird *Procurement Review* of 2003), accessed on 12 November 2005.
US Government Accountability Office, www.gao.gov, accessed on 12 November 2005.
The Center for Public Integrity, www.publicintegrity.com/default.aspx, accessed on 12 November 2005.
US Department of Defense, www.acq.osd.mil/, accessed on 12 November 2005.

Bibliography

Boulton, D. (1978), *The Lockheed Papers*, London, Jonathan Cape.
Brzoska, P. (1999), 'Economic factors shaping production in less industrialised countries', *Defense and Peace Economics*, 10 (2): 139–70.
Buckley, E. (2002), *Interview with the NATO Assistant Secretary General for Defence Planning and Operations*, 6 December 2002, www.nato.int/docu/speech/2002/s021206a.htm (accessed 25 November 2005).
Grimmett, R. (2005), *Conventional Arms Transfers to Developing Nations, 1997–2004*, Washington DC, Congressional Research Service, www.fas.org/sgp/crs/natsec/RL33051.pdf (accessed 30 October 2005).
International Institute for Strategic Studies (IISS) (2005), *The Military Balance 2004–5*, Oxford, Oxford University Press.
JDCC (2001), *British Defence Doctrine* (2nd edition), Joint Warfare Publication 0–01; Shrivenham; Joint Doctrine and Concepts Centre.
Jeshuran, Chandran (1989), *Arms and Defence in Southeast Asia*, Singapore, Institute of Southeast Asian Studies.
Kwankwanso, R. and Oritsejafor, R. (2005), 'Achievements in the Ministry of Defence', *Federal Ministry of Defence*, www.nopa.net/Defence/messages/4.shtml (posted 17 May 2005; accessed 20 November 2005).
Lewis, A. Frank (1969), *The Arms Trade in International Relations*, New York, Praeger.
Ministry of Defence (2004a), The Smart Acquisition Handbook (4th edition), www.ams.mod.uk
—— (2004b), *Annual Report and Accounts 2003–4*, London, Stationery Office.
Murray, D. J. and Viotti, P. R (1994), *The Defense Policies of Nations: A Comparative Study* (3rd edition), Baltimore, MD, Johns Hopkins University Press.
National Audit Office (2003), *Ministry of Defence: Through Life Management*, London, Stationery Office.
Sampson, Anthony (1977), *The Arms Bazaar: the Companies, the Dealers, the Bribes: from Vickers to Lockheed*, London, Hodder & Stoughton.

Siddia-Agha, Ayesha (1999), 'Pakistan's defense industry: an effort towards self-reliance', *Defence and Peace Economics*, 10 (4): 335–446.

Singh, Ravinder Pal (ed.) (1998), *Arms Procurement Decision-Making Volume 1: China, India, Israel, Japan, South Korea and Thailand*, Oxford, SIPRI/Oxford University Press.

Stanley, J. and Pearton, M. (1972), *The International Trade in Arms*, London, IISS/Chatto and Windus.

Stockholm International Peace Research Institute (2000), *Arms Procurement Decision-Making Vol. II: Chile, Greece, Malaysia, Poland, South Africa and Taiwan*, Oxford, SIPRI/Oxford University Press.

Stockholm International Peace Research Institute (2005), *SIPRI Yearbook 2005*, SIPRI/Oxford University Press, www.sipri.org/contents/armstrad/, accessed on 24 April 2006.

Taylor, T. and Neal, D. (2004), 'The delineation of defence projects in the UK Ministry of Defence', *Defense and Security Analysis*, 20 (2) (June): 155–77.

Thayer, George (1969), *The War Business: The International Trade in Armaments*, London, Paladin.

US Department of Defense (December 2004), *Defense Industrial Base Capabilities Study: Protection*, www.acq.osd.mil/ip, accessed on 20 November 2005.

14 Performance management and the Balanced Scorecard

Sylvie Jackson

Introduction

Over the past decade, the defence sector has begun to implement numerous performance management and measurement techniques that have migrated from the commercial sector where they have been used for some considerable success. These techniques are now *de rigeur* in the establishment of best practice organizational performance, by military and defence industry organizations alike.

When we discuss performance management here, we are talking about measuring the performance of organizations. Human Resource Management also uses the term, performance management, but there it refers to individuals' performance and the appraisal and review of personal objectives.

History of performance management

Measurement-based or fact-based management is not a new idea. A form of it was developed just after the Second World War, when a group of young ex-USAAF officers, who became known as the 'whizz kids', became powerful managers at Ford Motor Company through innovative use of company data. Robert MacNamara, one of the 'whizz kids' went on to become US Secretary of Defense and introduced the same management methods in the Pentagon during the Vietnam War. This approach to management, with its orientation to the industrial age is now largely in the past and strikes us as cold and impersonal – the mind-set of cartoon Dilbert's pointy-haired boss.

Performance based management today uses the principles from Total Quality Management that recognize the importance of employees with their knowledge of the organization and ideas for improving quality. They also recognize that measurements are simply essential to provide a rational basis for decisions.

Jac Fitz-Enz writing in Benchmarking Staff Performance in 1996, suggests that it is possible to measure any work process or practice, indeed it is imperative. He believes that measurement applies to individual professional practices as well as routine process work because without numbers it is not possible for managers to know what they are doing and therefore, how can they manage? Without measurement, managers are merely caretakers and administrators of the processes.

Public organizations have always been required to exemplify model practice as employers and in employment procedures. However, restructuring of the state sector has prompted changed employment and management practice. The ethos of public service was founded on accountability, impartiality and commitment to community values, now, it could be argued, it is about affordability, flexibility and organizational efficiency. Today, governments want proof that money has been well spent.

Jack Welch former Chief Executive of General Electric has been cited as saying the following about measurement in organizations:

> We always said that if you had three measurements to live by, they'd be employee satisfaction, customer satisfaction and cash flow. If you've got cash in the till at the end, the rest is all going to work. If you've got high customer satisfaction you are going to get market share. If you've got high employee satisfaction, you're going to get productivity. And if you've got cash you know it's all working.
>
> (Neely 1998: 10)

Four CPs of measurement

Managers will give a range of different reasons why organizations should measure their performance. Neely (1998: 71–89) in his book on Business Performance identifies what he calls the 4 CPs of measurement and their roles. The first of these is to *check position*. The role of measurement here is to understand where you are as an organization and where you are going. Measurement allows the organization to check whether its plans are working and delivering the desired results and also to track performance over time to ensure improvement programmes are working. Measurement systems are sometimes described as dashboards or control panels which give the analogy of the organization travelling on a journey to its goals or future desired state. Measurement can also allow us to check our position against other similar organizations, which allows us to see whether we are aiming for and achieving superior performance.

The second role of measurement is to *communicate position* both within the organization and externally to stakeholders and regulators. Internal communication is often used to recognize good work and thank employees and teams and/or to exhort them to achieve even higher levels of performance. External communication may be a legal requirement, in the form of annual financial accounts or reporting operational performance to regulators, or it may even be used as a way of marketing the organization to increase customer awareness or loyalty. Each of an organization's stakeholders is likely to have different interests in organizational performance, for example regulators have an interest in compliance with legislation, shareholders want to know about current and future financial performance, employees are interested in performance against the organization vision and values. Different communication methods and media are used for these different messages and audiences.

The third role of measurement is *confirm priorities*. This role follows on from checking the position of the organization, in relation to its journey to its goals and future desired state, and communicating that position to interested stakeholders, because it helps the organization to decide what it should do next and in what order. If progress is deviating from the plan, then corrective action can be taken, such as tighter cost control or identifying where to focus investment or supervision.

The fourth and final role of measurement is to *compel progress*. Simply measuring something will not improve performance, however it does communicate priorities because it sends a message to employees, that this is something that the organization cares enough about to invest time and cost in identifying its performance. Progress towards a target or goal is made explicit by measurement, so it is a very good way of establishing whether required actions have been taken to ensure improvement in performance. Some organizations use bonus schemes to reward employees on the basis of their performance, for example, the Civil Service employees in the UK MoD (but not the armed forces).

These measurement roles can help the organization to ensure compliance in reaching minimum levels of performance, act as a health check for long-term viability and allow for challenge of the appropriateness of an organization's strategy.

Measuring performance is not always straightforward. Fredland (2004: 211) cites the difficulties of measuring military outsourcing where he describes the 1997 Sandline contract with Papua New Guinea. Whilst Sandline were contracted to render the Bougainville Revolutionary Army militarily ineffective and repossess the Panguna mine, there was no clear explanation of what the first action means, leaving successful completion of the primary objective open to interpretation. In addition the contract included the following statement: 'the achievement of the primary objective cannot be deemed to be a performance measure for the sake of this agreement if it can be demonstrated that for valid reasons it cannot be achieved within the timescale and with the level of contracted resources provided.' This indicates that payment was based on the level of effort expended by Sandline and not on the result.

Measurement records

If we are to use measurement in our organizations, we need to keep records which document and explain the measurements. First, we need to detail the actual measure and the reason, or purpose, for taking the measurement. We will need to give specific advice about the formula for calculating the measure, the frequency of measurement (this may include specific timing or dates) and the source of the data. If there is a target for the measure, this may need to be included in the reporting of the measure, along with progress towards the target and reasons for any performance below the target. Finally, roles and responsibilities are required so that it is clear who collects the data and does the measuring, who acts on the data, and information about what happens to the measurement.

Measurement principles

There are a number of key principles about measurement which should be taken into consideration. Measurement provides information, but it needs to be acted upon. It is only useful if it enables judgments to be made which allow for effective change. Measurement is the key driver of improvement activity and this will entail the measurement being fed back to those with the authority to make changes and those undertaking the activity being measured.

As collecting data is expensive in time and effort, thought must be given about how it adds value and what will be done with the information. Use of data affects behaviour and must be appropriate. A warning comes from the British National Health Service. On 19 December 2001, the press reported that nine NHS Trusts had manipulated the figures for their waiting lists (a key measure). One NHS Trust admitted it had contacted patients to find out when they would be away on holiday. The patient's operation was then booked for this period and the patient's name was removed from the waiting list, even though they would refuse the date offered. A year later, 22 December 2002, there were further press reports (*The Sunday Times*) about measurement and the NHS. The revelation was that scores of dangerously ill patients had been forced to wait up to nine hours in ambulances outside casualty (Accident and Emergency) departments. In a practice called ambulance warehousing, these patients who were left in car parks did not count on waiting time statistics. The patients only became official once they were inside the hospital building, when they needed to be treated within four hours. Hospital chiefs privately admitted that there was a link between pressure from the UK Government Health Secretary to cut hospital waiting times and a surge in ambulance delays.

All too often, the use of league tables and the big stick (punishment) drive this type of behaviour because measurement is not used to encourage better performance. As defence managers are increasingly being urged to do more with fewer resources, we need to learn from mistakes in other organizations if we are to truly manage performance towards our goals, rather than simply collect statistics or, worse, encourage the wrong sort of behaviour.

> In the defence environment, Polyakov (2003: 8–10) writing about managing the challenge of illegal arms transfers draws attention to the importance of transparency of information about sales of arms between countries. He identifies Belgium, Sweden and Italy as countries who have published annual reports of arms exports for years, whilst some European Union countries have only recently implemented such a practice (e.g. France, Germany, The Netherlands, Spain, Great Britain and Denmark). He suggests that a high level of transparency allows for specific issues to be discussed in parliaments and therefore acts as an important instrument of control and analysis of government policy. The absence of such transparency in arms export decisions leads to accusations that countries (such as Ukraine) are violating international rules for arms trade and there is nothing to prove otherwise.

The Balanced Scorecard

The Balanced Scorecard is the most well-known and used performance measurement and management tool and is recognized as best practice for organizations. The UK MoD began using the Balanced Scorecard in 1999 in response to requirements from the Treasury Department to demonstrate that it was getting 'value for money' from the budget provided by the government.

History

In 1990, the Nolan Norton Institute, the research department of KPMG Management Consultants sponsored a one year multi-company study, called 'Measuring Performance in the Organization of the Future'. David Norton served as the study leader and Robert Kaplan, of Harvard Business School, acted as an academic consultant. (Kaplan also developed Activity Based Costing, which has a link to Resource Account Budgeting, in the UK MoD.) Representatives from a dozen companies – manufacturing and service, heavy industry and high-tech – met bi-monthly to develop a new performance measurement model. The companies represented included Apple Computer, CIGNA Insurance Services, Du Pont, General Electric, Hewlett Packard and Shell, Canada. The study was motivated by a belief that existing performance measurement approaches, which primarily relied on financial accounting measures, were becoming obsolete. This would mean a hindrance on organization's abilities to create future economic growth.

Writing in the Harvard Business Review (1996a: 75), Kaplan and Norton stated:

> Most companies' operational and management control systems are built around financial measures and targets, which bear little relation to the progress in achieving long-term strategic objectives. This emphasis on short-term financial measures leaves a gap between the development of a strategy and its implementation.

The study examined a number of organization case studies, one of which was Analog Devices, who had an approach called a Corporate Scorecard. In addition to several traditional financial measurements, the Corporate Scorecard included measures of customer delivery times, quality and cycle times of manufacturing processes, and the effectiveness of new product developments. A variety of other ideas and methods were considered by the study group, including shareholder value, productivity and quality measurements, but the focus stayed on the idea of a multi-dimensional scorecard. The participants in the study experimented with building prototype scorecards in their own companies and reported back to the study group. The conclusion of the study in December 1990 documented the feasibility and the benefits from such a balanced measurement system and was published in Harvard Business Review in 1992.

What is the Balanced Scorecard?

Kaplan and Norton (1996b: viii) explained the name 'Balanced Scorecard' in this way:

> The name (balanced scorecard) reflects the balance provided between short-and-long-term objectives, between financial and non-financial measures, between lagging and leading indicators, and between external and internal performance perspectives.

The Balanced Scorecard measures organizational performance across four broad business perspectives: Financial, Customers, Internal Business Processes, and Learning and Growth (later to become Innovation and Learning). Whilst these perspectives formed the original design of the scorecard, Kaplan and Norton have always held the view that the scorecard must be tailored to fit the particular organization if it is to be a valuable tool. Therefore, we see some scorecards with only three perspectives while others may have as many as six. These perspectives may also have different titles to the original design. Each of the perspectives has a series of objectives within them. The only stipulation that Kaplan and Norton have made is to keep the number of objectives within the perspectives down to below twenty, otherwise the scorecard will not be manageable.

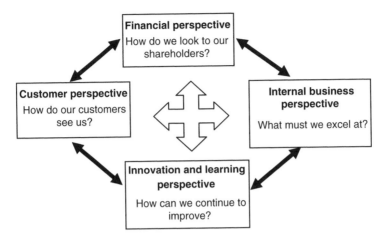

Figure 14.1 The Balanced Scorecard.

The Balanced Scorecard is shown in diagrammatic form in Figure 14.1.

Each of the perspectives indicates the type of objectives and measurements that they cover – usually having between two and five objectives each – which are effectively strategies or goals for achievement. Now we will look at what objectives organizations will typically cover in each of the perspectives starting with the top perspective into which all the others feed.

Financial perspective: how do we look to our shareholders?

Private Sector organizations are likely to choose objectives that include statements about revenue growth and mix with an emphasis on sales and profit. In the public sector financial reporting will be more concerned with how budgets are spent (see Chapter 12). All organizations (including the Public Sector and Government Departments) are interested in reducing costs and improving productivity and asset utilization which will mean they are more efficient. Organizations are also interested in ensuring they have an optimum investment strategy which will lead to long-term sustainability and potential time and cost savings.

Customer perspective: how do our customers see us?

Organizations in the private sector are interested in retaining customers and acquiring new ones, so objectives will emphasise these areas as well as market share, customer satisfaction and customer profitability. These are based on customer value propositions such as product or service attributes, customer relationships and the image and reputation of the organization. In defence, and other public sector organizations customers are less easily defined. Nevertheless, this perspective will be concerned about how the organization is perceived by others.

Internal business perspective: what must we excel at?

Private Sector organizations will have an emphasis on the three key business processes of innovation (or research and development) for new products and services; operations which builds and delivers the products and services; and after or post sales service which deals with any queries or complaints by the customer. Key measurements for processes are the time taken to undertake activities, the cost of undertaking the activities and the quality of the product or service. Service organizations do not have the same kind of measurements, as they do not have a tangible product. Organizations such as hospitals or airlines might use such measurements as: length of waiting times, accuracy of information, access to information, fulfilment of requests or transactions and effective communication.

Learning and growth perspective: how can we continue to improve?

This perspective is one of the hardest for organizations to identify objectives and measurements for. Typically, organizations choose employee skills and capabilities and information systems capabilities. Employee capabilities often include measurements of employee satisfaction with the organization as an employer and employee retention. Therefore measurements may seek to measure employee satisfaction regarding their involvement in decision making, receiving recognition for doing a good job, support levels from staff functions, encouragement to use their initiative and the availability of information to do their job well.

A Balanced Scorecard with its perspectives and completed objectives may look like that shown in Figure 14.2.

The Balanced Scorecard as a strategic tool

Undertaking further work with Rockwater and FMC Corporation allowed Kaplan and Norton to see that the Balanced Scorecard was more than a measurement system – it could also be used to communicate and align new strategies. With their additional experience from working with the scorecard in various companies, they stated that the Balanced Scorecard:

> translates an organisation's mission and strategy into a comprehensive set of performance measures that provides the framework for a strategic measurement and management system.
>
> (Kaplan and Norton 1996b: 2)

Today, the Balanced Scorecard is viewed as a framework that can translate strategy into operation, is used to ensure clarity of the strategy; and to communicate. It forms the basis of a more effective management process and links long-term strategy with short-term activity. Figure 14.3 indicates how it does this.

The first step is for the organization's managers to consider what is happening in the world and how this affects them. From this information,

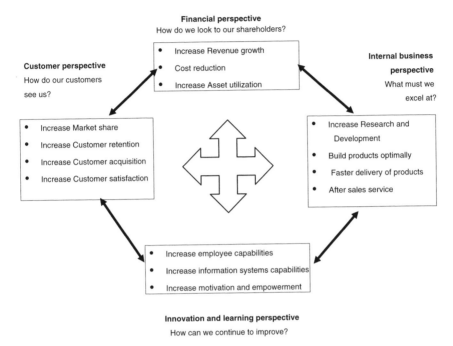

Financial perspective
How do we look to our shareholders?

- Increase Revenue growth
- Cost reduction
- Increase Asset utilization

Customer perspective
How do our customers see us?

- Increase Market share
- Increase Customer retention
- Increase Customer acquisition
- Increase Customer satisfaction

Internal business perspective
What must we excel at?

- Increase Research and Development
- Build products optimally
- Faster delivery of products
- After sales service

- Increase employee capabilities
- Increase information systems capabilities
- Increase motivation and empowerment

Innovation and learning perspective
How can we continue to improve?

Figure 14.2 A Balanced Scorecard with completed objectives.

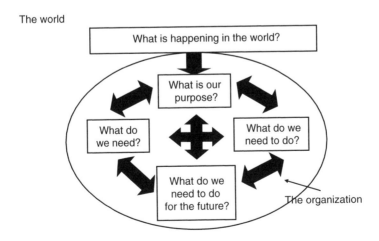

The world

What is happening in the world?

What is our purpose?

What do we need?

What do we need to do?

What do we need to do for the future?

The organization

Figure 14.3 The Balanced Scorecard as a strategy tool.

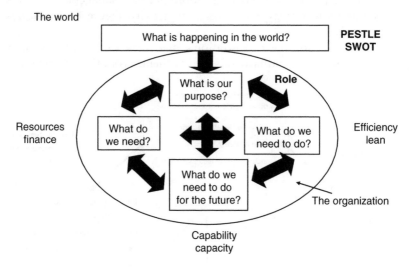

Figure 14.4 Tools, techniques and activities for the Balanced Scorecard as a strategy tool.

they can determine the organization's purpose or role. Once this is decided, they need to consider what resources it will need and the key activities or processes to achieve the purpose. Finally, the organization needs to ensure that it will have a future, and identify areas to work on to ensure future capability and capacity.

Figure 14.4 shows key activities and management tools and techniques than can be used in each of the areas. For example, PESTLE and SWOT are use to determine what is happening in the world and help us determine our purpose (these tools are covered in more detail in Chapter 9).

Kaplan and Norton claim a number of benefits from using the Balanced Scorecard now that it has evolved from an improved measurement system into a core management system. These include

- clarification of the vision throughout the organization;
- gains in consensus and ownership by the management team;
- the provision of a framework to align the organization;
- integration of strategic planning;
- a driver for the capital and resource allocation process;
- help for the organization to become more customer focused;
- and an understanding how knowledge enables business processes.

Strategy to action

In order to turn the Balanced Scorecard into a plan, the next step is to take the objectives and develop measures, targets and initiatives to achieve them. This material then becomes the strategic plan for the organization.

Table 14.1 Financial perspective of a Balanced Scorecard

Financial	Objectives	Measures	Targets	Initiatives
To succeed financially, how should we appear to our shareholders?	Revenue growth	Sales last year, versus sales this year	5% growth	Promotions
	Cost reduction	Staff costs + Equipment costs below last year	5% reduction	No recruitment Equipment replacement deferred for year
	Asset utilization	Use of buildings + use of vehicles	10% increase	Longer shift working
	Investment strategy	Number of new projects completed	10% increase	Prioritized list of projects implemented as budget available

Initiatives can be cascaded down the organization to appropriate levels for departments, teams or, even, individuals. The table above (14.1) shows how the financial perspective might be completed in simple format for an organization in the private sector.

The Balanced Scorecard used in Defence

The Balanced Scorecard was developed in the United States and therefore initial interest and usage has been in the United States and Europe. The US Department of Defense has been using the Balanced Scorecard for a number of years. As suggested by Kaplan and Norton, the Scorecard has been tailored to the organization needs and therefore the names and content of the perspectives have been changed from Kaplan and Norton's original design as depicted in Figure 14.1. The top level Scorecard with its perspectives and objectives is shown in Figure 14.5. As can be seen there is a specific 'people' perspective (force management goals), and the financial, resources and processes areas are covered in one perspective (institutional goals). The operational goals perspective is effectively the customer perspective, and future challenges covers innovation and learning.

The UK MoD introduced the Balanced Scorecard in 1999 to be used by the Defence Management Board and Top Level Budget holders. The Defence Management Board has stated that:

> The Defence Balanced Scorecard is a tool for managing, not just for reporting performance. It should allow the Defence Management Board to make sensible, informed assessments of how the department is doing, in order to decide where particular efforts have to be made.
>
> (Presentation at Defence Academy of the United Kingdom 2001)

Force management goals

Ensure Sustainable Military tempo	Maintain Quality workforce
Maintain Workforce satisfaction	Maintain Reasonable Force costs
Shape the force of the future	

| Streamline the Decision process, Drive financial Management & Acquisition excellence | Realign support To the Warfighter (including Defense agencies) |
| Improve the Readiness & quality of Key facilities | Manage Overhead & Indirect costs |

Institutional goals

DoD framework Balanced Scorecard

| Forces Management Risks | Operational Risk |
| Institutional Risk | Future Challenges Risk |

Operational goals

| Are they Postured to succeed? | Are they Employed Consistent with the strategy? |
| Are forces Currently ready? | Do we have the forces Available? |

| Drive Joint Operations (CONOPS) experiments | Define future Human skills And competences |
| Define & Develop Transformation capabilities | Develop more Effective organizations |

Future challenges goals

Figure 14.5 The US Department of Defense Balanced Scorecard. (Used with permission: US Department of Defense.)

The Defence Balanced Scorecard encapsulates the Defence Management Board's key objectives and priorities, including the Public Service Agreement targets (from the Government), over the full range of MoD business. In 2001, acknowledging the success in developing, implementing and using the Balanced Scorecard, Kaplan and Norton awarded the MoD 'Hall of Fame' status, making it the first public sector organization outside the United States to be given the honour.

Although the UK Defence Balanced Scorecard has four perspectives (as in the original design), the titles and content have been changed, or tailored, to reflect the role of the MoD, just as the US DOD has also tailored its Scorecard. In this case the customer perspective has become Purpose (of the organization), the financial perspective has broadened to cover all Resources, internal business perspective has become Enabling Processes; while the innovation and learning perspective has become Future Capabilities. The perspectives titles and objectives have changed each year as the Defence Management Board has matured in its use of the Balanced Scorecard.

The UK Defence Balanced Scorecard for 2005–07 is shown in Figure 14.6. You will also see that the financial perspective and customer perspective have changed places. This is because Kaplan and Norton suggest that the perspectives feed into each other: Innovation and learning feeds into the internal business processes perspective which, in turn, feeds

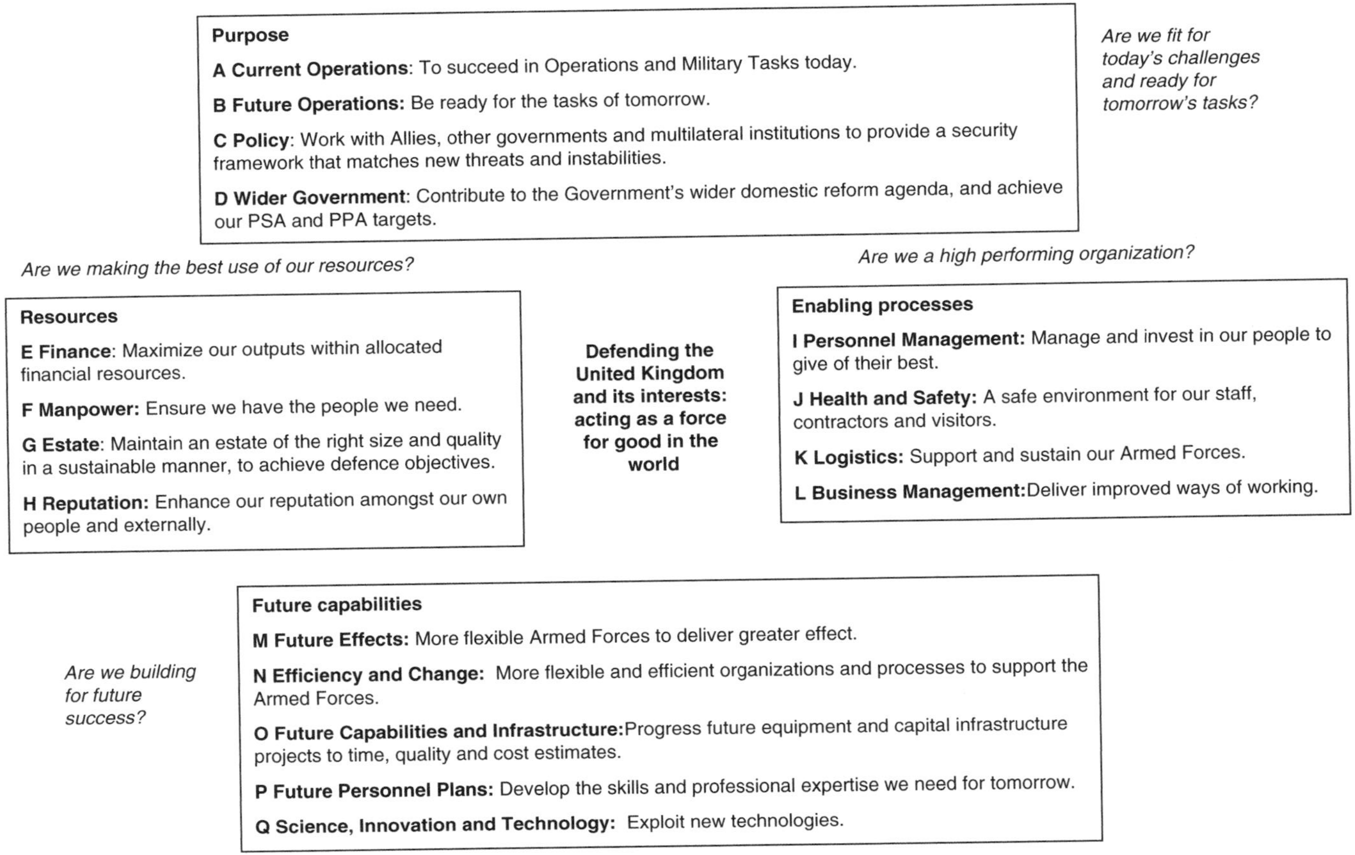

Are we fit for today's challenges and ready for tomorrow's tasks?

Purpose

A Current Operations: To succeed in Operations and Military Tasks today.

B Future Operations: Be ready for the tasks of tomorrow.

C Policy: Work with Allies, other governments and multilateral institutions to provide a security framework that matches new threats and instabilities.

D Wider Government: Contribute to the Government's wider domestic reform agenda, and achieve our PSA and PPA targets.

Are we making the best use of our resources?

Resources

E Finance: Maximize our outputs within allocated financial resources.

F Manpower: Ensure we have the people we need.

G Estate: Maintain an estate of the right size and quality in a sustainable manner, to achieve defence objectives.

H Reputation: Enhance our reputation amongst our own people and externally.

Defending the United Kingdom and its interests: acting as a force for good in the world

Are we a high performing organization?

Enabling processes

I Personnel Management: Manage and invest in our people to give of their best.

J Health and Safety: A safe environment for our staff, contractors and visitors.

K Logistics: Support and sustain our Armed Forces.

L Business Management: Deliver improved ways of working.

Are we building for future success?

Future capabilities

M Future Effects: More flexible Armed Forces to deliver greater effect.

N Efficiency and Change: More flexible and efficient organizations and processes to support the Armed Forces.

O Future Capabilities and Infrastructure: Progress future equipment and capital infrastructure projects to time, quality and cost estimates.

P Future Personnel Plans: Develop the skills and professional expertise we need for tomorrow.

Q Science, Innovation and Technology: Exploit new technologies.

Figure 14.6 The UK MoD 2005 Balanced Scorecard (Ministry of Defence, Departmental Plan 2005–09: 8. Used with permission).

into the customer perspective which feeds into the financial perspective. But, in the public sector the finances feed into providing the customer objectives, hence the switch round. In addition the content of the Defence Scorecard perspectives have changed: Purpose considers, are we fit for today's challenges and ready for tomorrow's tasks?; Resources considers, are we making the best use of resources?; Enabling Processes asks, are we a high performing organization? and Future Capabilities considers, are we building for future success?

Balanced Scorecard Reporting

Figure 14.7 shows an hypothetical example of a scorecard in reporting format. The perspectives and objectives are based on the UK Defence Management Board Balanced Scorecard from 2001 and the colours are purely illustrative to support an explanation as to how the objectives are interconnected.

If we start with the reporting period, you will see that these are quarterly reporting periods – they range from −3 to +7 with 0 being the current date. So, we look back at performance for one year and look forward to forecast performance through this year and to the end of the following year. The choice of reporting period is for the organization to decide.

Looking at the colours, we see red, amber, yellow and green – a variation of traffic lights. The colours have the following meanings: Red – critical

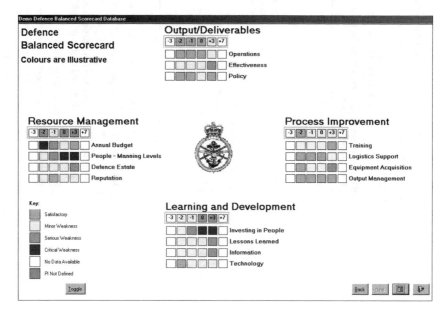

Figure 14.7 The Balanced Scorecard in reporting format (Presentation at Defence Academy 2001).

weakness, Amber – serious or major weakness, Yellow – minor weakness and Green – satisfactory. In the book, these colours show in greyscale, but the key will help with translation.

The Navy uses a fifth colour – blue which signifies 'satisfactory but at the cost of too many resources'. Some scorecards use a coloured flash in the corner to indicate that whilst the majority of measures indicate a certain level of performance, there are one or two measures that are significantly different. A Defence example of this might be manning, which might generally be yellow with a red corner to indicate there is a shortage of specialists such as medical staff, engineers or pilots.

If we look at how the scorecard has been used as a management tool, we see that in period −2, the budget (Resource Management Perspective) was showing critical weakness. Clearly some action was taken by the management board because the performance colours have gradually improved so that we are now predicting a satisfactory performance at the end of the year. If we look at the rest of the scorecard, we can also see the effect that those actions, to improve the annual budget performance, have had on performance for other objectives.

In the resources perspective

- Manning levels have moved from yellow to red with the same prediction for the end of the year. This suggests we have stopped recruiting.
- Estate is also predicted to worsen from yellow to amber. Perhaps less money is being spent on new building or maintenance of estate.

In the output perspective

- It is predicted that Operations performance will worsen from green to yellow, and, effectiveness from yellow to amber. Both of these are likely to be caused by less staff being available, due to the stop on recruitment.

In the enabling processes perspective

- For Training an improvement is anticipated. This is slightly surprising but may be due to staff having to be redeployed because of the stop in recruiting.
- Logistics Support is expected to worsen from green to yellow. This could suggest that less budget is being spent on the supply chain.
- A worsening performance, from yellow to amber is anticipated for Equipment Acquisition. Again, this suggests that less budget is being spent on equipment acquisition which may be slowing down the acquisition process.

In the learning and development perspective:

- Investing in People (a civilian award for performance in people management) performance deteriorated from amber to red and looks set to continue that way to the end of the year. Here, too, there is likely to be a link to the stop on recruiting.
- Lessons Learned is predicted to worsen from yellow to amber by the end of the year. It is likely that less time or resource is being used in this area.
- Another decline is expected for Information so that its yellow rating could become amber by the end of the year. This could also be due to less resource being used in this area.

So overall, quite a lot of objectives have seen, or will see, deterioration in performance as a result of the action taken to improve performance in the budget area.

Thus, the Balanced Scorecard report shows the Management Board that, although they have taken action to ensure the likelihood of meeting the budget by the end of the financial year, their methods to achieve that have had a detrimental effect on the organization's outputs, and on the resources and activities and future capability that are needed to achieve outputs in the future.

As well as its obvious purpose within the MoD, the Balanced Scorecard report is also used to brief government. It can offer compelling evidence in the argument for greater resources to achieve better effect.

For the Defence Management Board, the Scorecard approach provides a simple, clear statement of the strategic intent of the Defence Council and Defence Management Board. It offers a more comprehensive view of performance than any performance measurement tools used in the past. Its clear focus on outputs, rather than simply on financial measures, allow vivid insight into how the various components of performance relate to each other and to the delivery of key outputs.

Conclusion

This chapter has identified the important role of performance measurement and management in an organization by identifying its functions in checking position, communication, prioritization and compelling progress towards organizational goals. The Balanced Scorecard has been introduced as a useful tool to help organizations develop strategy and to review and manage performance. The Balanced Scorecard clarifies and communicates the Management Board's strategic intent, simply and effectively, in a one page diagram. The Scorecard has been shown to be in effective use in the UK Ministry of Defence and the US Department of Defense.

Questions to consider

1 Think about your own organization.
   a Are measurements used for the four CPs?
   b If not, how are measurements used, and what more could be done with them? Is there room for improvement?

2 What types of measurement records are kept in your organization? For example, do the people capturing data in our organizations really understand what happens to the data, who it is for and how it is used?

Suggested reading

Kaplan, Robert and Norton, David (1996), *The Balanced Scorecard*, Boston, MA: Harvard Business School Press.
Neely, Andy (1998) *Measuring Business Performance*, London: Economist with Profile Books.

Bibliography

Cavoli, C. (2004), 'The Balanced Scorecard and other thoughts on metrics', *Defence AT&L* (January–February), pp. 1–18.
Cracknell, D. and Rogers, L. (2002), 'Sick kept in ambulances in bed crisis', *The Sunday Times*, 22 December 2002.
Fitz-Enz, J. (1996) *Benchmarking staff Performance: How Staff Departments can Enhance Their Value to the Customer*, San Francisco: Jossey-Bass.
Fredland, J. E. (2004), 'Outsourcing Military Force: A Transactions cost perspective on the role of military companies', *Defence and Peace Economics*, 15 (3) (June): 18–32.
Kaplan, R. and Norton, D. (1992), *The Balanced Scorecard – Measures that Drive Performance*, Harvard Business Review: January/February.
—— (1996a), *Using the Balanced Scorecard as a Strategic Management System*, Harvard Business Review: January/February.
—— (1996b), *The Balanced Scorecard*, Harvard Business School Press; Boston MA, USA.
Ministry of Defence, *Departmental Plan*, 2005–09.
Neely, A. (1998), *Measuring Business Performance*, Economist With Profile Books: London.
Polyakov, L. (2003), *Managing The Challenge Of Illegal Arms Transfers*, Conflict Studies Research Centre, Defence Academy of the United Kingdom, Camberley.
Potter, M. (2001), *Presentation at Defence Academy of the United Kingdom*, Directorate of Performance and Analysis, 25 June 2001.

15 Change management

Putting strategy into practice

Derrick J. Neal

Introduction

We have been 'doing' change management for a very long time and it certainly predates the observation of Machiavelli when he wrote in *The Prince*,

> There is nothing more difficult to take in hand, more perilous to conduct, or more uncertain in its success, than to take the lead in the introduction of a new order of things.
>
> (Niccolo Machiavelli 1532)

Thus it might come as a surprise that the management literature is full of examples of our failure to come to grips with the subject. Very well respected writers on the subject of change management, including Kanter (1985), Pascale *et al.* (1993), Kotter (1995), Handy (1989) and Nadler and Nadler (1998), are consistent in their view, through empirical research, that in excess of 80 per cent of change programmes fail to deliver the envisaged benefits. This chapter will explore the theory of change management and its evolution over the last 20 years and contrast this with the lessons that should be drawn from experience. Finally, the chapter will put the subject into the context of change within a ministry of defence (MoD) and explore the successes and the continuing challenges. Whilst the ideas discussed will be of a generic nature, the complexity of the situation increases dramatically when the scenario moves to change management within a nation that is undergoing security sector reform. Given that this topic is covered elsewhere in this book the reader is urged to use the observations made in this chapter and reflect on the issues highlighted in the other chapters. Essentially, all organizations large, small, public and private, are involved in change management constantly and many managers would benefit greatly from having a better understanding of the issues within change.

The complexity of managing change

One of the difficulties with change management is its simplicity at one level and complexity at another level. The issues and concepts are easy to understand but their effective implementation usually spells the beginning of the problems. Because the issues and concepts are so obvious, senior managers may believe that they have the necessary skills, both in terms of management and leadership, to deliver the change. Senior managers certainly have the authority to make changes but, if their people skills are lacking, meaningful change is unlikely to occur. This usually leads to frustration and, to compound matters, managers find themselves addressing the wrong issues in trying to force progress, usually through directives.

How have we come to this state of affairs? In part this can be explained by the rapid growth in interest in strategic management in the late 1970s and early 1980s. At this time businesses in both the public and private sectors were heavily engaged in conducting strategic reviews and producing impressive strategy documents. The management consultancy business did particularly well out of this activity. However, academics such as Haspalagh (1982) reported that a large percentage of organizations never actually saw the strategies turned into effective performance improvement. Indeed, this led to the acronym SPOTS (strategic plans on top shelves) as this is where many ended up (although in one African state, the proposed change programme for the police ended up as a very effective door jamb!). The elegance of the strategy formulation process led to a false sense that the delivery of the strategy was no more than a formality. Failures in this regard led several large management consultancies to change their focus and to provide a service based on helping organizations to both formulate and implement the strategy, and today there are many management consultants heavily involved in change management implementation. Expectations often exceed capabilities, as highlighted by a range of reports by academics which details failure to deliver the full potential of the envisaged strategy.

The challenges of change management are common to private and public sector organizations. However, the consequences of failure are not the same. Typically, if a private sector organization fails to deliver an effective change management program, the very survival of the company may well be at stake. Most public sector organizations do not have this threat, if they fail to deliver change and, as a result their performance suffers, it usually results in an enquiry being held. Some of the top management may be replaced and departments is restructured, or given new responsibilities and we are told that the mistakes will not happen again – until next time. Failure within an MoD is much the same but if the failure impacts on operations this can result in the loss of life in the front lines. Given that all sectors of economies face the need to address changes in their organizations and respond to an ever changing environment it is appropriate to consider the approaches to change that are available.

Models for change management

Change models can be characterized by the number of steps involved in the process. Several examples of three-step models exist including:

- Lewin (1957)   unfreeze/change/re-freeze;
- Tichy and Devanna (1986)   awakening/mobilizing/reinforcing;
- Nadler and Tushman (1989)   energizing/envisioning/enabling;
- Egan (1988)   diagnosis/future vision/the strategy.

In addition to these, other researchers have proposed multi-step models. For instance, Kanter (1985) refers to 10 commandments; Beer *et al.* (1990) use six steps; Nilikant (1998) has a model with seven steps; and the often quoted Kotter (1996) model uses eight steps as shown below.

1   Establish a sense of urgency
2   Form a powerful guiding coalition to drive the change programme
3   Create a vision
4   Communicate the vision
5   Empower others to act on the vision
6   Plan for and create short-term wins
7   Consolidate improvements and produce still more change
8   Institutionalize the new approaches.

Further, a number of more conceptual models and approaches have been proposed including: the congruence model, see Nadler and Nadler (1998), the cloverleaf, Handy (1989) and the three circle model proposed by Adair (1997).

However, dynamic checklists should not be seen as a holy grail – it does not matter how comprehensive the list is if management are unable to turn each element into a reality through an effective process. The concern with these models is that management may tend to apply them as tools and as ends unto themselves (in a similar way to the argument made about the Planning School in Chapter 9) rather than as a way of thinking. Such a tendency is understandable when one considers how senior management might view the need for change. The McKinsey 7 S model, is helpful in explaining this point as it highlights the key dimensions, or levers, that need to be addressed:

- Strategies (H)
- Structures (H)
- Systems (H)
- Staff (S)
- Skills (S)
- Styles (S)
- Shared values (S).

The key point here is that three of the areas are defined as hard (H) and, as such, they are levers over which senior management have full control and where change can be made relatively quickly. Consequently, it is unsurprising that management address these areas first and, often misguidedly, think that the other levers, defined as soft (S), will take care of themselves. Unfortunately, this is not the case and frequently the problems associated with the delivery of change arise in these areas.

This issue is captured in the notion that the generic elements of any change programme have two dimensions, namely, content and process. All too often in large bureaucracies, with their hierarchical structures, the emphasis is placed on the content of change. In this regard management look at what it is that they want to change and this frequently results in new organizational charts, new titles and responsibilities and changes in the power available to individuals and/or groups within the organization. On paper this is change (see Figure 15.1) but in reality it is often the cause of yet another set of problems for management.

The missing link in this approach is the importance of thinking through the process of delivering change. The correct time for engaging in this aspect of change management *is not* after the strategy has been formulated; it should form part of the strategy formulation process itself. At each step of the strategy formulation the key question that needs to be addressed is: 'how will this be implemented?' It is this very act that forms the basis for true strategic thinking, as failure to work through this aspect is likely to

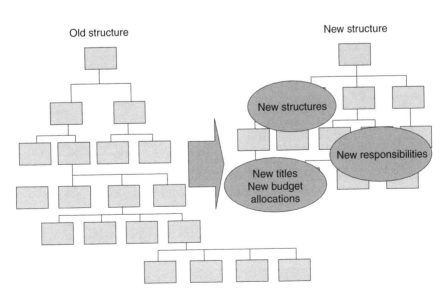

Figure 15.1 The content of change can cause more problems than it solves.

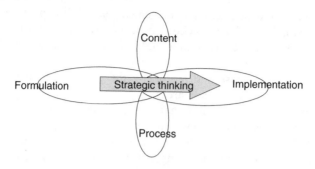

Figure 15.2 The concept of true strategic thinking.

lead to a strategic plan that has elegance but little or no hope of ever being implemented. The confluence of all four aspects is the very process of strategic thinking as shown in Figure 15.2.

Whilst this might seem like common-sense it is often difficult for senior managers to see their way through a number of the process challenges. In the belief that they are operating at a strategic level, managers find it too easy to jump to what they believe is the destination without giving enough thought or rigour to the issues associated with making the journey.

Given that the process of change is heavily weighted to people processes, managing expectations, and giving support and guidance to those making the journey, it throws the spotlight on the roles, skills and competencies of leadership within the organization.

Leadership and change management

Within the management literature a number of definitions of leadership exist including the following (which broadly equate with the definitions of political leadership outlined in Chapter 3):

> Leadership is about the lifting of people's vision to a higher sight, the raising of their performance to a higher standard, the building of their personality beyond its normal limitations.
>
> (Drucker 2001)

> The leader must have infective optimism. The final test of a leader is the feeling you have when you leave their presence after a conference. Have you a feeling of uplift and confidence?
>
> (Montgomery 1956)

> Getting extra ordinary things from ordinary people.
>
> (Harvey-Jones 1988)

When an organization is embarking on a major change programme it is all too easy to assume that those at the top of the organization have the requisite skills and competencies to shape and drive the change forward. Unfortunately this is not always the case. The traits and characteristics often credited to a good leader are,

- Honest under pressure
- Straightforward
- Open
- Keeps promises
- Sees mistakes as learning opportunities
- Promotes from within
- The organization is top of the agenda
- Excellent communicator.

When it comes to a change management situation one of the most important characteristics that is required is that of integrity. Those involved in the change have to believe in their leader. They need to see the leader as someone they can trust, respect and for whom they are prepared to go the extra mile, to make things happen. They need to believe that the leader is doing this for the good of the organization and not simply for personal gain.

Whilst these characteristics are important for most leaders in most situations they become critical when major change – transformational change – is being delivered within the organization. (The distinction between incremental and transformational change was raised in Chapter 9 under the concept of strategic drift.) Many researchers have studied this area and whilst they may use different words to describe the two types of change they are all essentially saying the same thing, as shown in Table 15.1.

The real problem begins when senior managers believe that they are dealing with incremental change when in fact the organization is in need of more radical transformational change. The key difference between incremental and transformational change is that, in the latter case, a paradigm shift – or culture change – is a requirement not an option. It is this dimension that requires management to deal with the soft Ss, as mentioned earlier in the context of the McKinsey model. Unfortunately, when managers reach for the levers under their control they naturally go straight for the hard Ss and hope that the soft areas will take care of themselves.

However, this issue pales into insignificance compared to the problems that occur when senior managers believe that the organization only needs incremental change and struggle to make progress in delivering change. One of the key problems here is that of frames of reference: that which is incremental change for one person is transformational change for another, as highlighted in the following example.

Table 15.1 Summary of research into the characteristics of incremental (first order) and transformational (second order) change. (Adapted from Lira 2004)

Author	First-order change (reformation)	Second-order change (transformation)
Lindblom (1959) Management theory	Branch change: a series of small, incremental changes that gradually move way from the current situation, step-by-step, by small degrees	Root change: a rational comprehensive approach, building from the ground up, starting from fundamentals each time, only relying on the past when experience is embodied in a theory
Vickers (1965) Management theory	Executive change: gives effect to policies by maintaining the course of affairs in line with governing relations, norms, and standards	Policy-making change: establishing the overarching principles that will create and communicate a new culture and system of values
De Bono (1971) Creative thinking	Vertical change: seeks to establish links between different aspects of the organization, so that one thing will follow logically from another	Lateral change: breaks from the past, and tries to find new patterns by restructuring
Greiner (1972) Planned change	Evolutionary change: gentle adjustments, aimed at maintaining growth while retaining the same overall pattern of management	Revolutionary change: major alteration, abandoning past management practices and establishing a new set of organizational practices as the basis for the next phase of evolutionary growth
Grabow and Heskin (1973) Planned change	Rational change: retains internal structures because it does not question the underlying assumptions	Radical change: a system change bringing a whole new cultural paradigm
Gerlach and Hines (1973) Change theory	Developmental change: a change within a current system that adds to, or improves, it rather than replacing some of its main features	Revolutionary change: brings in a new set of goals and means, taking the organization into a different direction
Skibbins (1974) Organization theory	Homeostasis: sees current forces, internal and external, as close to equilibrium so managers work to short-term goals, largely maintaining existing systems	Radical change: likened to caterpillars turning into butterflies; large scale change operations 'high spread, large scale processes are initiated, to bring about transfiguration of the organization'
Sheldon (1980) Management	Normal change: a constant tinkering of the various dimensions of the organization, to try to improve the fit between the organization and its environment	Paradigm change: concerns many or all dimensions of culture, reflecting a radical change in either the world or the world view
Ramaprasad (1982) Management theory	Minor change: simply improving current operations in attempts to boost efficiency	Revolutionary change: a redefinition of the entire system, which may occur at the conceptual, structural, or process level, or at some combination of the three

Christoph was the CEO of a medium sized company supplying uniforms for the Army. He was under pressure to improve the profit margins being generated by the company. His value chain analysis highlighted that most areas of the business were making good contributions but that the logistics and distribution departments were in fact hardly breaking even. With this in mind he decided to close these departments and to use outsourcing for the logistics function. From his point of view this was a relatively minor change that would improve the bottom line performance. However, for the staff left within the former logistics department, Yangos and Maria, now charged with managing a contract with a specialist logistics firm, this was clearly a *transformational change*.

When the situation outlined above occurs within an organization, and it may well be replicated many times within a large multi-national corporation or a large public sector organization, it is little wonder that all staff involved become frustrated at the lack of progress in delivering effective change.

One of the leadership factors that sets apart the military from most other public sector organizations is that officers are selected, in the first instance, for having leadership skills and competencies, and are continually trained to be leaders of men and women. With this in mind, it is no surprise that when change management is mentioned within the MoD the senior staff believe that they are particularly well equipped to deal with the challenge. Of course, in some instances, this is perfectly well justified but it may be more a case of luck on the part of the military having the right person in the right place at a particular time rather than good planning. The key point to be made here is that military officers are good leaders of men and women, especially within the military operations theatre. However, much of the change management that needs to be delivered today is in the business space and, unlike the operations scenario, the military do not spend their career training in order to make their contribution in a business management environment. Following the relatively recent move to the use of Integrated Project Teams (IPTs) in the equipment procurement cycle in the UK MoD it has only recently been recognized that staff moving into positions within IPTs (in particular the IPT leader role) have a need for specific training in project management.

The argument being developed is that several assumptions have been made in the UK MoD, that should be seen as danger signs; namely:

- that HQ can leverage the 'can do' culture that exists within a military operational environment into staff roles within the deep operations sphere (business space). Consequently much of the change management within this context tends to be under resourced.

- that military leadership skills are directly transferable to the deep operations staff roles, so that.
- management skills and competencies do not need to be developed in military officers in preparation for deep operations staff roles.

On all counts this line of reasoning is flawed. The failure to allocate appropriate resources to change management programs, in terms of finances, time, staff and training, has been a major cause of stalled and failed attempts to make meaningful progress within the MoD in recent years.

An additional problem is linked to the military mindset of attacking change management from a highly structured approach, through the creation of teams with bounded areas of responsibility and clear targets and goals. Whilst this can look good on paper it can also give a false impression that the organization is in control of the change programme. In the same way that military operations can have a tendency to develop a life of their own, often called mission-creep, so one can find that change management programmes develop change-creep. Projects develop a life of their own and additional resources are requested. These are well articulated in business cases, suggesting a raft of benefits that make agreement to the proposals an easy decision for senior managers. However, the reality is that often these cases are produced in response to a failure to deliver in other areas.

Considering change management in a broader context highlights the difficulties that need to be overcome. In the case of a developing nation or a country this is beginning to embrace a more democratic model of government it is clear that change represents a potential threat to many people.

Indonesia is a case in point where the nation is undergoing significant social change in many areas. Whilst the President and his government may state what changes are to take place, and have a desire to be seen to conform to the influences of the international community, it has to be recognized that some elements of society will resist the changes. The key elements here link back to the Machiavelli quote at the beginning of the chapter. To require change is to imply criticism of the current approach. It is also the case that in making changes those who currently benefit may lose power and influence whilst others (people or organizations) will gain power and influence from the change. Thus, in the case of Indonesia, the military (TNI) have historically had a major role in domestic security matters and in many ways have acted as a powerful police force in addition to being a military force. As Indonesia moves to a more balanced security infra-structure it follows that the creation of a professional police force is seen as a threat by the TNI. It is important that senior politicians recognize the people issues and the cultural issues of change management that need to be addressed if this change is to be successful. Unfortunately, it is often the case that the blunt instrument of new legal frameworks is used as a means of driving change with the inevitable consequence of significant unrest and trauma of people reluctantly accepting the new relationships.

Therefore, in any major change situation, such as the establishment of a MoD or the move to a more professional military, it is important for leaders and/or senior politicians to appreciate fully the time, resources and competencies that will be required to implement change.

Change management and transition management

Within any change programme managers need to demonstrate that a change management process has been put in place and be able to show that the people in the organization have fully engaged with change. All too often management spend a great deal of effort putting together highly detailed plans for delivering change, namely the changes in structures, responsibilities and the new strategy (the hard Ss in the McKinsey model), and simply expect the people to follow without questioning. Such an approach represents a focus on change management, but at least half of the challenge is to manage the process of transition. The lack of consideration of the people dimension is the major cause for failure of many change efforts.

The distinction can be shown diagrammatically as in Figure 15.3.

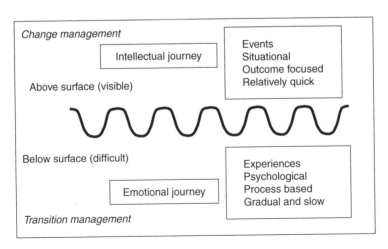

Figure 15.3 Characteristics and differences between change and transition management.

Conclusion

It is usually the people side of delivering change (transition management) that causes the most problems within delivering change to the organization. One of the ways of explaining this relates to the difference in speed between change and transition. It is often the case that senior management make the intellectual case for change and assume that it is understood and accepted by all in the organization. Having told people that change is going to happen, and having defined the desired end state, the senior team begin the race. Indeed this is often explained in the context of a marathon race and as such highlights the problems. For example, the senior management team have trained for this race (not in a physical or educational sense, but in terms of having had time to adjust emotionally to the new organization) through having had many discussions long before the staff is involved. Once the gun is fired the senior team are off, they may have already completed 20 miles before some of the low level staff have even begun the race. Other members of the organization may even be hanging around the start line not even aware that a race is taking place. Consequently, it comes as a great shock and disappointment to senior management when they feel that staff are not taking matters seriously and are not making the progress that they expect. Different parts of the organization will need to make their own journey and they will need to work through their own emotions both as individuals and as parts of the organization and it is the responsibility of management to recognize these needs and build them into the change process.

A major part of the transition process is for staff to reach the point where they are able to let go of things, and their old ways of working, and to move to the new ways of doing things. In order for this to happen they have to test the new environment and have to build confidence that it is not a threat and that, as a result, they and the organization will benefit. All of this takes time and needs support from senior management rather than more shouting and the issuing of instructions to do things faster.

When the concept of transition management is linked back to drivers for change and leadership issues, it becomes clear that good change management leaders need the necessary people skills if the organization is to embrace change as an opportunity rather than simply as a threat.

Questions to consider

1   Think about changes that have taken place within your own organization?

   a   To what extent were they successful?
   b   How did you feel about them?

2   Do you believe that the right change management skills/competencies existed where they were needed?

3 Thinking again of previous changes within your organization, what levers were being pulled: Hard? Soft? Or both?
4 What are the factors that are driving your organization to change and how do you think senior management should respond to these drivers?
5 Are the changes required in your organization incremental or transformational and how are they seen differently by different people within your organization?
6 Think about change(s) within your organization from the perspectives of change management as structure and process; Transition management as a people process; Which, if any, are you doing well?

Suggested reading

Drucker, P. (2001), *Management Challenges for the Twenty-First Century*, New York: Harper Business.
Kanter, R., Stein, B., and Jick, T. (1992), *The Challenge of Organisational Change*, New York: Free Press.
Kotter, J. (1996), *Leading Change*, Boston, MA: Harvard Business School Press.
Johnson, S., Libicki, M., and Gregory, F. (eds) (2003), *New Challenges, New Tools for Defense Decisionmaking*, Santa Monica, RAND Corporation.
Nadler, D. and Nadler, M. (1998), *Champions of Change: How CEOs and their Companies are Mastering the Skills of Radical Change*, San Francisco, CA: Jossey-Bass.

Bibliography

Adair, J. (1997), *The Action Leader*, London: The Industrial Society.
Beer, M., Eisenstat, R. and Spector, B. (1990), 'Why change programs don't produce change', *Harvard Business Review* (November-December): 158–66.
de Bono, E. (1971), *Lateral Thinking for Management*, London: Penguin Books.
Drucker, P. (2001), *Management Challenges for the Twenty-First Century*, New York: Harper Business.
Egan, G. (1988), *Change Agent Skills B: Managing Innovation and Change*, San Diego, CA: University Associates.
Gerlach, L. and Hines, V. (1973), *The Dynamics of Change in America*, Minneapolis, MN: University of Minneapolis Press.
Grabow, S. and Heskin, A. (1973), 'Foundations for a radical concept of planning', *AIP Journal* (March): 106–14.
Greiner, L. (1972), 'Evolution and revolution as organizations grow', *Harvard Business Review*, 50: 39–46.
Handy, C. (1989), *The Age of Unreason*, London: Business Books.
Harvey-Jones, J. (1988), *Making it Happen: Reflections on Leadership*, London: Collins.
Haspalagh, P. (1982), 'Portfolio planning: uses and limits', *Harvard Business Review* (January/February): 58–73.
Kanter, R. (1985), *The Change Masters: Corporate Entrepreneurs at work*, London: Unwin.

248   *Derrick J. Neal*

Kanter, R., Stein, B. and Jick, T. (1992), *The Challenge of Organisational Change*, New York: Free Press.

Kotter, J. (1995), 'Leading change: why transformation fails', *Harvard Business Review* (March/April): 59–67.

—— (1996), *Leading Change*, Boston, MA: Harvard Business School Press.

Lewin, K. Many books and academic papers make reference to the idea of 'unfreezing' and this can be traced back to references in (1958), *Readings in Social Psychology*, Holt, Reinhart and Winston.

Lindblom, C. (1959), 'The science of muddling through', *Public Administration Review*, 19: 79–88.

Lira, L. (2004), 'To change an army: understanding defense transformation'. Paper presented to *ISSS/ISAC Annual Conference*, 28–30 October, 2004.

Machiavelli, Niccolò (1532), 'The Prince', in *The Portable Machiavelli*, edited and translated by Bandanella, P. and Musa, M. (1998), New York and London: Penguin Books: 77–166.

McKinsey 7S model, www.valuebasedmanagement.net/methods_7S.html, accessed 20 March 2006.

Montgomery, B. (1956), *Montgomery of Alamein*, London: W. H. Allen.

Nadler, D. and Nadler, M. (1998), *Champions of Change: How CEOs and their Companies are Mastering the Skills of Radical Change*, San Francisco, CA: Jossey-Bass.

Nadler, D. and Tushman, M. (1989), 'Organisational frame bending: principles for managing reorientation', *Academy of Management Executive*, 3(3): 194–204.

Nilikant, V. and Ramnarayan, S. (1998), *Managing Organisational Change*, New Delhi: Response Books (Sage).

Pascale, R., Goss, T. and Athos, A. (1993), 'Reinvention roller coaster: risking the present for a powerful future', *Harvard Business Review* (November/December): 97–108.

Ramaprasad, A. (1982), 'Revolutionary change and strategic management', *Behavioural Science*, 27(4): 387–92.

Sheldon, A. (1980), 'Organisational change', *Organisational Dynamics*, 61–80.

Skibbins, G. (1974), *Organisational Evolution: A Program for Managing Radical Change*, New York: AMACOM.

Tichy, N. and Devanna, M. (1986), *The Transformational Leader*, New York: John Wiley and Sons.

Vickers, G. (1965), *The Art of Judgement*, London: Chapman Hall.

16 The governance and management of defence

Future challenges

Teri McConville and Laura R. Cleary

Introduction

One of the few constants in life is change, and the common challenge that all mankind faces is whether to embrace or reject it. Theorists have written extensively on how the process of globalization is affecting the social, political, economic, trade and technological environments of states, and how individuals and communities have had to learn to adjust to those changes. (Hoogvelt 1997; Held 2000; O'Meara *et al.* 2000). It has become almost a truism to say that the way to cope with new circumstances and environments is to be flexible; to meet change by changing.

For a time it seemed that defence establishments would remain islands of tranquillity, stable and unflinching against the pounding waves of change. However, in recent years that impression has been proved wrong. Events in Central and Eastern Europe, South America, Africa and South Asia have shown that the military is just as susceptible as the rest of society to the forces of change. In many cases they are overthrowing not governments, but perceptions that the military is conservative in nature, and willing only to defend the status quo. Armed forces around the world increasingly are embracing democratic reforms and good governance because they view them as the means to professionalize their forces and to make a real contribution to the wider security of the state.

That which has become known as the post-modern era is 'typified by a breaking down of accepted norms, [and] a relaxation of established structures' (McConville and Holmes 2003: xii), which can be profoundly uncomfortable. It is tempting and, perhaps, natural to romanticize earlier, more familiar times, and to lament their passing. However, systems, regimes and methods from the past belong there. Whatever else the future may hold it offers us all the chance of a new beginning. Beginnings bring opportunities and hopes and, provided that the lessons of the past are learned, the chance to strive for what might be.

Transformation as management

As with any journey, the road to what might be begins with a vision and a plan. The vision tells of the destination, and the plan of the route.

The vision will be based on perceptions of the national interest, encompassing 'what a state needs – security, economic well-being, and so forth – and what it aspires to become – a developed country, a regional power, the promoter of ideological preferences and so forth' (Cleary Chapter 3: 65). The vision for accountable, responsive and democratically appointed governments; for transparency in policy and practice; and for well-managed, efficient defence and security sectors is shared by numerous communities, states and regions around the world. It is the motivation for this book to be conceived, written and published.

The realization of that vision is neither an easy nor straightforward matter. It needs careful guidance, strong (transformational) leadership and competent management. While the fine details will differ between time, place and culture, the overall process will be strikingly similar wherever it occurs. To the extent that a nation or state will behave like an organization, the process of transformation can be tracked as an exercise in management, to recognize the common themes and challenges that it brings into focus.

Planning

The starting point on the journey to 'what might be' is wherever history has brought us. It may be the ending of an inter-ethnic conflict, or a new-found national identity. It may be the confusion of coming to terms with the demands of a global economy or of facing the, previously unthinkable, threat of terrorism. There is a terrible old joke that ends with the punch-line, 'Well, if I was going there, I wouldn't start from here!' For this journey, however, history has not allowed any choice about the starting point. Nevertheless, from that legacy, within limits, the future is something that can be shaped and moulded to the vision, provided that there is a plan.

That plan will form the strategic direction for the future. At governmental and international levels it will come in the form of policies. For the defence community in general policy needs to be translated into doctrinal principles that will, in its turn shape managerial strategy at the level of the specific unit, department or workgroup.

As Derrick Neal argued (Chapter 9), the first stage in planning has to be an honest, objective and thorough assessment of the security environment, both internally and externally. Honesty and objectivity are the fruits of managers and political leaders acting for the common good. They are difficult to attain if people in positions of power seek only to retain power for themselves, or are motivated by a narrow ideological framework that does not account for alternative views. Thoroughness can only be achieved if those scanning the environment have a comprehensive understanding of security issues, both within and beyond national borders and regional boundaries. This theme of 'security literacy' is recurrent as an outstanding challenge for defence transformation and security sector reform, for it is the basis of informed choice and ownership of security issues for leaders, managers and the electorate.

Organizing

For the effective implementation of any plan, it is necessary that resources are brought together with people who know how to use those resources to best effect, and that structures and procedures are appropriate for their use. These are frequently identified, to us, as the most pressing issues for future defence management around the world.

Too often, an emphasis on tight controls of government departments has produced over-regulated, rigid, mechanistic structures, that can undermine even the best efforts of those trying to deliver effective public services. People working hard within one particular sphere of activity can very quickly develop a distorted view of goals and priorities and misguidedly withhold essential information from others. To be responsive to changing circumstances defence, and other, organizations need to develop structures that are more like biological organisms, capable of adapting to fluctuations within their environment.

Changes in the security paradigm, the nature of threats, and the forming (or expansion) of regional alliances alter both the vision and the resulting plan for a state's security sector. They also call for changes in the structures that enable security and defence organizations to do their job. What the United Kingdom has called 'joined-up-government' requires a better balance between the various departments, agencies and forces; greater transparency in processes and procedures; effective communication (which includes communication with the wider population); and accountability concerning how resources are used, for working practices and for the results.

Flexible structures will only be truly effective if they are populated with skilled people (politicians, officials, officers, managers and other staff) who understand their role and are empowered to take decisions, and to act, based on their knowledge and experience. This calls for the careful management of that most valuable resource for any organization: its people. Space prevented Alex Alexandrou and Roger Darby (Chapter 11) from presenting anything but a brief guide to the relatively new field of human resource management but this is an outstanding matter for most organizations, public or private, that needs to be addressed. While it may still be possible to argue that the armed forces need to be different from the societies that they serve (Dandeker and Freedman 2002), movements away from conscription and the increasing need for professionalism, to cope with changing tasks and technological advances, require managers to give much greater regard to ethics and values, to find ways of empowering individuals, and to find ways of developing skills, knowledge and attitudes.

The scarcity of tangible assets, especially money, makes the task of governing and managing a testing one as, within and between public sector organizations, there is a potentially infinite demand for resources. The final decision about how resources are allocated across the public sector is a matter for policy makers, but it will be based on the advice of experts in various departments of government as well within specific organizations, and their departments. At the heart of these decisions are the principles of good governance (see Jeff Haynes contribution in Chapter 2), but they also need good management if an acceptable case is to be made for appropriate funding to any specific department or organization.

Where requests for resources are based on capability rather than some assumed threat or the desire to replace something that already exists (Taylor Chapter 13) decision makers are better able to make well-reasoned judgements and to establish priorities. Additionally, as Len Nockles and Teri McConville indicated, in Chapter 12, thorough and careful reporting on how assets have been used, and will be used, can help to establish the case for one department over another.

The need for improved processes and for managing information is clearly apparent. Annie Maddison (Chapter 10) warns that organizations are in danger of being swamped by information and that technology is not necessarily the answer – it may be part of the problem. From Sun Tzu to Lord Wellington, history provides myriad examples of the need to acquire information upon which to base decisions. What is different today is that the information is available in abundance so the managerial task, as with any resource, is to plan for and organize information as a resource, and to direct, co-ordinate and control its use, and this applies whether the information is security-related intelligence, specialist knowledge or more mundane facts and figures relating to, for example, the cost of supplies.

Command

Effective command, in this context, essentially concerns the direction and leadership of the defence sector. Direction ultimately comes from politicians who, in a democratic society, will be acting in accordance with national interests and whose authority rests upon the consent of the people. While the intent of national interest remains broadly the same the methods of achieving it have radically altered over the centuries. With the increasing emphasis on human, rather than national or regime, security and the pressure for co-operative, rather than unilateral, responses to challenges, risks and threats we have seen a gradual, but not always uniform, movement away from chauvinistic statements of national interest. It is a move called for by UN Secretary General Kofi Annan: 'A new, broader, definition of national interest is needed...which would induce states to find greater unity in the pursuit of common goods and values' (Annan 1999, cited in Kegley and Wittkopf 2001: 654).

The pursuit of those common goods and values must start, in the first instance, at home with an understanding of what the people want and need. This understanding is best achieved by means of transparent and accountable government, allowing the voices of the people and public servants to be heard. The recognition that good governance and security are linked is becoming more pervasive, when even the King of Bhutan, one of the last absolute monarchs, establishes a special task force to determine the necessary structural and functional changes to ensure a stable and responsive system of governance (Kuenselonline 2005).

The translation of a political vision into reality, however, is dependent upon both leadership and management skills.

Some notions of leadership have been addressed elsewhere in this volume (Chapters 3, 8, 11 and 15) so these common strands will not be repeated. Rather, the outstanding issue is the notion of what might be called the 'learning leader'. In times of change, no leader (politician, manager or commander) can have all the facts, all the options or all the answers for any situation. Instead the leader will bring together all the resources of the organization to inform decisions and to increase the pool of common knowledge. Learning leaders accept the human fallibilities of themselves and of others, and ask others to do the same. This is not to take a fatalistic

Table 16.1 Conditions for organizational learning

Sphere	Condition	Notes
Structural	Mechanisms for learning	Arrangement for the systematic collection, analysis, storage and use of information
Context	Tolerance for admitting error	The 'no-blame culture' where admitting mistakes is seen as a basis for learning rather than a cause for punishment
	Issue orientation	Concentration on substantive issues rather than political or personal interests
	Egalitarianism	Power-sharing, participation and equal responsibility for performance outcomes
	Commitment to learning	The organization values learning either in itself or as essential tool for effectiveness
Psychological	Doubt	Lack of knowledge, or uncertainty, that provides the stimulus for inquiry
	Sense of safety	To enable admission of error or doubt without risk of punishment
Behavioural	Transparency	Open disclosure of thoughts, intentions and reasoning
	Inquiry	Recognition of what is not known and taking steps to increase knowledge
	Disconfirmability	The open admission of error in the light of new knowledge
	Accountability	Taking responsibility for one's own actions and their consequences, and implementing lessons learned

Source: Adapted from Freidman, Lipshitz and Overmeer 2001, p. 761 ff.

approach to life and events (see Yorke 2003) but, rather, to come to terms with the existence of uncertainty and view every novel situation as a fresh opportunity to learn and to add to the body of knowledge within any particular organization.

Learning is a continuous process that involves all the systems, processes and people of an organization and brings together the totality of knowledge, skills and experience in pursuit of continuous improvement. The ultimate goal is an organization where learning is part of the daily experience; where the organization itself becomes the repository of knowledge. The conditions for organizational learning to occur will by, now be, familiar to the reader for they imitate the preconditions for good governance and management generally (see Table 16.1).

Within an organization, if learning is to occur, there must be a strategic plan that will establish cross-functional mechanisms for the management of information and knowledge; not just in some remote, specialist department, but throughout the organization so that there is a clear resource to which individuals can contribute and from which everyone can draw. Freidman *et al.* (2001) give an example:

> Within the Israeli Defence Force, pilots and their commanders meet immediately after each mission, not simply to debrief on the sortie but to analyse individual and group performance. Within these 'after action reviews' discussions are said to be forthright but pleasant with rank playing no role.
>
> This system has been taken up within the Ordnance Corps, where information derived from reviews is fed into the systems for project management. Two groups provide follow-up: one to work on specific problems concerning their Minerva tanks, the second to work on improving the after-action-review process.

If defence organizations are to look to their new beginnings and learn from the past (rather than simply repeating past errors) people need to feel safe so that they can admit what they do not know, or own up to previous mistakes, analyse them, and avoid them in the future. This 'no-blame' culture is difficult in the political sphere where, under the scrutiny of the public gaze, policy makers and leaders may fear for their own futures. It is, however, a necessity, not only to promote a spirit of enquiry (or curiosity) but as a basis for accountability and transparency.

Managers and other leaders need to put aside their own self-interests, and their regard for a personal power base, to concentrate on what is best for the nation, sector or organization. The ability to share power and responsibility with others gives those others ownership of the issues, empowering them to develop solutions and to take decisions. It also relieves managers of a considerable workload where, freed from minute details and sectional interests, they will be able to concentrate on the substantive matters that will make a real difference in how defence is governed and managed.

Co-ordination

The changing international environment presents opportunities for co-ordinating defence activities on national, regional, and international levels. At the national level, as has been discussed in Chapters 3–6, there is a need to achieve co-ordination, co-operation and compromise across the political spectrum, within government and between civilian and military personnel, if the defence establishment is truly to serve the people rather than a narrow elite. The concepts of co-ordination, co-operation and compromise are the hallmarks of democracy. They are also necessary requirements if one of the barriers to full democracy, 'the fault of understanding between the military world and the civilian world', is to be breached (Bachelet cited by Franklin 2005: 24).

The attainment of human security should be a state function, but states cannot guarantee this type of security on their own. Co-ordination, co-operation and compromise are also required at the regional and international levels. Increasingly, states are working together in order to support each other in their national change programmes. Below are just a few examples of that co-operation:

- At the national level, there is a move towards more joined-up government. In the UK this process is reasonably advanced, but in developing democracies, like Ghana and Ethiopia, there is an attempt to increase security literacy and thus co-ordination of security governance across ministries.
- National institutions are also forming bilateral and international agreements in the pursuit of best practice. As discussed in Chapter 5, national audit agencies from established democracies are mentoring those in developing democracies, and the International Organization of Supreme Audit Agencies has assumed a co-ordinating role.
- At the regional level, states are working together to ensure good governance. The African Peer Review Mechanism (APRM) has been established to foster the adoption of policies, standards and practices that lead to political stability and sustainable economic development. The APRM provides a means through which to share experiences and reinforce successful best practice.

The co-operation and support which is apparent between national governments and civil services is also mirrored in activities undertaken by armed forces. Few states are in a position to provide for the nation's security independently. For many states defence is not national, it is collective and armed forces are structured, trained and deployed for combined and multinational operations. In the last fifteen years we have seen the establishment of numerous multinational brigades and battalions: BALTBAT in the Baltic Sea region, SEEBRIG in South-Eastern Europe, ECOWAS in West Africa, and the SADC Peacekeeping Brigade in South Africa, just to name a few.

There are many reasons for the establishment of such forces. They may enable a state to pursue a particular ambition: to be a regional player or to demonstrate its capability and commitment to joint and combined operations so that it can join a larger alliance. Alternatively, it may be to reduce the overall cost of defence, by specializing in a particular capability. In contributing to the brigade or battalion, the state and its armed forces may hope to gain operational experience and thus greater professionalism. Whatever the motivation, there are a number of considerations that need to be addressed:

- How does participation in such a force contribute to the national interest?
- Are supportive policy and legal frameworks in place to make this ambition a reality?
- Can we afford to do this? Can we afford not to do this?
- How do we need to structure, recruit, train, deploy our forces to ensure that they are effective, efficient and not an embarrassment?
- Are our national rules of engagement compatible with those of the multinational brigade? Do we have rules of engagement?

These questions are illustrative, rather than exhaustive, but they do demonstrate the need for an interface between political leadership and defence management.

Control

Throughout this book 'control' has been used in the context of managing performance and the quality of organizational outputs. There is another context that presents one of the biggest challenges to those who want to improve the governance and management of defence. That is the issue of corruption in public services. This is an insidious problem, occurring at all levels of society, and, in the words of US Ambassador Victor Jackovitch (2001) could have a:

> corrosive effect on society at large. There is the danger that the population of a newly emerging state could begin to perceive criminality

and corruption as ineluctable elements in the process of transition. There are probably only two directions from such a point once it is reached: acceptance of criminality and corruption as permanent elements in society, or rejection of the entire transition process and of democratization.

The Ambassador further emphasizes that:

> ... the problems of crime and corruption are all the more acute when they directly involve the armed forces, law enforcement agencies, border police and customs. This is not only because these are important pillars of the state. It is also because these are the very institutions that are charged with the task of safeguarding the security of everyone else in the state.
>
> (Jackovitch 2001)

So, within the defence and security communities, tackling corruption must be a priority if 'what might be' is not to turn into 'that which went before'. As well as being valuable in their own right, transparency and accountability are powerful principles for safeguarding societies against corrupt practice. They apply equally to managers, for instance in assessing bids for contracts, as to politicians deciding upon policy issues, or to individual officials going about their work and dealing with members of the public. When activities, policies and procedures are subjected to scrutiny, and named individuals are held responsible for the way they do their work, and for the outcomes of that work, both the opportunity and the inclination for corruption are reduced. But these things will not happen unless there is the political will to combat the problem from the highest levels of power, within departments of state and throughout the public sector.

It was the English historian, Lord Acton (1834–1902), who said that 'power tends to corrupt and absolute power corrupts absolutely' (Oxford Dictionary of Quotations 1996: 1). Hence, effective control must ensure that no one person has sufficient power to rule or lead without the consent of others. Separating power between politicians, the state, the judiciary and other religious or secular groups not only removes opportunity for corruption from those who might seize excessive power for themselves, but also ensures that multiple views are taken into account in the formulation of policy, and that is the basis for democracy.

In closing

One of the forerunners of management theory, Fredrick W. Taylor (1856–1915), famously asserted that a manager's task was to find the one best way to do a job and to ensure that that was followed. History and learning have proved him wrong, for there is no single best way for any job, whether it be building a new helicopter or managing an entire security sector.

What is best in one time or place will be different in another context. Defence is a complex, dynamic and difficult task and, for no two countries, will there be a single best way to plan, organize, command, co-ordinate or control the defence function.

Within this short volume we have tried to share some of the commonly agreed principles and to give examples of good practice, and to offer you a few questions to think about. This, though, is only a broad outline. There is neither a clear formula nor a basic recipe for the governance and management of defence. There are though some common issues, such as the establishment of suitable structures, the harnessing of sufficient resources (money, material and information), attracting the best people to do the necessary work, and the delicate processes of managing change. There are also common challenges concerning the combating of corruption; improving security literacy and developing cultures for learning; and increasing transparency and accountability – both in the wider governmental sphere and, specifically, within the defence sector. As states move toward greater democracy, from authoritarian regimes or from near-anarchy, and as they come to terms with new defence tasks, the questions that must be addressed, and their answers, will be unique. Social, economic, political and technological factors will each have a bearing on the vision of 'what might be' and in determining the way to achieve that vision. There is no single, best way but, as we have attempted to demonstrate throughout this book, there is another way.

Bibliography

Dandeker, C. and Freedman, L. (2002), 'The British Armed Services', *The Political Quarterly*, 73 (4): 465–75.

Franklin, Jonathan, 'All I want in life is to walk along the beach, holding my lover's hand', *The Guardian*, 22 November 2005, 24–5.

Friedman, V. J., Lipshitz, R. and Overmeer, W. (2001), 'Creating conditions for organizational learning', in Dierkes, M., Antal, A. B., Child, J. and Nonaka, I. (eds), *Handbook of Organizational Leaning and Knowledge*, Oxford: Oxford University Press, 757–76.

Hoogvelt, Ankie (1997), *Globalisation and the Postcolonial World: the New Political Economy of Development*, Houndmills: Macmillan Press.

Jackovitch, V. (2001), 'Corruption with security forces: A threat to national security' *Address to the Global Forum on Fighting Corruption and Safeguarding Integrity*, The Hague; Ministry of Justice, www.fas.organisation/irp/news/2001/05/corrupt.html (accessed 20 November 2005).

Kegley, Charles W. Jr and Wittkopf, Eugene R. (2001), *World Politics: Trend and Transformation* (eighth edition), Boston, MA: and New York: Bedford/St Martin's.

Kuenselonline, 'Good governance crucial for parliamentary democracy', kuenselonline.com/article.php?sid=6188&PHPSESSID=b698e5a0eee8d2 (accessed 20 November 2005).

McConville, T. and Holmes, R. (2003), 'Introduction' to *Defence Management in Uncertain Times*, London: Frank Cass, xi-xviii.

O'Meara, Patrick, Mehlinger, Howard D, Krain, Matthew (2000), *Globalization and the Challenges of a New Century*, Bloomington and Indianapolis, IN: Indiana University Press.

Oxford Dictionary of Quotations (1996) 4th Edition, Oxford: Oxford University Press.

Yorke, J. (2003), 'The quest for certainty: coping with uncertainty', in McConville, T. and Holmes, R. (eds), *Defence Management in Uncertain Times*. London: Frank Cass, 1–27.

Index

Note: Numbers in italic indicates figures and tables.